THE REAL
PERSUASION

THE REAL
PERSUASION

PORTRAIT OF A REAL-LIFE JANE AUSTEN HEROINE

PETER JAMES BOWMAN

AMBERLEY

First published 2017

Amberley Publishing
The Hill, Stroud
Gloucestershire, GL5 4EP

www.amberley-books.com

British Library Cataloguing in Publication Data.
A catalogue record for this book is available from the British Library.

ISBN 978 1 4456 5950 3 (hardback)
ISBN 978 1 4456 5951 0 (ebook)

Typesetting and Origination by Amberley Publishing.
Printed in the UK.

FOR CLAUDE

'He loved her – she loved him; and, without any unseemly elopement, they lived down and loved down a pretty strong family opposition, and were married.'

The Letters of Mary Russell Mitford

Contents

List of Illustrations

12. Katherine Bisshopp. Crayon sketch. Castle Goring MSS/PD/100, West Sussex Record Office, Chichester.
13. Katherine Bisshopp, Robert Curzon, Harriet Curzon *née* Bisshopp and Assheton Viscount Curzon. Oil on canvas. Property of Parham Park Ltd, Parham House, West Sussex. Photography by Elizabeth Zeschin and Hugh Gilbert.
14. Hagley Hall, Staffordshire. Engraving by Samuel Lacey after John Preston Neale.
15. Robert Curzon. Oil on canvas by Richard Pentreath. By descent in the family of the sitter.
16. Harriet Curzon. Oil on canvas by Richard Pentreath. By descent in the family of the sitter.
17. Gorhambury, Hertfordshire. Engraving by W. Warwick after John Preston Neale.
18. George Richard Pechell, Royal Navy, MP. Lithograph by Edward Morton after Thomas Charles Wageman. © National Maritime Museum, Greenwich, London.
19. Katherine Bisshopp. Crayon sketch. Castle Goring MSS/PD/101, West Sussex Record Office, Chichester.
20. Hampton Court Palace, Middlesex. Aquatint by Edward Duncan after Henry Bryan Ziegler, in Hermann von Pückler-Muskau, 'Erinnerungsbilder', vol. 1. Property of the Erbengemeinschaft der Grafen Pückler on permanent loan to the Stiftung Fürst-Pückler-Museum Park und Schloss Branitz.
21. Royal Pavilion, Brighton. Aquatint from John Nash, *The Royal Pavilion at Brighton* (London: Ackermann, 1826). Royal Pavilion & Museums, Brighton & Hove.
22. Trial of the R.Y.S. Brig *Water Witch*. Engraving by C. Rosenberg after William John Huggins.
23. William, Henrietta and Adelaide Pechell. Watercolour by Mrs Mannin. Property of FitzRoy and Marigold Somerset.
24. Robert Curzon II. Oil on canvas. By descent in the family of the sitter.
25. Emily Curzon *née* Wilmot-Horton with her daughter Darea. Oil on canvas by Alexander Glasgow. Property of Parham Park Ltd, Parham House, West Sussex. Photography by Elizabeth Zeschin and Hugh Gilbert.
26. Edward Curzon. Photograph of a sketch. Parham Archive 1/5/6/9/28, West Sussex Record Office, Chichester.

Preface

Her father is a vain, foolish baronet, obsessed with his lineage but so careless with money that he is obliged to retrench by quitting his ancestral seat. Her sister is a fretful invalid with a good-natured husband and two disobedient sons. She herself falls in love with a handsome naval officer, and he with her, but her proud family judge his status and prospects to be inadequate. Heartbroken, the lovers part: he goes to sea while she leads a forlorn life at home. Years later he returns, having made a fortune in prize money, and after further misunderstandings he claims as his bride the woman he has never ceased to love.

This is the story of Anne Elliot in Jane Austen's *Persuasion*. It is also the story – true this time – of Katherine Bisshopp, the clever, beautiful daughter of an old Sussex family. To be sure, Katherine's sister Harriet is a more intelligent and likeable woman than Mary Musgrove, but along with her ailments and her unruly children she shares her fictional counterpart's tendency to make the most of poor health and claim the attention of her sister whenever she is ill.

'I cannot conceive a more perfect mode of writing any man's life,' declares James Boswell in his *Life of Johnson*, 'than not only relating all the most important events of it in their order, but interweaving what he privately wrote, and said, and thought.' This technique of interweaving has been adopted here, using the sisters' letters and journals and other family correspondence to bring the main characters into focus. Whether their subject is daily life at Parham, the Bisshopps' family seat, or the social round in London, Brighton and elsewhere, the writers of these hitherto unpublished documents use a fresh, unaffected language that is redolent of its time.

The central strand of the narrative is Katherine's eleven-year courtship with George Pechell, which causes harrowing despair and only ends when his improved circumstances and her dogged attachment overcome her parents' opposition. It is the happiest of unions and produces two daughters and a son. Pechell becomes a royal equerry, an MP for Brighton, and a vice-admiral. Both Katherine and Harriet endure severe trials as mothers, and Katherine's desolation at her only son's death in the Crimean War is only partly alleviated by her close bond with her daughters and their husbands.

The Bisshopp chronicle is interspersed with segments comparing it with the portrait Jane Austen paints of society in her letters and novels. In particular the extraordinary coincidence of character and circumstance between Katherine Bisshopp and Anne Elliot is demonstrated to the point of their marriages, while Katherine's subsequent experiences are seen as a possible future for Anne, whose story, according to Jane Austen's custom, closes as her conjugal career begins. The reality of history and the deeper truth of fiction together yield a detailed picture of the age.

This book is written in the belief that the past is brought most vividly before us not by the study of those who dwelt in the limelight of public fame, or whose achievements transcend their era, but by piecing together the lives of engaging but unremarkable people and letting them speak for themselves. The intention is to show rather than tell, where necessary to explain, but rarely to comment, in the hope that readers will feel closely acquainted with the heroine and her family and at home in their world.

*

It was while researching another book that I had the pleasure of making Katherine Bisshopp's acquaintance, and the generosity of FitzRoy and Marigold Somerset in letting me see family papers and showing me places and artefacts that illuminate her life gave me the impetus to set about documenting it. Their encouragement then sustained me through the years it took to complete the task.

The bulk of my work was done in the searchroom of the West Sussex Record Office in Chichester, and a more agreeable environment in which to carry out historical research would be hard to imagine. I am indebted to Caroline Adams for devoting so much time to guiding me through a complex body of material and making sure I saw every relevant document. I am also grateful to the other members of the searchroom staff, particularly the late Frances Lansley, who dealt with my final queries and requests.

Lady Emma Barnard and Lyndy Kessell made further items available to me during two enjoyable visits to Parham. Sandra Budd at Knepp Castle, Patricia McGuire at King's College, Cambridge, and the staff at Hertfordshire Archives and Local Studies allowed me to consult papers in their care. Martin Hayes of Worthing Library placed George Bason's compendious researches into the Pechell family at my disposal, and Mr Bason himself responded to my questions.

I am obliged to several historians of Sussex for information and advice: Sue Djabri, Mary Monnery, Janet Pennington, and Sue Peyman-Stroud. The late Timothy Frankland answered my written enquiries about his ancestors.

Caroline Adams, Lady Emma Barnard, Claude Piening and Marigold Somerset kindly read an early draft of the book, which has benefited from their comments. My most critical reader was Annie Campbell, whose suggestions led me to revise the text substantially.

The West Sussex Record Office has provided a third of the illustrations. Another third are from private collections, whose owners generously consented to their reproduction. Christian Friedrich, John Grodzinski, Krystyna Pickering and Karen Wraith assisted me in various ways with the other images.

Finally, I thank my editor Alex Bennett for his help and reassurance, and for always offering them so promptly.

Childhood and Youth

1782–1807

When Harriet Anne, the only child of William Southwell and his wife Annabella *née* Pye, of Frampton Cotterell in Gloucestershire, was united on 27 July 1782 with Sir Cecil Bisshopp, 8th Baronet, of Parham in Sussex, both were judged to have made a good match. The Southwells were a family of established dignity, recently enhanced by the success of Mr Southwell's elder brother in getting the ancient barony of De Clifford called out of abeyance in his favour. Miss Southwell was in her twenty-third year, a tall, strikingly attractive woman with rich chestnut hair and clear blue eyes. According to her friend Hester Lyttelton, it was her 'uncommon beauty' that had captivated Sir Cecil. She also had a lively temperament, a wide range of accomplishments, and a well-stocked mind.

Sir Cecil, six years older than his bride, seemed in every way worthy of her. He combined a pleasing exterior with a reputation for amiability and, for a man not yet thirty, he was enviably well set up in life. In 1779 he had inherited the Bisshopp baronetcy and Parham, a fine Elizabethan house with a 10,000-acre estate, and a year later he entered parliament as member for New Shoreham. Miss Lyttelton declared herself satisfied with Miss Southwell's prospects of marital comfort, and although that young lady experienced some 'blue devils' on parting from her beloved parents, the excellent sprits she displayed in public after the wedding seemed to realise the most sanguine hopes of those who cared for her. Soon the young Lady Bisshopp was inviting friends and relations to her new home and rejoicing at the impression it made on them.

Located in the parish of the same name, a few miles south of the village of Pulborough, Parham was built in the 1570s and 1580s by Sir Thomas Palmer, the son of a wealthy London mercer who acquired extensive lands in Sussex following the dissolution of the monasteries. Constructed of honey-grey stone in a flattened 'H' shape and set in a deer-stocked park, the house faces south towards the chalky Downs that fill most of the twelve miles between it and the sea. To the northeast it is sheltered by a ridge, and to the west a plain extends to the fast-flowing River Arun. In 1601 the Palmers sold the house to Thomas Bisshopp of Henfield, a lawyer and politician who was created a baronet in 1620, and his descendants lived there for three centuries, gradually altering and adding to the original structure. In the early 1700s the fifth baronet modernised the house with segmental gables and sash windows, and it was in this form that Sir Cecil and Lady Bisshopp knew Parham.

Eleven months into their marriage the couple celebrated the arrival of a son. Five successive Bisshopp baronets had been called Cecil, and the boy received the same name. In September 1784 there was a second son, Charles, who was given to the care of the Southwells while his parents went with the infant Cecil on a long tour of France, Italy and Switzerland. During their travels Lady Bisshopp became pregnant again, and it was in Geneva that her first daughter was born, in September 1787. She had always hoped for a girl, and little Harriet Anne, who would take after her in appearance and character as well as sharing her name, became her favourite. Katherine Annabella began life at Parham in December 1791, and a third girl, Caroline, was born in 1797 but lived only eleven days.

The Bisshopps relished the two and a half years of their European tour. They took several servants and rented houses as they went, and there were few pleasures they denied themselves in the way of plays, operas, balls and excursions. Lady Bisshopp, who all her life abhorred cold and wet weather, luxuriated in the warm south while Sir Cecil indulged his fashionable artistic and antiquarian leanings by purchasing marbles, books and paintings. In Rome he had their portraits done by Angelica Kauffman and shipped them home with his other treasures. 'You and yours are all I regret in England,' wrote Lady Bisshopp to her mother from Turin, 'for except in being separated from you I have never met with one unpleasant circumstance abroad.' Even after the birth of little Harriet they were in no hurry to return.

At home and abroad, Lady Bisshopp kept up a regular correspondence with her mother, and this is our main source of information on the early years of her marriage. Her letters are full of filial love, and she spent so many hours writing them that Sir Cecil was sometimes jealous. As for Mrs Southwell, she held her daughter to be quite perfect; there were no words, she said, to express how much she honoured and esteemed her. She delighted in picturing how lovely she looked in a new gown, relayed every golden opinion of her that she heard from others, and was half out of her wits with joy at the thought of seeing her again after her tour. Her friends had plenty to listen to on her favourite subject: 'I want much to see the Throck[morton]s,' she wrote one day, 'for I never converse so comfortably about your sweet Ladyship as with them.'

The Southwells themselves were not a uniformly contented pair. Mr Southwell, like most of the men in our story, was averse to writing letters, so we only have the perspective of his much younger wife, who was often out of patience with him. His faults, it seems, were indecision and hypochondria. 'Mr Southwell *as usual* talks dayly of going to Tunbridge or some water drinking place *but as usual* quite undetermined' is typical of her tart remarks. He was a fussy eater, dilatory about seeing friends, insistent but vague on the subject of his infirmities, and given to sudden, inconveniently timed urges to quit London for the good of his health. However, after his death in 1795 his widow missed him, disliking her solitude and feeling too 'dull' to entertain or go out alone. His daughter missed him too, and cherished the one fragment of his handwriting in her possession.

Lady Bisshopp also corresponded vigorously with her many female friends, married and unmarried. The aim in each letter was to cram several pages with news of visits and counter-visits, births and deaths, flirtations and marriages, often with each sentence beginning a fresh topic. Receiving such a letter was always a treat; writers were praised to the skies for their best performances and warmly chided when they were slow to pick up their pen. There is a marked feminine bias in subject matter – with men playing supporting roles or ignored altogether, and a tender, romantically tinged tone towards recipients that was common among educated women at this time. 'My sweet pheasant' is what one friend always called Lady Bisshopp, and Hester Lyttelton went further: 'My dear pretty soul, to say how much I love thee more than life poorly expresses what my heart would shew.'

Lady Bisshopp's epistolary style was mischievous but not malicious. Her love of gossip extended itself to conversation, and her bouts of 'chit-chat' could fill an evening. Not that her mind was trivial; rather she was an intelligent observer of life with a real interest in politics, literature and the arts, an *esprit savant* as one friend put it. Nor was she vain, either of her mental gifts or of her beauty, and her mother's uncritical adoration did not spoil her character. She could be forthright in her opinions and felt entitled, as a virtuous woman, to criticise persons whose selfish or licentious conduct wrecked the happiness of their families. The loose morals of the age provided plenty of targets for such criticism.

Because his own letters were infrequent and short, and because those his wife exchanged with her mother and friends say little about their menfolk, it is not easy to get a sense of Sir Cecil's character during these years. Lady Bisshopp's correspondents speak of him with regard but no obvious affection, and it is clear that he was less naturally companionable than she, though he liked society well enough and was good at organising balls. He enjoyed the role of bountiful lord of the manor, readily issuing invitations to Parham and sending gifts of figs, pineapples and venison to friends and acquaintances, influential politicians and members of the royal family. He appears to have been an affectionate husband and father: he was overjoyed at Cecil's birth and watched over him night after night during a fever a few years later; and when Harriet was born in Geneva he transmitted the news to Mrs Southwell, adding that even if the girl developed every quality she could never equal her mother.

Unlike Lady Bisshopp, Sir Cecil did not harmonise well with his own family. Relations with his father had been so frosty that his education, first at Cheam School and subsequently in Bordeaux and Toulouse, had been superintended by his grandfather, the sixth baronet. He was on poor terms with his brother Hugh, a commissioner of customs and gentleman usher to Queen Charlotte, and with his sister Susannah, of whom little is known. His only family correspondent was his mother, who had left her husband long before his early death. Her letters show respect for Sir Cecil as head of the house and gratitude for little attentions, but her tone is curiously bland and impersonal – partly from an avowed feeling that her retired existence offered little in the way of anecdote, and partly, as she delicately hinted more than once, because he rarely wrote to her. After she died in 1791 Sir Cecil had no regular contact with his own relatives.

As a young family the Bisshopps of Parham presented a smiling group portrait. At its centre were the children, healthy and pleasing to behold. Lady Bisshopp was proud to have breastfed them all and took a more active role in their care than was customary for women of her rank. Cecil, the eldest, was blessed with a full measure of the 'Bisshopp beauty', and from an early age his fine appearance was a theme of family letters. Known as 'Whisk' or 'Jig', he was an energetic, mettlesome boy, quick to take fire but quickly bored. Charles was not as comely: his face was pitted by smallpox and he had a tendency to gluttony that spoilt his figure and earned him the epithet 'Pancakes'; but he was a kind, even-tempered boy and the pet of his grandmothers. A few years at Winchester College revealed that neither brother had any aptitude for study, a disappointment for Lady Bisshopp, who nonetheless saw that their frank, straightforward characters gave her 'great reason to be satisfied with them'.

Harriet's resemblance to her mother declared itself early, so that her nickname 'Little Me', though possibly coined by herself, seems apt. Not only did the girl look like her mother, with regular features, clear white skin, wide-spaced blue eyes and rich medium-brown hair, she also developed the same charm and grace of manner. Taught at home by her mother and by governesses, she learned her lessons well and easily acquired the essential feminine accomplishments. She learnt to sing, play the harp and pianoforte to a good standard and could compose letters in French by the age of ten. In addition she was an amateur astronomer, with her own telescope mounted in the house. We hear nothing of drawing, but it is unlikely that it was neglected; perhaps, like needlework, it came later.

Harriet was expected to write regularly to her mother when they were apart, and the replies she received mixed encouragement with gentle correction. In early 1798 she accompanied her mother's friend Lady Stawell and her eighteen-year-old daughter to Bristol.

LADY BISSHOPP TO HARRIET
LONDON, 8 FEBRUARY 1798

My dearest dear Puss – I received your comical letter yesterday, with which I am extremely well satisfied, as you seem to have written exactly what you would have said if you had been with me. You did very right not to stay too long in Mrs Howard's dressing room on account of the piano forte. I only require you to practise your three hours whenever you can do so without being troublesome to any body else, and when you are settled at Bristol I am sure you will be able to do so, and particularly on your harp, which may be moved into any room where you can be alone ...

Your Papa and I miss you very much and talk of you all day long. Grandmamma is very well and desires her love to you. We hope you do not forget to recommend yourself to God every night and morning, and to think of poor dearest in your innocent prayers. I have had a very kind letter this morning from Lady Stawell, in which she speaks of you most affectionately, and I am sure you cannot be too grateful to Lady S. and Miss Legge for the notice they take of you. I shall be glad to hear of your arrival at Bristol, and pray continue to send me the most minute accounts of every thing you see and of all the people you meet. Frisky desires his duty. Your poor little fish is dead, but I have sent this morning to buy a companion for the living one. I have not heard from either of your brothers since you left us. God bless you my dear Harriette. Believe me ever most

Affectionately yours
H. B.

LADY BISSHOPP TO HARRIET
LONDON, FEBRUARY 1798

My dearest Harriette – I have written twice to you, the last time yesterday directed to Lady Stawell, Bristol Hot Wells, and I beg she will send to the Post Office for those letters. You don't keep your promise of writing often to me, and the letter I have received today is very ill and vulgarly written, and much less agreeable in all respects than your two former letters. I should have liked some account of your journey and when you got to Bristol, and whether you have a pretty lodging, whose room you sleep in etc., in short a great many particulars about yourself Lady Stawell and Miss Legge, instead of Mrs Sneyd and her tiresome children. William of Wick*ham* is spelt thus, with a *ham* not Wickam.

Pray send me word immediately whether you have your harp and piano forte. I think it quite time lost writing silly letters to your brothers. If you practise three hours every day and write often to me, walk out and divert yourself, and clean your teeth and nails, I am sure your day will be fully employed. Pray play to Lady Stawell with proper attention all those difficult passages in Clementi's last lesson, and give me an account of the progress you make; and do try if you have any time to make some pens. I regret so much Cecil and you not having succeeded in that talent, for I cannot get any tolerable pens any where. Adieu, pray get your harp and work hard, and try to write well, and distinctly, and make the proper stops. Buy some very good hard pens and believe me ever your affectionate mother

Harriet Anne Bisshopp

LADY BISSHOPP TO HARRIET
LONDON, FEBRUARY 1798

My dearest Harriette – You are a dear love for writing so constantly, and I am quite impatient for the hour of four o'clock today that I may appear less ungrateful to dear Lady Stawell, as at that hour she will receive my packet, and indeed I could not write Saturday, but after having dispatched a long letter to each of you yesterday I think it is very pretty of me to write again today. I beg you will tell me about Clementi's lesson, and how the harp goes on. I wish you not to practise more than three quarters of an hour at a time upon either, but if you begin the day with a practise you will have time enough to employ your three hours and with spirit ...

I am much pleased with your description of the prospect from your window, and your Methodist parson, and *extempore* sermon, which you should have called it, not by heart, as one can only repeat a thing by heart which has been learned by rote. Do you comprehend the difference? Pray keep it in your knowledge box. As for the text, I should have been glad to know *what* and not *where* it was, it is like *the maids* to say it was in the 21st Chapter of St Luke. I only tell you all this my sweetest Puss-tuss to divert and not discourage you, for your letters after all are amazingly easy and sensible for your dear white paws (*I hope the ongles are clean*) to write at their age, and you are a love of a little girl ...

We learn less of Katherine as a child. Our first sight of her is in 1798, aged six, with her father about to fetch her home from Mrs Southwell's house in London. Despite having a cold she is such an amusing companion, emptying a box of necklaces and earrings and throwing them about, that her grandmother does not want to give her up. A few years later we glimpse her with Harriet, who kisses their mother's portrait while writing her a letter: 'Kate *being a monkey* has done the same; she is now *grining* at her *wit*.' Imitation of her sister was a large part of Katherine's upbringing, especially once she began the same system of home education. She equalled Harriet as a reader, sang and played the same pieces on the pianoforte, and at five years old was twanging the strings of her own harp. Physically they were less similar. Like Harriet, Katherine was blonde as a little girl, but her hair turned much darker, and while her sister and mother had bright blue eyes, hers were an equally radiant green, hence her nicknames 'Kitten' and 'the Cat'. She had a smaller frame, and at intervals in her growth was too thin, so that gains in weight were noted with satisfaction. Harriet watched over her progress with loving officiousness, and despite the four-year gap they were very close.

The image of carefree family life in an idyllic setting impressed itself on visitors to Parham, among them Anna Tonelli, a Florentine portraitist who came in 1795 to fulfil a commission for two pastel drawings of the rising generation. One of these, showing Harriet and Charles poring over a book, is lost; the other, of Cecil with a protective arm around Katherine, still hangs in the house. Signora Tonelli made further visits, and the outdoor teas, strolls in the park and card games that filled her leisure hours became fond memories. In 1800, while travelling with another British family in India, where she was miserable, she replied warmly to Sir Cecil's invitation to come again on her return: 'How happy I shall be when the time of my banishment is over! And more happy in having the hope to see Parham again! I am extremely obliged to you for your kind offers, and for ever I shall remember yours and Lady Bisshopp's goodness and friendship to me.'

The demands of parenthood, running a household and entertaining did not dull Lady Bisshopp's appetite for letter-writing. There was now a man, too, among her correspondents: the historian, topographer and archaeologist Sir Richard Colt Hoare. He had married her intimate friend Hester Lyttelton in 1783 and, when she died in childbirth two years later, Lady Bisshopp's letter to him and his anguished response founded a lifelong friendship. His urbane and erudite letters, describing the scenes of his travels in Italy and Ireland and his landscaping work at Stourhead in Wiltshire, breathe a tender reverence for the companion of his wife's youth. As an old man he sent her copies of some of his books: 'Accept them as one of the many remembrances of you which still exist, and ever will, I hope, in my heart.'

Sir Cecil's main occupation was making improvements to Parham. He paved the great hall, remodelled the dining room, and converted what had been a storeroom into a saloon in the neo-classical style. He spent a large sum on a new library and in 1794 had a catalogue of its contents compiled and printed (this includes a quantity of French erotica with titles like *Les Disgraces des amours, Aventures secrettes et plaisantes* and *Les Libertins en campagne* – it would be interesting to know whether Sir Cecil bought or inherited these works). He constructed a range of offices and stables around a courtyard to the north of the house, laid out pleasure grounds to the west, and enhanced the 260-acre park. Later he rebuilt the parish church of St Peter, a short walk from Parham's south elevation.

In 1795 Sir Cecil did his patriotic duty in the face of the threat of French invasion by raising a troop of yeomanry. Before his marriage he had been a captain in the Sussex militia, and he drew on this experience to drill his eighty-strong force of local farmers twice a week in various locations around Arundel. Sometimes they exercised in Parham Park, and on one wet day in 1796 in the long gallery at the top of the house. Each man provided his own horse, breeches, boots and spurs, but was otherwise armed and accoutred by Sir Cecil. The activities of the Parham Troop, as it became known, were regulated by an orderly book, with fines for non-attendance, insubordination and drunkenness, and field officers of the Kent and Sussex districts made regular inspections. The captain of the troop took his duties seriously, and only when Napoleon was exiled to Elba did he disband it.

As a politician Sir Cecil was less zealous. From 1780 he was one of two Tory MPs for New Shoreham, but he did nothing to bring himself to notice and lost his seat ten years later. In 1796 he won it back, and in 1802 came in again with his friend Timothy Shelley. As the two men were unopposed there was no canvassing, but they still had to meet the costs of putting up hustings, remunerating election officials, and providing the customary drinks and dinner on election day. The bill of £610, shared between them, shows what an expensive ornament a political career was. Sir Cecil retired from the House of Commons in 1806, not having spoken once in the final decade of his attendance.

While parliament was sitting Sir Cecil was often in London alone, but he and Lady Bisshopp went together for court functions and the Season. They first had a house near the Southwells in Spring Gardens, off The Mall, then one in Baker Street, and in 1802 they took a twenty-one-year lease on a new house in Stratford Place, off Oxford Street. Stratford Place would be the base for Harriet and Katherine's first forays into the fashionable world, but until then they usually remained at Parham with their governesses Mrs Gines and Marianne La Housse and received letters from their mother or, if he was in London without her, from their father.

SIR CECIL BISSHOPP TO HARRIET
BAKER STREET, 6 FEBRUARY 1802

My dear little Harriett – I am very much obliged to you for all your kind little notes and letters and beg you will send me more. I am quite well again, am sorry I cannot come to Parham to-morrow (Sunday) as I propose going to the levee on Wednesday next. If you wish me to bring you and your sister gloves from my old shop [in] Leicester Square you must send me one of each, or I shall be happy to bring any thing wanted. I cannot find the *book*. All the house is very clean and comfortable. Have been in your room, quite clean, *rather cold*.

I drive to day in Covent Garden to go after to the play to hear Mrs Billington in Love in a Village. I do all my writings at breakfast, which keeps me at home till 2 or 3 o'clock, then depart for the House or dinner, sometimes the play. I wrote a little letter to Cecil, I hope the grey hounds are well ... Love to your dearest Mamma and pretty little Puss. [It] is very dirty and damp walking

out, and generally cold air. Write to me and I will write to you
and bring any thing you wish to have.

Believe me to be

  My dear little Harriet

Your affectionate father
Cecil Bishopp

Thus far our portrait of the Bisshopps has exuded a warm domestic
glow. It is the portrait they painted themselves, as when Sir Cecil
invited an acquaintance to visit Parham and 'see an old family
mansion and find a hearty welcome'. Occasionally the pleasant
routines of manorial life were broken by sorrow or anxiety: as well
as the loss of baby Caroline in 1797 Lady Bisshopp suffered at least
two miscarriages, and some of the other children's illnesses briefly
appeared dangerous. Such things occurred in almost every family,
however, and the engrossing bustle of everyday life soon drew their
sting. But there were two other distresses that grew more acute as
the years passed and eventually inflicted an ugly rent across the
picture we have been admiring.

The first of these distresses was pecuniary, and the blame for
it lies squarely with Sir Cecil. During the two centuries they
had owned Parham the Bisshopps had maintained their wealth
and standing, and the fourth and fifth baronets had married
Oxfordshire heiresses through whom much property passed into
the family. Sir Cecil's income from his combined estates was in the
region of £10,000, and he inherited no significant debts. His wife
further enhanced his position; there is no marriage settlement in
the archives, but as the only child of moderately wealthy parents
she must have come with a good portion. All Sir Cecil had to do
to ensure a life of untroubled ease was cast an occasional eye over
his finances and avoid gross excesses in spending.

He did neither. The list of pictures at the back of the Parham
library catalogue includes works by Caravaggio, Poussin, Titian
and Murillo, presumably the harvest of his Grand Tour, and even if
some of the attributions are optimistic the outlay would have been
considerable. Meanwhile the Bisshopp estates were neglected, and
Robert Hurst, the Horsham lawyer engaged as his agent, wrote to
Sir Cecil in Geneva to draw his attention to the parlous state of
the Oxfordshire properties in particular. He ignored this warning;
indeed for at least a year he did not reply to it. Things barely

improved after his return, and he was served with a subpoena in relation to a contract for timber, which he could have avoided if he had attended to the matter.

For a long time this pattern of nonchalance and prodigality continued. Lavish entertaining, the extensive work on the house, gardens and park, and such luxuries as the library catalogue, bound in leather for private circulation, gradually degraded Sir Cecil's finances, and a letter to Robert Hurst of 1792 shows him borrowing to meet immediate obligations. In 1802 he had to sell the Gloucestershire property that had come to him on Mr Southwell's death seven years before. This must have irked Mrs Southwell, and not surprisingly she left her own possessions to her daughter, free from the 'controul, incumbrances or engagements' of her husband.

Lady Bisshopp was slow to apprehend the dangers of Sir Cecil's extravagance, not least because her own grasp of finances was none too thorough. Her greater worry, and the second threat to family concord, was the volatility of his moods – the legacy, perhaps, of a loveless childhood. A natural desire to conceal problems in her marriage makes it hard to know exactly when she became aware of this flaw in his character. Aside from one ambiguous remark there is no hint of anything amiss in the correspondence of the 1780s, but in the 1790s the painful truth emerges: her initially pleasant husband was growing unaccountable in his behaviour, losing his composure at the merest trifle, and flying into rages that frightened her. Then, just as abruptly, he would calm down and act as though nothing had happened.

Lady Bisshopp's friend Lady Stawell, whose husband neglected her for a life of selfish pleasure, offered her sympathy. 'You and I have great comfort in telling each other our grievances,' she wrote in one letter, and in another she advised her to spend some time away from Parham, 'for where one is on the spot to hear every thing that is disagreeable it does not prevent the evil but encreases it, and by absence it may wear itself out'. The writer's own situation was worse, for Lord Stawell was deliberately cruel, scolding her constantly and imprisoning her at home by depriving her of carriage and horses. She was released from her torment by an early death in 1804.

Likewise admitted to Lady Bisshopp's secret was Lady Stawell's sister Lady Bromley, who extended the same sympathy: 'I don't think I have any more to say than that I love you very much and partake of every thing that afflicts you. God bless you, we must comfort each other in these earthly trials.' One wonders how often the passionate friendships of women were intensified by conjugal woe; certainly these bonds became precious to Lady Bisshopp as she lost her esteem for her husband and spent ever more time away from him. In his quieter moments – when, in family parlance, he was 'tame' rather than 'fierce' – she could pity him, and at least he was not a cold-hearted bully like Lord Stawell. Still, his nickname 'Grumpus' suggests a more engaging sort of crosspatch than his wife and children often felt him to be.

In May 1803 hostilities with France, suspended the previous spring, were resumed. By this time both Cecil and Charles were wearing the king's uniform. In 1795 Cecil, aged twelve, had joined his father's militia as a cornet, and this early taste of soldiering made him keen to join the regular army. Four years later he entered the prestigious 1st Regiment of Foot Guards as an ensign, and it was not long before he was promoted lieutenant. He went on half-pay in September 1802 to join Rear-Admiral Sir John Borlase Warren's diplomatic mission to St Petersburg to congratulate Tsar Alexander I on his accession. On his return the following spring, he joined the 47th Regiment of Foot as a captain before exchanging back into the Guards with his former rank. The next few years offered only dull barracks duty in Windsor, but his love of army life and eagerness for preferment remained strong. In time he would have the opportunities he craved to show courage in his country's service.

His military duties kept Cecil from Parham for long periods, and although fond of his family he cherished the freedom this gave him. His letters home and a journal of 1801–1802 reveal a bluff, hearty young man with a love of the hunting field, practical jokes and all-male jollification. He enjoyed the society of women too, and his good looks and easy charm qualified him for the pleasures of flirtation. Occasionally he felt an urge to improve himself, and his chosen method was to learn German, but his application never lasted long and he did not penetrate far into the mysteries of that language. As a letter-writer Cecil had a colourful, light-hearted style and a line in self-deprecation, especially about his clumsiness and tendency to rush his fences. He readily conceded that his prose was inelegant, but was needled if reproached for this by his clever mother. 'You must not … expect from me so long or so entertaining an account as some people who are more *bright* than myself might do' is the opening of a letter to her from St Petersburg.

Sir John Warren, who did Cecil the signal favour of appointing him to his suite, was celebrated for a string of bold naval actions against the French. He had a tenuous family connection with the Bisshopps, but the real bond was the friendship of his wife Caroline and Lady Bisshopp. In Russia Lady Warren took Cecil under her wing and was sorry when he had to go home in case of renewed war with France.

CAROLINE, LADY WARREN TO LADY BISSHOPP
ST PETERSBURG, 13 APRIL 1803
… I shall sadly miss his gay good humoured face, and I told him yesterday that I hoped he never would forget the value of good and discreet conduct, for that he left us and *this place* with the greatest applause possible from all parties, Russian, French and English, and that he had not once either said or done the least thing that Sir John or I could disapprove. I told him that I hoped it would act as a spur to him upon all occasions, having conducted himself so well for 7 months. Poor dear, he took this parting sermon very kindly indeed, and, as I said in my last, he only requires your kind advice to make a very good figure in life, just for a year or two more to be with you or some one like me that he has confidence and regard for …

Meanwhile Charles had joined the navy as a midshipman at the age of twelve. It was a tough existence, eating and sleeping below deck and enduring the same privations as ordinary seamen, but a boy of his background could expect to become an officer in due course, and his family placed great faith in the connection with Sir John Warren, who as a naval man could do even more for him than for Cecil. By the beginning of 1798 Charles was serving aboard HMS *Canada* with Sir John, and in March he was present when she seized an enemy cargo worth £40,000. Such 'prizes' were every sailor's dream because ship and cargo were sold by an agent and most of the proceeds disbursed to the captors. In October Charles saw action in the Battle of Tory Island, off the coast of County Donegal, in which Sir John acquitted himself so skilfully that it became known as 'Warren's Action'. As with Cecil a few years afterwards, Lady Warren was all solicitude for her friend's son.

CAROLINE, LADY WARREN TO LADY BISSHOPP
PLYMOUTH, 1 JANUARY 1798

... I can give you an excellent account of Charles, who is spoken highly of by every one. Really it is remarkable how much he takes to the profession and pleases all parties. I sent for him on Xmas day and made him say his catechism to Miss Hatfield and took him to church *in a motherly way*. There is now a school master on board, and I have ordered that he shall attend Charles for an hour every morning, added to which I shall put him under the care of Mr Goodwin the chaplain ...

Indeed Charles is a most fortunate boy to have fallen into the best society that ever was found in a ship, as all the midshipmen are very steady and very fond of him. He is the youngest, and of course the favorite. The purser Mr Pryn and I take care about his cloaths etc. There is so much to learn in fitting out the ship that I very seldom see him, as that would be needless attention to take him from his duty. Every morning at 9 he sets out in a boat with the order book under his arm to copy out the several orders from the admiral's ship, which is good practice both as to writing and spelling. In short, I dont think he can be in a better way than he is in every respect, and it is a great comfort to me to see it so, not only because I love you, but really for the boy's sake ...

As Charles approached manhood it was clear he would never be as handsome as his brother, and Lady Bisshopp's concern that he would not grow tall was borne out. He was still overweight, but not sensitive about it and happy to apply his nickname 'Pancakes' to himself. In 1801 he sailed in Sir John's flagship HMS *Renown* to the Mediterranean, where she joined a squadron that cruised around in quest of French ships. The letters he sent his mother from Port Mahon, Valletta, Naples and Alexandria are almost devoid of anecdote but reveal an affectionate, curiously gentle nature. He wanted her to be proud of him and informed her minutely of his successes. However, when she urged him to secure extended leave and seek the polish of good society at home he countered that the only way of 'getting forward' in the navy was to remain on active service. Charles was in earnest about his career, and in his quiet, steadfast way as ambitious as Cecil. In early 1803 he passed his examination to become a lieutenant and was promoted the same year.

Harriet was growing up fast, and more than ever the delight of her family. In looks, accomplishments and manners she was a paragon, and if her little girl's cleverness had not ripened into mental powers to match her mother's this was hardly noticed. To the elements of her education she added the skills required to alter clothes and beautify the home. These she picked up very easily, prompting a teasing remark from the friend who taught her to paint velvet: 'I am not surprised that you succeed so well with the velvet. I always told you you would, but you are so accustomed to do everything well that you were quite astonished that you did not *excel* your *mistress at the first lesson.*' Above all, Harriet was a talented musician. She enjoyed playing the harp and the pianoforte for an audience, and her singing was so good that it remained a staple of evening parties long after it had ceased to be the adornment of a pretty young woman.

Her brothers were very proud of her. Charles called her a 'sovereign queen' who outshone any finery she wore and told her that he and Cecil believed her character to be close to perfection. Lady Bisshopp was filled with joy and, as her mother had done with her, she told Harriet how much she admired her. Her letters still contained titbits of general information, advice on how to behave and spelling corrections, for she was a born pedagogue, but very early she treated her daughter as a confidante, even on the subject of her volatile father. 'Poor Grumpus is quite tame,' she wrote to the sixteen-year-old from London, 'and commends his dinner every day.' Harriet more or less ran the household when her mother was away and received her directions about servants and neighbours. Naturally she looked after Katherine, and at seventeen she was asked to see that Charles, three years older, cleaned his teeth daily while at home on leave. She was, her mother told her, 'the woman of business'.

For all the strains in their parents' marriage the girls had an agreeable childhood. Sometimes they were taken to London to see Cecil and Mrs Southwell or to attend children's balls, but mostly they were at Parham, where Katherine finished her education. Her accomplishments were similar to Harriet's. Both were fluent in French and also learnt Italian, for Anna Tonelli had repaid the family for their hospitality by corresponding in Italian with Lady

Bisshopp, who then taught it to her daughters. Katherine drew well and, like Harriet, was adept at painting velvet; Charles said he would commission her to decorate the cabin of the first French 74-gunner he captured. She was probably a less gifted musician, but remained keen enough to learn the guitar and the organ as an adult. Together the sisters kept a musical notebook with scores for an 'Aria Napolitana', the 'Duke of Devonshire's Waltz', 'Rousseau's Dream' and a 'Hungarian Air'.

Aside from literature, which they liked equally, Katherine was a more avid reader than Harriet. 'You cannot think how agreeable and intelligent dear Kate is become,' Lady Bisshopp told Harriet. 'She not only reads, but really thinks it over, and compares and remembers, and takes down all the different historians that give accounts of the same event.' Her strongest interest was in the history of art. 'I often wished for dear Kate beside me, when viewing the pictures at the Louvre,' wrote Lady Warren from Paris. 'She would have explained them all historically to me.' She was fascinated too by architecture, and it became a family jest to speak of the house she would build once she had studied enough examples to fix her taste, and of course made a sufficiently splendid marriage.

While Harriet and her mother were of above average height, Katherine grew decidedly tall, and as she was still thin she began to stoop. Moreover her colour was too high, and Harriet joked that she looked as if she had been dropped in a rouge box. Lady Bisshopp was not one to countenance such imperfections in a daughter: 'Kate is very well, only her shoulders are grown round and her nose red for want of my drilling, but when I get her to myself I hope to set all to rights.' She drilled away, and the shaping hand of nature did the rest: the ungainly girl became a graceful, slender beauty, with her long legs – the 'belles jambes' of family letters – displayed to advantage in the simple muslin gowns of the day. Most striking of all, framed by almost jet-black hair, were the penetrating green eyes that gave rise to her feline pseudonyms. 'I do not think it easy to improve upon your eyes, sans compliment!' Harriet told her. Katherine was the more intrepid of the sisters; both learnt to ride, but in adulthood Harriet shunned this and other forms of exercise, whereas Katherine enjoyed all outdoor pursuits open to women.

Lady Bisshopp had done her best by her children and was rewarded by the love they all felt for 'Snugest', as they called her.

Her marriage, on the other hand, grew more and more frustrating. Sir Cecil's refusal to attend to his finances turned into a refusal to do anything very much, and she took on responsibilities that ought to have fallen to him. In particular he neglected to seek the patronage that his sons' military careers required. After some badgering he had petitioned the Duke of York for Cecil's Guards commission, but subsequent bids to bring the young soldier to notice came from his mother, which was awkward as her correspondents must have wondered why they were not writing to the head of the family. Charles fared no better, and Lady Warren delicately pointed out that Sir Cecil, who was after all an MP, might do more for him than rely on her husband's good offices, on which there were other claims.

Sir Cecil's temper grew worse. He remained capable of kindness and warmth, but his bad patches were fearful and, mortifyingly, he now flared up in front of acquaintances, even strangers. At Parham the atmosphere was heavy, as Cecil, visiting on leave in early 1802, noted in his journal: 'Found Snugest, Grandmamma and the Little Me at tea, Grumpus was setting by himself in the end parlour.' A week later he came again and saw the same arrangement 'in consequence of a scuffle between the parties'. In the same year Lady Warren commiserated with her friend for a life 'full of every vexation and perplexity that any woman ever suffered'. The force of this statement makes us wonder how much we do not know. Did Sir Cecil, in addition to shouting and storming round the house, sometimes raise his hand to his wife? If so, pride and reticence prevented the survival of written testimony.

It was fortunate that Lady Bisshopp had her children to cheer her, and soon one of them provided some very pleasant news. In January 1804 Cecil wrote to her in mock bafflement of a rumour that he was to marry Lady Charlotte Townshend. There had been whisperings at balls, he said, and apparently even the queen had gossiped about it. He did not remain coy for long; the story had substance, promises were exchanged, and in February Sir Cecil and George Townshend, Earl of Leicester opened a correspondence about the financial settlement. The Townshends were an old Norfolk family and Lady Charlotte, the earl's eldest daughter and a pretty, kind-hearted girl, was a fine catch. Cecil's friends, on hearing of the proposed alliance, congratulated him heartily.

However, the lovers had to be patient. Sir Cecil's initial terms were so little to Lord Leicester's liking that he dismissed them out of hand; to do otherwise, he told his daughter, would injure his fortune and her sisters' prospects. The fathers stalled for a year and then inched towards an accommodation through a thicket of trusts, mortgages and jointures. At last a deed was drawn up and the couple were married in April 1805. The Bisshopps presented them with a Worcester dinner service and offered Parham for the honeymoon, from where the bride sent a letter to her mother-in-law: 'If you think me very idle in not writing more frequently you must blame dear Cecil, as unless I write over night he never allows me to ever think of a letter till the post bag is ready to depart, but he is such a good creature I must not complain and I must own myself a very happy mortal in belonging to him.'

The newly-weds settled in London and Cecil resumed his military duties, now at St James's Palace. Lady Bisshopp and Mrs Southwell grew fond of Charlotte, and her special friend in the family was Harriet, to whom she wrote chirrupy letters with social and domestic news and information about flower painting, the restringing of a harp, and the pattern for a cap. A few months in Shropshire in 1806 gave her and Cecil a taste for country life, and they searched for a house of their own in Sussex. Before long they settled on Holmbush, not far from Horsham. The Parham and Holmbush households visited each other often, and Charlotte's place in the Bisshopps' hearts was confirmed.

Charles had been unable to attend his brother's wedding, for he was still patrolling the seas in search of enemy vessels, but he received reports of it and at the same time of Harriet's entry into the fashionable world, wearing a bracelet he had sent her as she danced merrily through her first Season. She was, said her sister-in-law, in a fair way to becoming 'the most dissipated young lady in London'. Meanwhile Katherine, who idolised her as much as the rest of the family, willingly ceded the limelight and amused herself with childish things. She had a passion for collecting and cataloguing, and owned a cabinet of curiosities to which Charles promised to contribute some foreign items.

1807

In July Sir Cecil was honoured with the task of welcoming Princess Charlotte of Wales, the eleven-year-old only child of the

Prince of Wales, to Worthing, where she was to take a seawater cure. Leading his yeomanry troop, he met the royal party in the village of Findon and escorted it into the festooned streets of the town to the merry strains of two volunteer force bands. A few weeks later, just before the princess's departure, Lady Bisshopp and Katherine visited her and her governess Lady de Clifford, who was Lady Bisshopp's aunt. Harriet was unwell and stayed at home.

LADY BISSHOPP TO MRS SOUTHWELL
PARHAM, 2 SEPTEMBER 1807
My dearest Mother – I begin my letter by informing you that four partridges left Parham this morning to wait upon you in London. They ought to be carried to your house tonight, but if by any chance they should not be arrived you will send to the White Bear in Piccadilly ...

Last Saturday, Katherine and I went to Worthing to call on Lady de Clifford, as they were to go away on Monday. Lady de Clifford received us by herself, and sent word to Princess Charlotte who was upstairs with her sub governess Mrs Udney that we were come to wait upon her, and she seemed very glad to see us as I found she had a list of people who were to be admitted and that we were among the number. I like the little girl very much, and the more as she is quite unassuming and playful in her manner like any other child. She is very short of her age, and they hoped bathing would make her grow. I think she has a very pretty countenance but Lady de C. seemed to be quite glad I thought so, as she said the mob often said she was a plain child, and indeed she has no cherry cheeks to attract admiration but is very well made, and I think will be a pretty woman ...

In September Cecil and Charlotte came from Holmbush, and after they left Sir Cecil and Lady Bisshopp set off with their daughters, servants and pets for Worthing, intending to follow the princess's example and seek the benefits of sea air and saltwater bathing. We know that this stay proved disappointing from Harriet's journal, which she now began in earnest. The house they took was unsatisfactory, the weather was poor, and the salubrity of the sea failed to make itself felt.

HARRIET'S JOURNAL

25 September. – We set out for Worthing, Mamma and Anne in the post chaise, Kate and I on horseback … Rode on to the top of Washington Hill, when we put the pug in the carriage, but after a little while it rained so fast that we were obliged to get into the chaise and make George ride Betty and lead Pesy. When we arrived at Worthing Brown was not with us so we were obliged to send George back after him. Our house is no. 1 Collonade, very small. Grumpus arrived soon after us in the curricle. Kate and I slept together in a very stuffy little room. The other servants came in the cart.

26 September. – Kate went out to bathe in the sea. Mama, Kate and I breakfasted in the parlour, walked to Stanford and begged Mrs Stanford to ask Mrs Lindupp to move the bed out of the second drawing room, which Grumpus has taken possession of for his dressing room. Kate and I are to sleep in a front room and have the room we slept in last night for a dressing room.

27 September. – My father, Mama and Kate went to Broadwater Church. My head was so bad as to prevent my going, so I staid at home with the dogs … Kate came home in the chariot from church with Papa, she had fainted and been ill. He returned to hear the sermon. I gave Kate some cold meat and a glass of port wine as the best thing I could think of to do her good. She had hardly eat any breakfast … Dr Witter called on us and went with us to Spooners Library, where we read in the newspapers that Peter Burrell is to espouse Miss Drummond of Perth. I am glad she has not got Lord James. Papa subscribed to the library and we brought home Mrs Rowes Letters, and Brydones Tour through Sicily and Malta.

28 September. – Kate went down to the sea but it was so rough the women would not bathe her.[1] After breakfast I tuned my harp and wrote to my grandmother … Walked on the sands with Kate, Janett and Anne and the dogs. I went out in my grey velvet pelisse, but finding it too hot came home again and put on my muslin cloak.

29 September. – A very rainy day, therefore we could not go out all day. Last night Kate and I walked up and down in the front of the house for some time. Snugest was ill with a pain in her face and teeth. Dined upon goose it being Michaelmas Day.

Played on my harp. In the evening we went to Spooners for some books, and got some trash to amuse us for the night.

These meagre pleasures were cut short five days later by the news that Cecil's wife Charlotte, after a very short illness, had died of scarlet fever. The Bisshopps were dumbstruck. 'A short fortnight ago,' wrote Harriet, 'she left us blooming in health and flourishing in youth and the most luxuriant beauty. Who could have immagined that she was to return a corpse in a few days? To Cecil she was the most tender best of wives, to her sisters a friend that nothing can ever replace, to me and to dear Kate and to Snugest an affectionate and faithful friend.' Charlotte had died at her father's house in Richmond, Surrey, and Cecil was comforted there by Charles, who was on leave and rushed to his brother's side.

Letters sped between Richmond and Parham, where the Bisshopps had returned, full of expressions of grief and arrangements for Charlotte's funeral in Parham Church and interment in the family vault. Harriet covered shoes for herself and Katherine in black velvet and their mother prepared a room for Cecil so that he did not have to occupy the one he and his wife had lately shared. Harriet felt Charlotte's death as a warning for herself: 'Oh my God let this awful lesson of the uncertainty of human happiness be of use to me, and prove a salutary example when I am run away with the vanities of the world. May I reflect on the almost sudden death of my sweet beloved, lamented Charlotte and be better for this sad affliction.'

Then came more bad news.

HARRIET'S JOURNAL
9 October. – In the evening Kate and I walked out in the pleasure ground. As we were returning home we met Mama, who told us that Charles was just come alone. I was exceedingly frightened and thought he was come to tell us Cecil was ill. However he came out of the house and walking with us up and down on the gravel, and told us that a friend had sent him word that his ship, the Muros, was ready to sail and was to leave England the first fair wind. He received this account at Richmond. She is bound to Halifax or if unable to get thither, she is to go to Bermudas and from thence to the West Indies. Charles has long wished to go to the Leeward Islands. As there is no preferment to be obtained for seamen at home it is quite necessary for those who wish to get on

in their profession to go out. Charles is first lieut. of the Muros, she is the Alcide, the prize he brought in himself.

When he found it would be impossible for him to take the appointment and stay with his brother, he wished to give up going and remain to comfort poor Cecil, but Cecil seeing how desirable it is that Charles should go sent him off to Portsmouth to see the state of the case himself. When he arrived there he found the Muros waiting for a fair wind, and finding he had not any time to spare he came to Parham to see and consult with us what he should do. We were obliged to perform the hard task of persuading him to leave us, perhaps for ever! He dined and after drinking tea with us took leave of us all. I cut off some of his hair. He said he should return if possible to us on Sunday and attend dear Charlotte's remains. It is a sad trial to our poor dear mother and indeed to us all to part with him just now, especially as we have so lately and nearly felt how uncertain it is when we part with our friends whether we may ever meet again. I felt so overcome with grief and pain that I retired to my room and went to bed very early.

The next day, Saturday, Charlotte's hearse arrived, accompanied by two mourning coaches and other carriages for her family. Cecil followed on Sunday for the funeral. He controlled his feelings during the service, but his resolution failed him at the sight of the freshly dug grave and he embraced Harriet in a flood of tears. When he departed the rest of the family returned to Worthing, where the girls tried to cheer themselves up by ordering new dresses, but Harriet was tearful and irritable and Lady Bisshopp exhausted after having made all the funeral arrangements and written countless letters. Sir Cecil, who had done next to nothing, for once led a more sociable life than his wife and daughters.

Charles had not attended the funeral, and his family could only assume HMS *Muros* had already sailed. Indeed she had, though on the first day adverse winds prevented her clearing the Isle of Wight, from where Charles wrote his last letter on English soil. He thought Halifax, Nova Scotia and Bermuda would be his first ports of call, followed by Jamaica, a good base for the disruption of Spanish trade with Cuba. Letters would take a long time to arrive from these places, and the Bisshopps knew they would have to wait patiently for news. They did so at Parham, having decided to spend the winter there after completing their profitless stay in Worthing.

On 2 December Lady Bisshopp told her mother that Katherine had just had a birthday: 'Katherine desires to tell you with her love and duty that she was sixteen yesterday, and hopes dear Granny drank her health in a dish of coffee.'

1808

Mrs Southwell had been a widow for thirteen years and during that time her life had revolved around her daughter and grandchildren, the 'sweet loves' as she called them. She stayed at Parham for weeks or months at a stretch, and on their visits to London the family always saw her. When she was alone she wrote chatty letters to Lady Bisshopp and to Charles, who had been in her charge as an infant and remained strongly attached to her. In 1805 he said he was glad she enjoyed 'such a flow of spirits'; indeed the only serious trial of her old age was the deterioration of her eyesight, which made reading and writing difficult. However, in early 1808 her health declined fast, and she died in London at the beginning of April with her beloved daughter at her bedside.

A month later death struck again. As expected the *Muros* had sailed for Halifax, from where Charles wrote that his voyage had been pleasant so far but that he was keen to move on to warmer climes. His convoy accompanied a ship laden with Canadian timber to Bermuda, and by the middle of winter he was cruising off Havana. In a letter of early April that she did not live to read, Charles told his grandmother: 'I am thank God in the best possible health and spirits, chasing Spaniards every day in the finest weather you can possibly conceive.' Then a mishap occurred during an attack on a Spanish battery near Havana.

CHARLES BISSHOPP TO LADY BISSHOPP
NASSAU, NEW PROVIDENCE, 7 APRIL 1808
My dearest Mother – It is with considerable concern that I find myself unable to date this letter from on board ship as usual, the Muros having unhappily been wrecked on the coast of Cuba about a fortnight ago. The circumstances under which the ship was lost did not in the least endanger our lives, and the Spaniards were not active enough to collect a sufficient force to make us prisoners, but allowed us not only to escape, but likewise to set

our ship on fire, which we did so effectually that it burnt for three days notwithstanding all their endeavours to put it out. We shaped our course with our boats for the Florida shore, where having got hold of a Spanish prize we found our way here. I am ordered with fifty of the men to Jamaica, for which place I sail to morrow ...

It is understood that all the officers will be under the necessity of returning to England. Thus shall I have the pleasure of seeing you at least three years sooner than I expected. I long to get to Jamaica as I shall then receive whatever letters you may have written to me, for I have not received a single one since I left England. I have written to you repeatedly, so much so that I expect I have fully recovered my lost credit in that particular ... I hope my dearest Mother that you have enjoyed the most perfect health since I left you, and as I dreamt the other night I saw poor dear Harriet perfectly well I conclude that it is so. Give her and dearest Kate a thousand loves from me, I beg my duty and regards to my father. Believe me my dearest Mother that into whatever region I may steer my course I shall remain ever most affectionately yours

Charles Cecil Bisshopp

Charles sailed to Jamaica in a government schooner, and on the way he played a leading role in the capture of a French privateer, the *General Ferrand*, his largest prize to date and a feat that brought him an official commendation. His joy was short-lived, for on arriving in Jamaica he showed symptoms of yellow fever, and although he rallied briefly it was obvious he would not recover. After an illness of just three days he died on 10 May. 'I feel how vain it is,' one of his senior officers wrote to Sir Cecil, 'to preach consolation to a parent in the situation in which Lady Bisshopp and you will be placed on the receipt of this letter; but let me assure you that my departed friend was attended by the most eminent physician in the island; that he had two excellent nurses who watched him from the first to the last moment of his existence; and that his sufferings appeared to be alleviated by my personal visits.'

Charles was buried in Kingston. His pocket watch and a lock of his hair were sent to Parham, but these items and the sad tidings that accompanied them did not arrive until the end of June. Because of a lack of letters in the ensuing weeks we can only imagine the family's grief. At least they could reflect that devotion to duty, not just bad luck, had curtailed Charles's life: he had shown great bravery in the attack on the *General Ferrand* and personally seized her letter of marque (a government licence to take enemy prizes), and the resulting exhaustion, together with the extreme heat, had deprived him of the strength to fight off the fever. It must have pained them, though, that he could not be laid to rest in the Parham vault. He had loved his home, as his mother reminded Harriet two decades later: 'Dear Pancakes used to return after his different travels still saying he never saw any place in any country like Parham! I hope I shall not make you melancholy.' Instead a memorial tablet was made for the church honouring him as a 'gallant officer, and amiable and excellent young man'.

The death of Charles made the news that Cecil's regiment, the 1st Foot Guards, was to join the force sent to fight the French in Portugal and Spain even more ominous than it would otherwise have been, and he received what he called 'agonising letters' from his mother. After years of kicking his heels he was eager for active service, but he was now his parents' only son and everyone knew the operation in the Peninsula was hazardous. It was, therefore, a welcome distraction from gloomy thoughts when Princess Charlotte, whom Lady Bisshopp and Katherine had seen in Worthing the previous year, came to Parham during a stay at Bognor. She dined with the family and was driven round the park, and later the chair on which she had sat was stitched with her coronet.

Neither of the deaths of 1808 is recorded in Harriet's journal, which she had neglected since the previous autumn; nor is the marriage – her own – that gave the Bisshopps some much-needed cheer. It is unclear when she first met the Hon. Robert Curzon, but he visited Parham in September 1807 and the following February Lady Warren alluded to their courtship. Obstacles there were none, for the two families were equally delighted at the prospect of their union. 'I can hardly believe my good fortune when I feel that I shall possess such a treasure,' Robert wrote to Lady Bisshopp. 'Will you have the goodness to say every thing kind and affectionate to her for me. I want words to express what I feel.'

Robert's father Assheton Viscount Curzon was a fairly new peer. Born in 1729 as a baronet's second son, he sat for many years as MP for Clitheroe, a position he used to no other end than to press for his own ennoblement. He was given a barony in 1794 and a viscountcy in 1802, though an application for an earldom was turned down. He was married and widowed three times, and Robert was the son of his second wife Dorothy, a sister of the first Earl Grosvenor. The heir to Lord Curzon's title was Penn Curzon, a grandson from his first marriage, but Robert too was well placed: he had taken over the representation of Clitheroe in 1796 and was the heir to Hagley Hall in Staffordshire, where he lived with his father and his unmarried sister Elizabeth. The Bisshopps knew the Curzons well, and Lady Bisshopp's friends Lady Bromley and Lady Stawell, the latter deceased, were Lord Curzon's daughters by his first marriage and thus Robert's half-sisters.

Although thirty-four years old to Harriet's twenty, Robert was as much loved as loving. Indeed a mature husband, who promised to continue the mixture of adoration and guidance she had received from her mother, suited her perfectly. It is to her credit that she was no more spoilt by praise than Lady Bisshopp had been; instead, in keeping with her less forceful nature, it bred in her a tender meekness and a desire to please that Robert would turn into rewarding dispositions. He was no romantic hero: a shortish, fair-skinned man of average build with blue eyes, a small, thin mouth and a rather long nose. His abilities were unremarkable and his personality a little stolid, and Katherine was later surprised at how much Harriet missed him when he was away from her; but there never was a kinder, gentler man, or one more devoted to the woman at his side.

The fathers soon agreed terms. Lord Curzon gave Robert £1,000 a year and Sir Cecil gave Harriet £6,000 as a lump sum, an unspecified allowance and a small house in Welbeck Street, Marylebone – rather to the surprise of his son, who remembered how niggardly he had been with him. Engagements at this time were generally short, and this one might have been shorter but for the tardiness of lawyers in sending papers to be signed. While they waited for a date to be fixed Robert wrote love letters to Harriet, of which the sole survivor, sent from London, adopts the fond but rational tone that one senses she liked best: 'It is not agreeable when ones body is in one place and ones mind in another. My mind was with my sweet H., I almost imagined I could hear her soft voice and light step tripping across the hall as I sat after my solitary meal. How is the dear head and beautiful ankle? Not strained again

I trust. It seems quite an age since we parted and will be another till we meet again.'

The wedding took place on 14 October in Parham Church; the Bishop of Chichester officiated and the bride, resplendent in white satin and lace, was the admiration of all beholders. Cecil was absent, having shipped out to Spain, but several members of the Curzon family made the journey to Sussex. Like her brother in 1805, Harriet had Parham for her honeymoon, and from there she despatched 'famous accounts of herself' to her mother in London, while Robert sent Sir Cecil his 'most grateful thanks for having bestowed upon me a being so perfect as Harriet'. Sir Cecil, who had been affable throughout, replied graciously: 'I do assure you *though I was always proud of Miss* I am perfectly satisfied with having bestowed her upon you, and feel quite sure you will long be happy together.'

Thanks to her daughter, Lady Bisshopp's 'year of sorrow' held its share of joy. But once the excitement of the wedding had died down she felt a little lonely. Charles was dead, Harriet married and Cecil in Spain, so only Katherine was still with her. 'God bless you,' she wrote to Cecil, 'I often think of your dear merry face. We miss you here very much, and every time the door opens I seem to expect one of my dear absent children.' It was not easy to correspond with Cecil; some letters went in the diplomatic bag, others were carried by fellow officers, but a few still went astray. Those Lady Bisshopp received only amplified her concern, filled as they were with long marches, torrential rain, dirty billets, appalling food and plagues of fleas, but Cecil scorned these hardships: 'I never was in better health and find that campaigning agrees very well with me.' He was a soldier to his fingertips, and relished the rapid changes of scene and the comradeship of his fellow officers and men. The only thing lacking was contact with the enemy, and this came when his regiment joined the army of Sir John Moore in retreat towards Corunna.

After Harriet's marriage, Katherine, who had rarely been separated from her and had even shared a bedroom with her at Parham, was downcast. 'I shall do all I can to comfort her for the loss of her angelic sister,' her mother wrote, though she too could barely pass an hour without thinking of her departed favourite. However, a visit to Hagley was planned for December and before that the Bisshopps went to Oxford, where there were many fine buildings for Katherine to admire. Her impressions are contained in the journal she now commenced.

KATHERINE'S JOURNAL
5 November. – Mamma wrote to Dr Nott[2] requesting him to breakfast with us and show us Oxford afterwards. Soon after eight he came to the King's Arms where we were, and as Mama was not dressed I went down to him. He said he would return at 11 to show us All Souls but was engaged till that hour. After breakfast Papa was not ready, Snugest and I desired a man from the inn to show us the way to Christ Church College. On our way we looked in at Oriel College and the man was very stupid, but fortunately I had an account of Oxford. We proceeded thro' Canterbury Gateway in to Peckwater Court, which I did not admire, to the Great Quadrangle at Christ Church. It would be quite beautiful if it was not for the heavy stone balustrade at the top. Mama and I went up the beautiful stairs and looked in at the hall thro' the open doors. This is the finest room in Oxford but did not appear to me so very large, I suppose because we did not go in. The ceiling is in drops like the hall at Parham ...

We then returned to the inn where Mr Nott soon joined us, but unfortunately Grumpuss was out of the way so we were obliged to go without him. S[nugest] and I proceeded with Dr Nott to All Souls and in the way Snugest and he settled that Oxford was much more beautiful than Rome. I never saw anything so pretty as the outside of this delightful college, the library is perfection 200 feet long, 30 wide, 40 high.

Mr Nott showed us the Pentatuke in Hebrew, the Koran on the bark of a tree, the Sanscrit manuscripts which are (I believe) an account of the Hindoo wars, an Illuminated Persian missal which he said was a very bad specimen and the famous Persian epic poem by [Ferdowsi].[3] Just as we were going out Papa arrived ...

We afterwards proceeded to the Radcliff Library, which contains nothing but books of medicine and consequently there are but few. In the principle room are two handsome Roman candlesticks of stone. I suppose they are 6 or 7 feet high, they were given by Sir Roger Newdigate and found in the ruins of Emperor Hadrian's palace at Tivoli. Mamma, Dr Nott and myself went up upon the leads to see the view of the town from that point. It is the finest thing I ever saw. Papa did not come up because the staircase is so narrow and like a ladder. We then took leave of Mr Nott.

They then had a chance to see Harriet and Robert. The young couple were making such slow progress to Hagley that the Bisshopps had caught up with them. They converged at Barrington Park, Gloucestershire, the home of the Dutton family, who were related to the Curzons by marriage.

KATHERINE'S JOURNAL
5 November. – We changed horses at Whitney, and Snugest and I were in a great fuss for fear of it being too late for dinner as Mr Dutton is very particular and does not like waiting. At length it grew quite dark and we arrived at Barrington after having been through seven gates within the space of about half a mile. We found dear Little Me ready dressed in the hall waiting to receive us. We were soon joined by Mr Dutton, who was very happy to see us and said we were not to dine until six o'clock and that we should just have time to dress ... Anne could not find any thing so I was obliged to put on an old worn out gown half way up my legs and arms. How that one came to be uppermost I cannot conceive. I was obliged to go into the drawing room alone as Mama was ready before me so in I marched, shook hands with many and Mr Curzon. He immediately asked me which of the colleges at Oxford I liked best. I said All Souls, which most fortunately happened to be the one he admired the most. We went into dinner, the house delightful. In the evening tea, prayers, and while every body played at cards I sat on the couch and talked to dear Harriet. Supper brought in and we went to bed. I slept with Mama, a very comfortable room on the ground floor on the right of the hall, Papa opposite.

Next day the Duttons took their guests to an ancient church 'colder than anything ever was' to hear a hymn in honour of Robert and Harriet and then to a paper mill on the nearby River Windrush. At luncheon Lady Bisshopp was taken with a fit of giddiness and had to lie on the sofa, and after dinner the men fell asleep, leaving the women to their own devices. Two days later they all drove the short distance to Sherborne House, belonging to the titled branch of the Dutton family. Only sixteen, Katherine was already quite pert in her remarks on those she met: Lady Sherborne she found 'rather a handsome woman with plenty of rouge and powder and frizzy hair'; her daughter Miss Dutton had a 'wonderful long chin'; and Mr Naper, another relation, was a 'stupid dapper youth'. Mr Naper liked her more than she liked him, and at Barrington he held skeins of cotton for her, but so clumsily that he kept dropping them.

The sisters contrived to spend many hours alone at Barrington and Sherborne. Then the Curzons continued to Hagley and the Bisshopps visited Kirtlington Park, the Oxfordshire seat of Sir Henry Watkin Dashwood.

KATHERINE TO HARRIET
KIRTLINGTON PARK, 17 NOVEMBER 1808
My dearest Harriet – I was prevented writing to you yesterday as I had intended as we went to Blenheim, but today I will give you an account of myself ever since I have been here. We found Anne Dashwood very happy to see us, *very smart* and very agreeable as she always is. A Mr Annesley staying in the house, he is a clergyman and brother to the man who lives at Bletchington near here, a very agreeable man. This is a most beautiful place, the outside of the house is modern, with steps up to the door something like the centre of Kedleston, and two low wings, which form the offices. The park is beautiful and the country round it frightful which sets it off very much. You come in to a large hall, to the left is a library, a large room 20 feet high with a coved ceiling and books from the ground as high as the doors. The next room is the drawing room, which is full of pictures, a Rubens wife, a beautiful portrait of Lady Dashwood by Sir Joshua Reynolds etc. The ceiling painted to represent monkeys hunting, which is very comical. The next room is the dining room, then a great saloon without a floor which has never been finished, a billiard room much in the same state, then Sir H.'s dressing room and two little rooms which bring you again into the hall. There are two great staircases exactly alike on each side of the hall. When I build a house it shall certainly be like this in the inside; the outside I think very ugly ...

Katherine was very taken with Blenheim Palace, especially the library and Capability Brown's park with its famous cascade. Back at Kirtlington she was introduced to a Mr Hulse, 'son to

Sir Something and Lady Hulse who give balls', a short, fat man with a disagreeable manner. She was placed next to him at dinner on two successive evenings and complained that he plagued her to death.

The Bisshopps did more sightseeing in Oxford and then meandered on. In Birmingham they followed a group of Quakers to an assembly room and heard a lecture by the educational reformer Joseph Lancaster. They also went to a factory and were shown the processes of plating knives, casting medals and setting false stones. Visits to factories and workshops in Birmingham's jewellery quarter were popular among well-heeled travellers, and manufacturers turned the practice to account by ending the tours they gave in the adjoining shops, where their guests could buy specimens of the wares they had just seen being made. In one of these shops Sir Cecil bought Katherine a silver brooch in the shape of a racehorse for her seventeenth birthday. The following afternoon they arrived at Hagley and 'found Harriet looking beautiful'. Some of the neighbouring families had been invited, and the daylight hours of the next two weeks were spent walking, riding and driving out.

Aside from a few inconsequential jottings Katherine now abandoned her journal for several years, but the sisters' lives are amply documented in her letters to Harriet and in Harriet's journal, which she resumed in the autumn of 1809 and kept sporadically for the next decade.

1809

Hagley Hall was located near the market town of Rugeley in central Staffordshire.[4] Contemporary engravings and later photographs show a house in a medley of styles, with gables, bays, rooflines and chimneys in jaunty profusion, facing downhill and set in well-wooded parkland. It was probably built in about 1620 by the judge Sir Richard Weston, and passed through several hands before being purchased by Assheton Curzon in 1753. He constructed a new stable block and remodelled the house, adding a south wing with an octagonal drawing room. He also improved the grounds and hired unemployed miners to carve a network of grottoes, including a chapel, out of the red sandstone bedrock. Like Parham, it was a house with a strong hold on the affections of its occupants.

Given the friendship between the Bisshopps and the Curzons, Harriet had almost certainly seen Hagley before her marriage. As she knew, the commanding presence there was the eighty-year-old

Lord Curzon, a firm but benevolent patriarch held by all in high esteem. His daughter Elizabeth, Robert's sister, ran the household. Other members of his large family often came to stay, including his widowed daughter Esther with her son Sir Robert Bromley, and his widowed daughter-in-law Sophia, Baroness Howe in her own right, who came with her daughter Marianne and her son Penn, Lord Curzon's grandson and heir. Not far away was Kedleston Hall, the palatial home of Nathaniel Curzon, 2nd Baron Scarsdale, who was the son of Lord Curzon's elder brother.

Harriet had been nervous about her reception by Robert's family, but they liked her exceedingly. Lady Bisshopp received a pile of glowing testimonials, and Lord Curzon wrote a letter to his daughter Esther 'full of Harriet's perfections [of] mind and body and accomplishments from one end to the other'. Nonetheless, the young bride worried about getting into 'scrapes', and when in doubt she applied to her mother: 'I am sure I never intend to do anything wrong, on the contrary I am to the greatest degree anxious to behave quite right, and as you my dearest Snugest have always done, shewing me a bright example of goodness and propriety in every way.' There were few things Lady Bisshopp liked better than giving advice, and she coached her daughter on small matters of conduct while reminding her that a married woman must look to her husband for guidance, and that her mother could only be his adjutant.

Most important for Harriet's happiness was her husband's love, and this she possessed absolutely. He showed it when they were together and expressed it in wooden but heartfelt letters when they were apart. She must have been surprised when Lady Howe told her that Robert, like all the Curzon men, was not partial to writing: 'The females of the family have engrossed all the passion for writing to themselves. I have many times wished the male part of the family liked it a *little* better than they do.' In fact Harriet received a constant stream of epistles, beginning in January 1809 when Robert went to London to attend parliament and declared his head was so full of her that he could not understand the speeches. Nor did his assiduity diminish over time: 'You are such a dear to write to me every day, which is all my delight and comfort,' Harriet told him two decades later.

After their stay at Hagley the Bisshopps travelled to Parham, stopping at Holmbush on the way. Charlotte's death had raised the question of whether the expense of the place could be justified. At first Cecil resisted giving up his home, but his mother persuaded him to sell the lease and during his absence in Spain she wound down his household.

KATHERINE TO HARRIET
HOLMBUSH, 4 JANUARY 1809

... We set out from London Monday fully intending to dine at Holmbush, but by the time we got to Crawley it was past five and so extremely foggy and the road across the forest so deep that we thought it would be better to snore at the inn than be overturned and break our necks. So there we stayed, and to my great joy there was an old *scratchy harpsichordal* piano forte on which I thrummed with great success, and found the music of Comus by Dr Arne and Handel which is charming, and a song called Grizzle Snugest was delighted with. But only conceive my dear Little Me my horror and amazement when I got up, the whole country covered with snow and not a track to be seen. However we were lugged here by four horses and two South Saxons who drove us, and arrived at 12 o'clock.

We immediately began with the help of Emery and Ann Jenkins, took down all the caricatures etc. etc. Cecil has directed all his glass to be sold, but Snugest has taken the cut glass for you as there is very little of it. It is packed up and will go to Welbeck Street directly. We have been hard at work upon all the things here, and take our departure tomorrow. Poor Snugest is tired to death with trotting about and is going to bed. I had so many things to say in my last letter I forgot to tell you how much Snugest and I were entertained with your account of Lord G. L. Gowers visit to Hagley. I wonder whether any body will ever find out what colour my peepers are. Don't you remember Mr Curzon's saying the other day they were the same as yours, while you know they are green as emeralds, the true cat hue ...

Towards the end of January news of the gallant but desperate action at Corunna reached England, and the Bisshopps waited to learn of Cecil's fate. Robert delayed his departure from London to get the latest details, but all was confusion: 'I have been on the tramp all morning to all the public offices to gain intelligence concerning the Guards. They at present know no more than what you see in the papers.' At last he found out that Cecil's regiment had distinguished itself and he himself was safe. The evacuation of 26,000 troops was chaotic, and for a while Cecil's whereabouts were uncertain. Eventually he wrote from Plymouth, and to celebrate his return the family put off their mourning for Charles.

During Cecil's months in Spain there had been some friction between him and Lady Bisshopp, for his forthright, independent nature rebelled against her fretting and interference. He saw the need to part with Holmbush, but disliked the way she made it her own concern, and unlike Charles, who had levelled the charge against himself, he strongly denied that he was a lazy correspondent. Then there were the family's requests: historic coins, current Spanish money, stained glass for Parham, an Andalusian pony for Katherine. He countered that if they looked at a map they would see he was nowhere near Andalusia, and warned them that unless they sent out Cobbett's *Political Register* with greater regularity they would get nothing. And why had he not received a piece of Harriet's wedding cake, which he wanted to share with his friends in her honour? These half-serious flashes of irritation were forgotten when the news arrived that he had escaped injury or worse at Corunna.

KATHERINE TO HARRIET
PARHAM, 30 JANUARY 1809
My dearest Harriet – You have of course by this time received Snugests letter in which she tells you we have heared from Cecil. His letter was dated the 24th and he said the Guards were to march from Portsmouth to Chatham. He should make the best of his way hither and be at Holmbush in about a week, so we expect him almost every minute. What a blessing it is he is safe, the anxiety poor dear Snugest suffered is not to be described ... Nothing could be more kind than dear Mr Curzon was, he wrote to Mamma every day to tell her all he could learn about the Guards. I suppose you are as pleased as Punch now he is returned to Hagley. Only think of poor Donald's being taken prisoner at Villa Franca. I will certainly let you know as soon as Jig arrives.

I am delighted with your Italian letter my dearest Little Me, it was so good of you to take the trouble of writing it to me.

I intend in the course of time to follow your bright example, but I fear it will be a most sad performance ...

Snugest is well enough to walk about and do every thing like any body else tho' she is extremely giddy at times when she exerts herself too much. I make her take as many pills as possible and I hope she will do well, but she has suffered so much about poor Cecil that it has thrown her back very much and brought on the giddiness again just as she was in a great measure recovering ...

We have been to wait on Mrs King and they have been here all in proper order. George King is very sprightly and agreeable and has cut off some of the *wool wig*. The Smyths have been extremely kind in sending us a letter they had received about the troops coming home before any body else knew of it, so we were obliged to go thro' the waters and thank them. We found Mrs Aldridge staying there. They all attacked me at once on different subjects, one asked after you, another after Cecil, while a third on the other side of me intreated to be informed how the roads were. This bewildered me so completely that I forgot all the pretty things I intended to have said, and as I was going home thought over all the *sprack* observations I might have made pour me faire valoire. This you know is one of the miseries.

That glory of his sex Pug is very well, but his zenith is certainly past and gone. This sad truth is confirmed more and more every day by the numerous grey hairs on his phiz ...

Mamma begs you to write in Italian de temps en temps. The only criticism she made was she thought con*chiu*deró would have been better than con*clu*deró. I inclose Cecils letter. The piano forte is safe in old Joneys house. I cannot think why he took it there, however it will now go to Welbeck Street. Kindest love to dear Mr Curzon,

Ever your most affectionate,
Katherine Annabella aux belles jambes!

KATHERINE TO HARRIET
PARHAM, 15 FEBRUARY 1809
Ten thousand thanks my dearest Little Me for the pattern of the handkerchief. My bones are to be adorned by a piece of tormented muslin in the same form, at which Anne is stitching most indefatigably.

We returned hither Monday and Cecil went to Chatham. I have not the least idea when we shall see him again as by the ill luck of his having been so long getting into any port all the other officers have got their leave before him. He is looking tolerably well and seems to have borne the fatigue better than one could have expected. He had the Opthalmia for one day only. It is settled that Holmbush is to be parted with, which is a great blessing. I am sure you will think nothing could be more kind than Snuggests going there with Cecil in the middle of the night ...

Our domestic seclusion has been interrupted by the arrival of the Hopcrafts so we are obliged to sport the proper and look civil all the evening. I had last night the happiness of entertaining young Hop for a considerable time, Snugest being gone to bed and Grumpus retired to his *usual retreat*, so I spouted politicks and shall be for ever obliged to the Spaniards for having given me such ample subjects for conversation ...

One day last week Grumpus and I rode to Fryern and found Mrs King with all her hair about her ears, at which Lady K[ing] was extremely annoyed. Grumpus told her his young ladies always kept a little comb and brush at hand, which they made use of upon the arrival of any visitor, and advised her to do the same.

Snugest says I do nothing but write to you and I cannot make her believe I have not dispatched an epistle since the Italian letter I wrote a fortnight since ...

Adieu my dearest Harriet, kindest love to Mr Curzon. I think of you all day long. Whenever you write again pray let us know what you wear, and particulars about your head and health.

Snugest desires her love. Your most affectionate

K. A. Bisshopp

Before returning to his regiment at Chatham, Cecil went to Holmbush one last time. Parting with the house was a wrench, he told Harriet, and he nearly changed his mind about selling the lease even though a buyer had been found. A few months later he learnt of the plan to send an expeditionary force to the Netherlands, ruled since 1806 as puppet state by Napoleon's brother Louis. Cecil wanted to be on the staff, and through Robert's good offices he was appointed aide-de-camp to General Thomas Grosvenor, a nephew of Robert's late mother. In July 40,000 men crossed to the swampy island of Walcheren and established a position there. Cecil was present at the siege and surrender of Flushing in the south of the island in August, but by that time British troops were succumbing to malaria and the expedition was called off.

Though disappointed with this outcome, the young guardsman had again enjoyed his campaign, and his claim that he would be glad to come home is belied by the exhilarated tone of his letters from Walcheren. On his return he found his family back at Parham after the Season, during which Katherine had been presented at court and received the attentions of a certain Mr Jevron: 'In London he was continually "taking the liberty to look in",' she told Harriet, 'and in vain I watched for the hour when he would be on the right side of the door. He outdoes Mr Mobray. I believe he must have inherited several pairs of sitting breeches!' In August the Curzons came to stay. It was an especially tender reunion for Lady Bisshopp as Harriet had just told her she was pregnant. Harriet said she hoped that if the child was a boy he would console them for the loss of Charles, and if a girl she would take after her grandmother.

In early October Cecil came home on leave, briefly making the family party complete. Then the Curzons set off on a roundabout journey back to Hagley, visiting friends along their route. For several weeks they stayed with the Duttons at Barrington Park, which was astir with preparations for a ball to celebrate the 49th anniversary of George III's accession.

HARRIET'S JOURNAL

25 October. – I was awakened early in the morning by the ringing of bells, which continued with little interruption the whole of the day. I did not go to church with the rest of the party. Mr and Mrs Dutton gave a dinner to all the charity children of Barrington and the poor of the parish. In the evening the servants and tenants had a ball and supper in the house. They danced in the dining room, which was decorated with red and white roses and laurels in wreaths and festoons, and the front of the house illuminated. The ball was opened by Mary and Mr Curzon, Mr Dutton and Mrs Ireland, who came with the Dr^5 early in the evening. I did not dance of course but amused myself with looking on. Supper was laid out in the hall. On the table were placed some coloured transparent lamps, with God save the King in large letters on them, and stuck round with laurels, which had a very pretty effect, and all the ornamental dishes, such as tarts etc. had G. R. on the top. I left the company at supper about eleven o'clock and went to bed, but I understand the dancing was kept up till five o'clock next morning.

At Barrington Harriet received a deluge of letters from Katherine and Lady Bisshopp, and was as prolific herself. Happy though she was, she missed her mother: 'I wish I could transport myself now and then to see you, and then hop back to my Bob.' Lady Bisshopp said she wanted to kiss her 'white snout', and Katherine plied her with news and questions. In the following letter she uses Harriet's new nickname, probably derived from an unflattering item of clothing.

KATHERINE TO HARRIET
PARHAM, 15 NOVEMBER 1809
My dearest of Frights – I will obey your commands about the minionette and jessamine. Moody will be quite happy with my employing him as the arrival of the new man has I believe caused a schism in the garden ...

As I have been so elaborate in my account of Jigs dinner at Lord Darnleys I hope you will tell us all about Mrs Dugdale's at Mr Repington. What did she say about the Townshends, and does she mention which of them she likes the best? Pray tell us all about it.

I am glad you are well my dearest Little Me, pray sleep away. It is very fine and we are going to Mrs Hindes. Snugest takes the Accomplished in the chariot, and I had intended to have taken a charming trot after the carriage, but Grumpus chooses to go and takes me in the curricle, so there's an end of that.

I am sorry you do not go to Mrs Dugdales, she is such a love, but it is not worth shaking the brat for. I am glad my little friend Mrs Millar looks pretty. Anne Dashwood says she has ordered her birth day dress, it is to be garter blue and silver embroidered with the rose, thistle and shamrock in compliment to the King's jubilee. I think it will be famously ugly.

My love to Mr Curzon in which Pug joins. Yours truly affectionately

K. A. Bisshopp

Lady Bisshopp was still grieving for Charles, and it dismayed her that it had not yet been possible to settle his affairs and, in particular, to claim the prize money for the *General Ferrand* and other captured vessels. She had been told that about £1,000 was to be paid, not by the admiralty but by prize agents in The Bahamas, who would transfer it to a nominated office in London. However these agents, who enjoyed too much independence and liked to invest the sums they held for as long as possible, turned a deaf ear. According to Lady Bromley's son Sir Robert, a naval officer and future vice-admiral, it was a tiresome business claiming prize money even at home, and from the West Indies one was lucky to get anything. The amount in question was not enormous, but it had been won by Charles's gallantry and the Bisshopps were angry at being treated so shabbily. It was only through perseverance and the intercession of friends that they at last received the money in late December, twenty months after Charles's death.

1810

As her pregnancy advanced Harriet feared she might be too weak to make the journey from Hagley to London, where she wanted to lie in. There was also uncertainty about when she was likely to 'produce', as Lady Bromley put it. From her mother she received the didactic love that always warmed her heart. She was 'as near perfection as a mortal can be', Lady Bisshopp told her, but must maintain her credit in the 'awful change' she was about to undergo. The Curzons set out in early January, travelling in short stages, and arrived at their house in Welbeck Street, where Lady Bisshopp and Katherine joined them. 'You have nothing now to think of but the joy of bringing a man into the world,' Lord Curzon wrote to Harriet, and for the next two months she waited for this event.

HARRIET'S JOURNAL
23 June. – My dear boy was born on the 16th of March after a tedious and painful labour of 21 hours. Thank God I got through it very well, and was blessed with a very fine child, who will I hope be a comfort and grow and increase in favor with God and Man. My prayers to the Almighty for him are that he may be like his father, and become like him the blessing of all his family, the comfort of his parents in their old age, an ornament to his

country and above all things a good man. I suffered a good deal in my lying in, however I was very happy in being permitted to nurse my baby, and being able to do so without any difficulty. It was a source of great satisfaction and pleasure to me.

My dear husband was obliged to leave me a few days afterwards, to accompany his father into Staffordshire on business. This separation was the more painful to me at this moment when I most needed his society and missed his kind and indulgent attentions, besides his great and increasing goodness to me during the time I was with child, and the week immediately after my confinement made me feel the difference most bitterly when he left me. Nor can I ever forget what I suffered, fearing my foolishness would hurt my milk and make my child ill, and at the same time I was too weak to get the better of it. This circumstance was extremely unlucky as it retarded my recovery at the time and laid the foundation for the lowness of spirits, debility and constant nervous irritability I have been struggling with ever since, and shall most probably feel in a great measure during my whole life.

However I had a very great consolation in my dear mother and dear Kate, who were so good as to devote their time entirely to me, and give up every amusement and gratification that could interfere or prevent their passing the greatest part of every day with me. I must however remember with some degree of pleasure that although I was wretched that my Bob must go, I was not so wrong as ever to request him to stay with me, knowing it was his duty to attend his father, and that by doing so he would avoid some late nights in the House of Commons. He returned to me Friday and found me still in my room, as I had not yet been able to go down stairs. However I was by no means worse, and although agitated at seeing him I did not I trust give way too much to my feelings.

Robert had written loving letters to his wife every day of his absence, and when he returned in early April he devoted himself to her. She went downstairs for the first time, and a few days later she was 'churched' (blessed after recovery from childbirth) in the Oxford Chapel in Vere Street. She continued to feel low, and was sometimes near collapse, but rallied in time for her baby's christening.

HARRIET'S JOURNAL

23 June. – On Friday the 11th May he was christened in our house in the back drawing room by our kind friend the Bishop of Chichester. We intended to have had the ceremony performed in the Parish Church of St Marylebone, but Lord Curzon had had an accident, a hurt on his shin, which made it impossible for him to go thither. Therefore for his convenience it took place in our house at about two o'clock. Lord Curzon, my father and Lady Bromley are the sponsors. There were present besides them and ourselves Mama, Kate, Cecil, Elizabeth, Baroness Howe, Mrs Dugdale, Marianne, Mary Dutton and Penn ...

My little boy was named Robert, after his dear father, whose bright example I hope he will follow, and I hope it will please God to bless our endeavours to give him a good education, to enable him to go through his trials in this world in a manner that may ensure him a neverfading eternal crown of glory in the world to come. May he always conduct himself like an Englishman, and never do any action that can tarnish the lustre of his name and family ...

On the following Monday my child was innoculated with the small pox by Mr Hill, a surgeon of great skill and humanity who has distinguished himself by discovering a method of inhaling vital air. I was particularly fortunate in all our family on both sides agreeing with me in preferring the small pox to vaccination. I was afterwards told I had been much blamed by some people for having *the cruelty* to give such an illness to such an infant, and indeed for giving it at all, but that is no matter. Little Bob went through it very favourably, and I have now no further anxiety on the subject.

Towards the end of June Harriet and Robert travelled with Little Bob to Parham, and a week later the Bisshopps left the house in their care and made their way to Oxford, where Sir Cecil was to receive an honorary doctorate in civil law. Encaenia, the ceremony in the Sheldonian Theatre at which such degrees were awarded, was an elaborate affair, and the one that took place in July more so than usual as it also installed the former prime minister Lord Grenville as chancellor of the university. Cecil was granted leave to attend and, like Katherine, intended to make the most of Oxford. There was plenty to tell Harriet, who was alone with her baby at

Parham, Robert having gone to Hagley for the appointment of teachers in two schools of which he was a trustee.

KATHERINE TO HARRIET
OXFORD, 4 JULY 1810

... I will now give you an account of all we have been doing. Jig arrived Monday evening, he had great difficulty in getting post horses and came one stage with Sir Sydney and Lady S[mith] and the Miss Rumbolds. Tuesday yesterday we got up at seven o'clock, Snugest put on a blue silk cap and flower and the new cotton and silk gown. I was full dressed in white muslin and lace etc. coral neckless and Lady Greys comb, white gloves and fans and white silk tippet. We then proceeded in the coach with Jig to the theatre, where there was a most terrible croud. We all waited till the doors were opened and there was a most amazing rush of all sorts of people, and the constables beating those back who were not to go in. I never heard such a screaming piece of work, however we got in at last and having only lost one of the hair broaches, one coral bracelet and my gown all torn.

It was a most beautiful sight, all Lord Grenvilles family, Fortescues etc. wore feathers and diamonds. Lord Grenville and the noblemen, doctors etc. came into the theatre in procession at eleven, the Chancellor took his seat and all the old doctors forming a circle the ladies set behind them. We were in the front row and *kicked* the doctors. The Rumbolds sat behind us, Mrs and Miss Ashurst on each side and Lady Ely opposite the students in the upper gallery, and all strangers, men etc. down stairs, so the men were completely divided from the women.

We sat nearly at the end of the circle and saw Lord G. entirely. He began with a Latin speech and afterwards admitted 20 new doctors, consisting only of peers and privy councillors, and made a Latin speech to each. I think all the people here seem to dislike the Grenvilles, as when Lord Buckingham and Lord Temple were made Dr's they all hissed very much; Mr Tierney was admitted with much difficulty. It was a very pretty sight. Dear Snugest is talking away to me all the time I am writing, but I hope you will make this out some how. After this we went through listening to 3 Latin speeches of about ½ an hours length each, one long English sermon about the arts, and last of all a most delightful poem spoken and composed by Mr Chinnery, the subject was the dying gladiator.

After this we had a great crash of sounds, and Braham at it as loud as he could bawl, about the clouds. We then adjourned, having set there from nine o'clock till half past two. Sir Sydney Smyth was in high favor and was most violently cheered and applauded as he entered the theatre. Papa is quite delighted, he dined with Lord Grenville etc. and is to be part of the shew tomorrow.

Jig brought Col. Murphy to dine with us, and in the evening we went to the ball at the town hall, when we found an immense croud of about 800. I danced with my little friend Mr Vane and half a dance with Mr Henry Tredcroft, who was with us in the morning and would have been affronted if I had not taken a trot with him. Snugest and I were so tired we could not stay to dance with Heneage Finch and came home soon after one ...

KATHERINE TO HARRIET
OXFORD, 5 JULY 1810

My dearest Fright – I am so afraid I shall not have time to write to you tomorrow that I am determined to make a beginning before I go to bed, and go on telling you what we have been about. Yesterday at five o'clock we went to the concert at the [Sheldonian] Theatre. The music was quite charming, Braham, Catalani, Mrs Ashe etc. and the Hailstone Chorus, which I enjoyed extremely. Snugest and I were alone and talked to nobody but Mr H. Finch. This will give you an idea how very stupidly all the people go on here, as nobody makes any parties together, but all go about singly and any how. Anne Ely tacks herself to a Mrs Barlow, who takes her in at St John's College, we have all called on each other repeatedly and never met comfortably till today we took possession of her in the carriage for two minutes.

After the concert we came home and dressed and carried Jig and Col. Murphy and Mr Augustus Curzon, Lord Scarsdale's son, to a ball at the Star Inn which was very select. Mr and Mrs Curzon invited us and gave up their rooms for it. I danced with Mr Fortescue, Lord F.'s son, who is remarkably agreeable but terribly short, and Mr Foley, who Snugest knows all about and says he is the son of the member for something and has a large property somewhere. I stood with the Wyndhams and Rumbolds.

We came home soon after one and got up before seven to go to the theatre. Snugest wore a blue gown and cap, I had on my yellow gown. I was rather nervous as Grumpus was to take his degree. Some of the new doctors are so terribly hissed, but it all went on very well as Papa was extremely applauded. Those admitted besides him were Sir Sydney Smith (who was so much applauded poor man he was obliged to stand and bow for several minutes together), William Lyttelton, Mr Fremantle and about 20 others. After this we heard 14 speeches. Lord De La Warr spoke in English verse better almost than any body and Lord Apsley in Latin, all flummerizing Lord Grenville, who sets with all his family in feathers and diamonds behind him and bears it as well as he can. After the speeches Catalani sang God save the King, very fine in broken English and all the others the chorus. Then Lord Grenville got up and walked out with all the red doctors after him, the Coronation Anthem playing. This is a very fine sight I wish you was here to see.

I hope you and the dear brat enjoy Parham all to yourselves and that you are not annoyed very much at Bobs absence ...

During the next days they watched a balloon ascend from the gardens of Merton College and went to a race meeting: 'I liked it while the horses were running,' Katherine told Harriet, 'but it is very dull between whiles.' There were several more balls, at one of which the steward chose Katherine to lead off the dancing. At Blenheim Palace she trod a measure with a Mr St John, who was tall and agreeable, and tried to avoid the less acceptable Mr Hulse: 'I thought he looked as if he would ask me to dance so I maneuvered for an immense time, and when I thought I was three rooms from him, to my astonishment I heard his odious little voice by my elbow so I danced with him after all.' This brought the Oxford jaunt to an end, and while Cecil travelled northwards to make some visits the others returned to Sussex.

Katherine had attracted a throng of admirers in Oxford, and many who asked her to dance found her engaged. Her family nickname 'Kitten' was in general use, and one man cut a cat's face from a sheet of paper and playfully asked his friends to compare it with hers. Katherine did not consider herself a beauty, and regretted she could not gain weight. 'Here I am, still "tall and strait as a poplar tree",,' she told Harriet, 'and despair of ever being the shape of an S like Lady Lucan, which you know Lord Curzon thinks the acme of perfection.' But others judged her looks differently, and her vivacity held its own appeal. She liked receiving attention, but her feelings were not stirred and her tone in writing of her admirers was light-hearted. This tone she maintained until she met the only man she ever loved.

Handsome Cecil, when not carousing with military friends, had also flirted in Oxford, and according to Katherine he passed whole days with the Miss Rumbolds. His wife's death in 1807 had grieved him deeply, for she had made him completely happy, but there was no danger in such a vital young man that his feelings would become morbid. Even before he left for Spain in 1808 he courted Catherine Tylney-Long, a nineteen-year-old and Britain's greatest heiress, 'a most charming young woman' in his judgement. They went yachting together and he escorted her to a ball, but his deployment brought the romance to an end and it was not resumed. Nor was his gallivanting with the Miss Rumbolds, who now disappear from view.

For Harriet at Parham letters of Oxford gossip were very welcome, for although Little Bob was flourishing she felt nervous and depressed. In particular she worried that she might have shown too much emotion when her husband left her, and he needed to set her mind at rest by assuring her she had behaved impeccably. At Hagley there had been endless enquiries about her, he said, and he had replied that she was more charming and lovely than ever. Meanwhile her mother gently admonished her: 'You know how I hate preaching, yet my Sweet I cannot forbear saying that it is a *leetle* wrong of dear you to be low because you are alone, when you know at the same time that you are the idol of so many hearts.' After eleven days of isolation Harriet took Little Bob and his nurse to Welbeck Street, where she was reunited with Robert. They made the best of the summer weather by strolling through the parks and streets, seeing the Exeter Change menagerie, and admiring the view from Westminster Bridge.

1811

In the final months of 1810 George III, who had suffered previous bouts of insanity, succumbed to the derangement that possessed him for the rest of his life. A regency bill was brought before parliament and, on 6 February 1811, the forty-eight-year-old Prince of Wales was sworn in as regent. To the surprise of many he kept his father's Tory ministers rather than turning to the Whigs with whom he had always publicly allied himself.

In April Cecil began a brief career as MP for Newport in the Isle of Wight. Four years earlier he had stood for his father's old seat of New Shoreham and come third in the poll. This time failure was impossible as he had been chosen by Sir Leonard Worsley-Holmes, who managed Newport in the Tory interest, to replace Viscount Palmerston, who had just vacated it to represent Cambridge University. For some reason Sir Leonard preferred candidates not to visit the constituency in person, and so Cecil did not meet his electors. However, even without a contest the candidate's expenses amounted to hundreds of pounds, and on election day we find him urging his father to send his quarterly allowance without delay. A benefit of his new status for Cecil, or rather for his correspondents, was the parliamentary privilege of franking. Before postage stamps were introduced in 1840 letters were paid for on receipt and, if they had been carried a long distance, could be quite expensive, but letters from MPs were delivered without charge.

Politics did not distract Cecil from his real vocation, and in the summer he obtained six months' leave from his home-fixed regiment to return to the Peninsula, where he hoped to join the staff of the army under Viscount Wellington. He sailed for Lisbon in July, but his onward journey to headquarters at Fuente Guinaldo, west of Salamanca, was delayed by the late arrival of his horse on another ship. To fill the time he joined the social round of Lisbon's British colony. His first impressions of the city were bad – 'without exception the hotest and dirtiest hole I ever was in' – but a course of sightseeing and entertainments changed his mind. When he and his horse reached headquarters he was told a post might be found, but only if he committed himself to remain indefinitely, for which he would have to extend his leave from the Guards.

The rest of the family spent the summer flitting from place to place. In September Katherine rode from London with her friend Mary Poulett, Mary's father Lord Poulett and a Mr Burke to Wanstead House, Essex, the 'English Versailles' belonging to Catherine Tylney-Long, whom Cecil had courted in 1808. The young folk sought to foster a romance between Lord Poulett and the heiress's mother, both of them widowed: 'Miss Long shewed us the view from the top of the house, and it was Mr Burkes joke to leave Lady Catherine and Lord Poulett together down stairs, that he might propose to her, but it would not do as Lord P. fagged up the ladder after us, and in about ten minutes up panted poor Lady Catherine. The journey almost killed her and she said she had never in her life been up there before.' This was Miss Tylney-Long's last carefree summer. The following year she took the disastrous step of marrying William Pole-Wellesley, a wastrel who squandered her vast fortune and abandoned her for another woman. By her death in 1825 Wanstead's contents had been auctioned and the house demolished for its building materials, all to pay off her husband's creditors.

Also in September, Lady Bisshopp and Katherine went to Bognor for their third meeting with Princess Charlotte. In a few years the princess would be the nation's darling, but at fifteen many thought her an awkward, wilful hoyden. Katherine disagreed: 'Her manners are extremely improved and she is perfectly quiet and *stately* and just what a princess ought to be.' At the Abingdon Races the Bisshopps found a wife for Cecil, a Miss Metcalfe – 'very fat and rich', his father noted – and courted her on his behalf; there was another man in the lists, and Cecil was told to hurry home to win her. This he had no desire to do, for although he still had no appointment there was plenty to divert him in Spain, and he wrote long accounts of dinners with senior commanders and visits to the sites of recent battles. He noticed how finely shod Spanish women were and offered to have black silk shoes made for his sisters if they sent their measurements. He also told Katherine that several officers had enquired after her in flattering terms; she replied that she was glad they had not forgotten her.

While Sir Cecil followed his son's progress on a handkerchief map of Spain and Portugal, Harriet and Katherine sent him cheerful letters. His best correspondent was his mother, who numbered her digests of news so that he would know if one went astray. She told him his father-in-law Lord Leicester, afterwards Marquess Townshend, had died leaving his money to his mistress: 'Poor Lord T. has died as he latterly lived, most disgracefully, and as the newspapers observed on the subject [it is] shocking that a nobleman should have it in his power to rob his children to enrich a prostitute.' Among other titbits, William Pole-Wellesley had fought a duel with Lord Kilworth, his rival for the hand of Miss Tylney-Long, who affected indifference to both; a former admirer of Harriet's had secured an heiress and joked that he had married ten thousand acres and the most charming of her sex besides; and the poetic scion of a prominent Sussex family had utterly degraded himself: 'Sir Bysshe says that young Shelley his grandson had best hang himself, having married the daughter of a coffee house keeper, a girl of 16.'

As the weeks passed Lady Bisshopp began to urge Cecil's return. The expected dissolution of parliament would allow him to stand for New Shoreham, which as a local seat was preferable to Newport, and his help was needed in the management of the Parham estate, so long neglected by his father. 'I am sure no family object can be so well pursued in your absence,' she wrote. But Cecil wanted to stay in Spain and get on the staff. At last he got a temporary post as aide-de-camp to General Hulse, who commanded an infantry brigade, and served him with the rank of brevet major during a French attack before Ciudad Rodrigo in late September. 'Altogether I have been very fortunate,' he informed Robert, 'Hulse's A. D. C. and brigade major having been so ill they have not been able to do anything. I have been the only effective man he has had.'

As her fears for him increased, Lady Bisshopp's pleas grew stronger and she admitted it was for her own peace of mind that she wanted him home. In early October she heard of the recent action, and her feelings were acute: 'I wrote to you a few days ago, and since that we have been tormented by accounts of a battle supposed to have been fought on the 28th or thereabouts. I trust in God you are at this moment in health and safety, and if it should please the Almighty to bring you safe back again after having been present at a glorious and victorious action, how we shall all rejoice!' Ultimately it was his dashed hopes of a permanent staff post that brought Cecil home. He sailed in December, having sent ahead two pipes of port for the Parham cellar and made arrangements for his sisters' shoes to follow.

Once again the Curzons spent the autumn at Parham. Sir Cecil was in good humour and there were none of the leaden atmospheres that often filled the house. They were 'all frisky', Harriet told Cecil, though she herself had toothache. When the Curzons left for Hagley they as usual chose a circuitous route, taking in as many friends as possible. Robert, who had someone to see in Havant, set off first and arranged to meet Harriet at New Park, the home of the

Estcourt family near Devizes. In getting there she experienced the miseries of travelling with a small child.

HARRIET TO LADY BISSHOPP
NEW PARK, 7 NOVEMBER 1811

My dearest Snugest – Here we are thank God safe and sound and quite well, after a very disagreeable journey. The first part as far as Chichester we performed with great success, but my first vexation was the servants would not go to the Fleece, but took me to another inn as Badcock does not keep post horses, but I hope it does not signify. Then it rained and when we arrived at Southampton I was so tired and out of spirits that it was quite a relief to find Maria Grosvenor was not at home, which we learnt at the inn, and indeed I believe I should have been ill if I had walked to her and looked at her house and made the agreeable, which I could not have refused doing as it was a very fine evening. Poor Little Bob was very good and did not cry poor fellow, but the roads were so bad and wet that the swinging motion of the carriage made him sick, and we were obliged to get out by the sea side near Portsea, and when we got to Southampton Akerman was so tired and the inn so full that I was obliged to exert myself to get Bobbins fire and bed ready, and upon those occasions Bettison is never any use as she generally gets out of the way and is very cross.

However yesterday morning we set out again in the rain and went on without any adventures to Salisbury, where Little Bob dined, and as the distance here from thence is 23 miles in one stage, the greatest part of the way over the plain and consequently nothing to look at, I was in hopes he would have gone to sleep, but no such thing, and though he was very good I was obliged to amuse him, and poor love he broke my necklace and black miss was thrown about. Then we walked down a steep hill and at the bottom fortunately discovered that the lynch pin was come out of one of the wheels, and we trotted on in the cold till another could be knocked in.

Altogether I was quite knocked up and exhausted and ready to cry when we arrived here, and found to my sorrow they did not expect us till today, therefore no fire lighted [in my] and my chicks room, and we were not to dine till six o'clock. It was then about 4 so I was obliged to comb out my hair and set in the drawing room and look good for an hour and a half before I could go and dress. Then my black spots would not go on and I was obliged to take it off and pull the sleeves to pieces before I could get ready, and my dear Bob the greatest of all dear loves waiting for me ...

In December Katherine turned twenty, and the marks of affection she received from her mother and sister prompted a bittersweet reflection: 'I have enjoyed myself so much for the last three years that I must always regret they are past and can never return, and [I] cannot expect to "do it again" as dear little Bob says.'

Living in Jane Austen's World

The year 1811, in which Cecil Bisshopp sought adventure in Portugal and Spain and his relatives sought amusement in various parts of England, saw the publication of a novel written by a Hampshire clergyman's daughter. Its title was *Sense and Sensibility*, and it was favourably reviewed in the *British Critic* and the *Critical Review*. The following years brought five more novels from the same anonymous author, the last two appearing a few months after her death aged forty-one in 1817. Steadily her reputation grew, and now, two centuries later, the period of British history in which she passed her uneventful adult life is more strongly associated with her than with anyone else.

And yet the picture Jane Austen paints of her country and her age is far from complete. Geographically, she concentrates on the southern counties of England rather than the United Kingdom as a whole; socially, she restricts herself to the gentry and avoids the nobility, the labouring class and, with some exceptions, the middle class. The same picture is painted in Jane Austen's letters, with the slight distinction that the novels exhibit the higher gentry, which comprised landowners and people of established wealth and included baronets, whereas the letters mainly focus on the 'pseudo-gentry' to which she herself belonged, that is to say families with small private incomes or breadwinners in respectable professions. Much of her knowledge of the higher gentry derived from long sojourns at Godmersham Park in Kent, the seat of her brother Edward Knight, who had been adopted by rich, childless relatives. The world of the Bisshopps is the world of the Knights and, in the novels, of the Bertrams in *Mansfield Park* or the Darcys in *Pride and Prejudice*. Indeed Sir Cecil Bisshopp's annual income of £10,000 is the same as Mr Darcy's.

In surveying this world, there is no need to rehash the information about dress, furniture, carriages, food and parlour games that is provided by the many Jane Austen companions. In any case, the trappings of everyday life are cursorily treated in her fiction, and appear to impinge very little on the human dramas unfolded therein. Her choice of location too often seems arbitrary, and her Hertfordshire, Northamptonshire, Somerset and Surrey are in most respects interchangeable. Sussex, the Bisshopps' county, contains Norland Park, the home of the John Dashwoods in *Sense and Sensibility*; and it is the setting of *Sanditon*, the comic novel about the fashion for seaside resorts that Jane Austen was forced by her final illness to abandon.

More important are the customs that governed the lives of the landed gentry. For much of the year they were on their estates, in the handsome country houses that, for the most part, still stand today. In these houses they followed regular but not inflexible routines, pursued healthy outdoor activities, and ate hearty meals, surrounded always by an efficient body of servants. It was a privileged life, but not altogether an idle one. The lady of the house would supervise her cook and housekeeper and look into her domestic accounts. She was likely to make clothes for and visit the poor, engage in other charitable work, entertain guests, and maintain a large correspondence. If she had daughters, she often took charge of aspects of their education. Her husband's main duty was to manage the estate and look after his tenants. He might beautify his house and grounds, involve himself in parish matters and other local administration, or act as a magistrate. He could also serve as a member of parliament, for which he received no salary.

Nonetheless there was plenty of leisure, much of it devoted to socialising. Within a locality the prominent families were forever drinking tea, dining and dancing in each other's houses or coming together for excursions, and the compulsive gregariousness of Sir John Middleton in *Sense and Sensibility* scarcely seems exaggerated. Fortunately the etiquette of such gatherings was relaxed. In the hospitable home of the Musgroves in *Persuasion* a large family and their guests form constantly changing groups around the cosy profusion of sofas and chairs, tables and flowers stands, books and the pianoforte. In a letter to her elder sister Cassandra, Jane Austen describes a similar scene during a visit to a neighbouring family in Hampshire:

> We had a very pleasant day on monday at Ashe; we sat down 14 to dinner in the study, the dining room being not habitable from the Storm's having blown down its' chimney. – Mrs Bramston talked a good deal of nonsense, which Mr Bramston & Mr Clark seemed almost equally to enjoy. – There was a whist & a casino table, & six outsiders. – Rice & Lucy made love, Mat: Robinson fell asleep, James & Mrs Augusta alternately read Dr Jenner's pamphlet on the cow pox, & I bestowed my company by turns on all.[6]

In Jane Austen's novels the social round is sometimes presented as an escape – not invariably successful – from tedium or irritation within the family group. The Bisshopp ladies too must have been glad of a release from being cooped up with the moody Sir Cecil. But all this activity was more than an agreeable distraction for people with time on their hands. It allowed individuals to acquire the outward conduct and moral values of their peers, worked to suppress selfishness and create bonds of solidarity among the gentry as a class, and expressed its role as an arbiter in the art of living. The notion of polite society as an ideal of civilised taste and manners would not have emerged without the normative influence of constant social interaction in domestic settings.

This influence was extended by the growing convenience of travel, which enabled families to embark on more frequent visits in different parts of the country. These visits often took the form of tours, such as the Bisshopps' meanderings in Gloucestershire and Oxfordshire in 1808, or a journey the Austens made to Gloucestershire, Warwickshire and Staffordshire to see their Leigh connections in 1806. For generations most families of the higher gentry, like those of the nobility, had spent a few months each year in London, but now it was possible to go there as necessity or inclination dictated. An array of seaside and inland watering places were also gaining in popularity, challenging the supremacy of Bath as the resort for salubrious conviviality. We have already seen Katherine in Worthing, and will follow her to Hastings, Brighton, Clifton and Harrogate. Jane Austen enjoyed a stay in Lyme Regis in 1804, and ushered most of the cast of *Persuasion* there a decade later. Thus, in circles larger and smaller, social activity was almost ceaseless.

For girls growing up in a country house like Parham, life was pleasant. Like their brothers, they spent their earliest years in a well-ordered nursery. Some mothers, like Lady Bisshopp, suckled their own children, but nurses and nursery maids provided the bulk of their care. Girls were taught by a governess, perhaps with their mother's help, and typically the rudiments of their education were English literature, French, history and arithmetic, with smatterings of geography, science and religion. Needlework formed an essential part of any girl's upbringing, and music, dancing and drawing masters could be brought in as required. Formal education finished early, sometimes before the pupil was twelve years old, and if she wished to learn more she read informative books and spoke with grown-ups.

Jane Austen was more modestly circumstanced than the Bisshopps and did not have a governess, but a similar programme of education was provided by her father and then boarding schools, and she supplemented it with a voracious diet of reading. She had a drawing master and under her mother's guidance became a fine needlewoman, excelling particularly in satin stitch. The assistant organist at Winchester Cathedral was engaged to give her pianoforte lessons, and she played with pleasure all her life. The novels suggest that Jane Austen's views on the education of girls were fairly conventional. She looked askance at knowledge for its own sake and purely ornamental displays of skill. The rote learning of the Bertram sisters under the guidance of Miss Lee in *Mansfield Park* does nothing except nourish their complacency, and the accomplishments of Charlotte Palmer in *Sense and Sensibility* or the Musgrove sisters in *Persuasion* are merely a gloss on their youth and prettiness. We are not intended to think less of Elizabeth Bennet in *Pride and Prejudice* for her relative lack of accomplishments, and the long list considered essential by her rival Caroline Bingley is simply an expression of snobbery.

If a girl was naturally studious like Katherine Bisshopp, her family might encourage her as long as she did not make a show of her learning or neglect more obviously feminine pursuits, both failings of the smugly bookish Mary Bennet. Polite society could accommodate a young woman like Katherine, who liked history well enough to compare different scholars on the same period, alongside those like Catherine Morland in *Northanger Abbey*, who dismisses the subject as 'the quarrels of popes and kings, with wars or pestilences, in every page; the men all so good for nothing, and hardly any women at all'.[7] Katherine's enthusiasm for art and architecture was also perfectly acceptable. Jane Austen shared these tastes, and liked to attend art exhibitions when staying in London, but she was too disciplined a writer to dwell on such subjects in her novels.

The transition between girlhood and matrimony was often short. Harriet Bisshopp married when she was twenty-one years old; many brides were not yet twenty. It is said that the eighteenth century saw the rise of companionate marriage in the higher classes, with young men and women finding partners they loved rather than submitting to dynastic alliances. Allowing for the varied reasons people have for entering the wedded state in any period, the trend was certainly towards marriages of affection, as Harriet's and her brother Cecil's may be called. However, they both made socially unproblematic choices, and anyone who did otherwise soon ran into difficulties, for families of the gentry and nobility were rarely indifferent to questions of status and money. As soon as a proposal was accepted the matter took a distinctly unromantic turn as parents, assisted by lawyers, began negotiating the financial aspects of the union.

Once the marriage settlement was drawn up, there was no reason to tarry. Weddings were simpler affairs than they subsequently became, and little planning was required: the bride's dress was less spectacular, guests often limited to family members, and a reception after the service not always provided. Elaborate nuptials were thought vulgar, and it is telling that the brash Augusta Elton likes more show than Emma Woodhouse and George Knightley put on at the close of *Emma*:

The wedding was very much like other weddings, where the parties have no taste for finery or parade; and Mrs. Elton, from the particulars detailed by her husband, thought it all extremely shabby, and very inferior to her own. – 'Very little white satin,

very few lace veils; a most pitiful business! – Selina [her sister]
would stare when she heard of it.'[8]

More time-consuming than organising the wedding was
assembling the bride's trousseau, the clothes she needed for the
first years of her married life. This might mean several shopping
trips to London and consultations with seamstresses. After the
wedding came the honeymoon, which was usually short, not
always made by the couple alone, and sometimes not made
at all. Harriet and Cecil were lucky to be given the use of the
family home without the family being present. They were better
off than Elinor Dashwood and Edward Ferrars in *Sense and
Sensibility,* who after their wedding move straight into Colonel
Brandon's house for a month while the parsonage they are to
occupy is renovated.

Marriage is the happy ending of all Jane Austen's novels, and
we learn little or nothing of her heroines' experiences thereafter.
She herself remained single, and, whatever other reasons there
may have been for this, several passages in her letters reveal
her fear, tinged with disgust, at the long years of childbearing
endured by many wives. 'Poor Animal, she will be worn out
before she is thirty,' she wrote of her niece Anna Lefroy.[9] Harriet
Curzon was spared this fate, bearing two children and suffering
one miscarriage, but the arrival of her first child was followed
by what appears to be postpartum depression. This condition
was recognised at the time, but Harriet felt she must try to hide
her anxiety and desperate need for her husband's support. New
mothers had difficult decisions to make about nursing their
children, earning, as in any era, the disapproval of others who
had different ideas.

Boys, like girls, had their earliest lessons in the nursery. From
then on their paths diverged, and boys' education centred on
the classics. First they were sent to a small private school or the
house of a gentleman scholar like Jane Austen's father, who had
boarders throughout her childhood. After this, depending on their
temperaments, they would either be taught at home by a tutor or
attend one of the public schools. Cecil and Charles Bisshopp went to
Winchester, and in the novels Henry Crawford was at Westminster
and the Bertram brothers at Eton. No great ability was required to
enter these establishments, nor even to progress from them to Oxford

or Cambridge, England's only two universities. In *Northanger Abbey* John Thorpe and James Morland have been to Oxford, and two less intellectually gifted men would be hard to imagine.

For Cecil and Charles the question of university did not arise as they were eager to embark on military careers. Of the options for employment open to a young gentleman, the armed forces offered the most prestige, as Mary Crawford explains in *Mansfield Park*: 'The profession, either navy or army, is its own justification. It has every thing in its favour; heroism, danger, bustle, fashion. Soldiers and sailors are always acceptable in society.'[10] Traditionally, eldest sons of families like the Bisshopps pursued no profession at all, but during the wars with France patriotic zeal and a lust for adventure led many to become officers in the army, marginally the smarter of the services. Not that an army career was all fighting the enemy: there was plenty of home duty tackling smugglers and civil disturbances as well as spells in barracks. Cecil had some dull times, but he did not lose his enthusiasm for soldiering. Moreover, the pay was welcome to a man from a financially weakened family, although its advantages were offset by the need to buy an officer's commission in the first place.

Jane Austen's fullest representation of soldiers and their ways is in *Pride and Prejudice*, where the arrival of Colonel Forster's regiment in sleepy Meryton brings excitement and danger. This regiment belongs to the militia, raised in wartime for home defence, rather than the regular army, but an air of raffish glamour permeated both branches. There is not much to choose between the dastardly George Wickham, who elopes with Lydia Bennet while serving under Forster, and Frederick Tilney, the dissipated dragoon captain in *Northanger Abbey* who captivates Isabella Thorpe, shatters her engagement, and then forsakes her. Something of Jane Austen's brother Henry, a charming, slightly roguish officer in the Oxford Militia, went into these portraits. Cecil Bisshopp certainly had an inclination for romance. Both he and Henry Austen were widowed early and spent the next years flirting hard with every woman who took their fancy.

Never would it have occurred to Jane Austen to say that the army was 'if possible, more distinguished in its domestic virtues than in its national importance'; but this is just what she says of the navy at the close of *Persuasion*.[11] Her higher esteem for the maritime service owes something to her pride in the achievements of her brothers Francis and Charles, who both eventually became admirals. It is also true that until the final years of the long struggle with France the navy played the more distinguished role, becoming the object of a strong national pride. What Jane Austen principally cherished, though, was not seafaring itself or victories over the French, but the honesty, bravery and enterprise she found in naval culture and the excellence of sailors like her brothers as family men in peacetime.

The navy enters her fiction in the form of William Price, who blows a bracing sea breeze across the staid world of Mansfield Park. Like the Austen brothers and Charles Bisshopp, William has served in the Mediterranean and the West Indies. Without vanity he tells entertaining tales of his adventures, and his uncle Sir Thomas Bertram discerns 'proof of good principles, professional knowledge, energy, courage, and cheerfulness' in what he says.[12] Not that sailors forgot their own interests in carrying out their duty. The lure of prize money was strong, and William Price hopes to win enough to alleviate his family's poverty and buy a cottage for himself and his sister Fanny. If he captures enemy vessels laden with treasure he will match the achievements of Charles Austen in the years 1800–1808 and Charles Bisshopp in 1798 and 1808. With luck his prize money will be paid out more promptly than Charles Austen's, which in one instance took five years to reach him, or Charles Bisshopp's, which came to his parents nearly two years after his death.

In an example of the family feeling Jane Austen so admired in naval men, her brother Charles used his first prize money of £30 to buy topaz crosses for her and Cassandra. This must have given her the idea for the 'very pretty amber cross' William Price sends Fanny from Sicily, which she wears at the ball in her honour at Mansfield Park. Charles Bisshopp was a similarly devoted brother, and in 1805 he used his prize money to purchase a bracelet in a Mediterranean port for Harriet, who wore it during her first Season. With his solid virtues and his deep attachment to his mother and siblings, Charles is every inch a Jane Austen naval man, and in his short life he achieved what Henry Crawford admires in William Price: 'the glory of heroism, of usefulness, of exertion, of endurance.'[13]

Socially the navy was the less elitist, more meritocratic of the services. Army commissions were purchased, but in the navy each man joined as a midshipman and could rise no higher without passing an examination. Sons of noblemen preferred the army, and although three quarters of naval officers were gentlemen by birth, the rest included men of very modest beginnings. Nonetheless, good connections were as helpful as in the army. Both sailor Austens had influential patrons, an arrangement so open that when they supplied the text for their entries in the *Royal Naval Biography* they mentioned them explicitly and gratefully. Knowing the system allowed Jane Austen to describe Admiral Crawford's intervention in gaining William Price's promotion to lieutenant. As for Charles Bisshopp, he leaned heavily, as we have seen, on Sir John Warren.

Persuasion, of which we shall say more presently, closes with a reference to 'the tax of quick alarm' paid by anyone belonging to the navy.[14] During the conflict with France mortality from enemy action, disease, shipwreck and fire was high. For families with sons serving overseas in the navy, or indeed the army, anxiety about their welfare was exacerbated by the slowness of communications. Letters took an age to reach home, but even they brought more up-to-date information than reports from theatres of war in the press. Jane Austen's letters show her family went through the same frustration and confusion as the Bisshopps in trying to ascertain the location and safety of their military scions, and when and where they might arrive on home soil again. At least the sailor Austens wrote regularly, as did Charles Bisshopp; his brother Cecil was not as diligent.

Had Charles lived longer, the archive of Bisshopp correspondence would be less thoroughly feminine in character. The truth is, though, that women tended to produce more and longer letters in this period than men. In *Mansfield Park* Mary Crawford laughs at the laziness of the young Bertram males and her own brother Henry in this regard:

What strange creatures brothers are! You would not write to each other but upon the most urgent necessity in the world; and when obliged to take up the pen to say that such a horse is ill, or such a relation dead, it is done in the fewest possible words. You have but one style among you. I know it perfectly. Henry [...] has never yet turned the page in a letter; and very often it is nothing more than, 'Dear Mary, I am just arrived. Bath seems full, and every thing as usual. Your's sincerely.' That is the true manly style.[15]

Even if men wrote regularly, like Robert Curzon, their letters are usually less circumstantial and less entertaining than those of women.

The art of corresponding with friends and family was sometimes represented as a conversation by other means. 'I have now attained the true art of letter-writing,' Jane Austen once told Cassandra, 'which we are always told, is to express on paper exactly what one would say to the same person by word of mouth.'[16] Her contemporary and fellow-novelist Mary Russell Mitford expressed the same view: 'Letters should assimilate to the higher style of conversation, without the snip-snap of fashionable dialogue, and with more of the simple transcripts of natural feeling than the usage of good society would authorize.'[17] In adopting this style, Jane Austen drew on an inheritance from her clever mother, whose letters are full of wit and high spirits. Cassandra's probably were too, and it is a pity they are not preserved.

Like her novels, but in a chattier way, Jane's letters reveal her sense of humour:

We were all at the Play last night, to see Miss O'neal in Isabella. I do not think she was quite equal to my expectation. I fancy I want something more than can be. Acting seldom satisfies me. I took two Pocket handkerchiefs, but had very little occasion for either. She is an elegant creature however & hugs Mr Younge delightfully.[18]

Often she takes aim at the frailties of human nature: 'Charles Powlett gave a dance on Thursday, to the great disturbance of all his neighbours, of course, who, you know, take a most lively interest in the state of his finances, and live in hopes of his being soon ruined.'[19] Or again: 'The death of Mrs W.K. we had seen; – I had no idea that anybody liked her, & therefore felt nothing for any Survivor, but I am now feeling away on her Husband's account, and think he had better marry Miss Sharpe.'[20]

Her letters are not always amusing. There are swathes of monotonous chatter about social calls, clothes, domestic happenings and prices, and she scurries from one topic to another:

We live entirely in the dressing-room now, which I like very much; I always feel so much more elegant in it than in the parlour. No news from Kintbury yet. Eliza sports with our impatience. She was very well last Thursday. Who is

Miss Maria Montresor going to marry, and what is to become of Miss Mulcaster? I find great comfort in my stuff gown, but I hope you do not wear yours too often. I have made myself two or three caps to wear of evenings since I came home, and they save me a world of torment as to hair-dressing, which at present gives me no trouble beyond washing and brushing, for my long hair is always plaited up out of sight, and my short hair curls well enough to want no papering. I have had it cut lately by Mr. Butler. There is no reason to suppose that Miss Morgan is dead after all. Mr. Lyford gratified us very much yesterday by his praises of my father's mutton, which they all think the finest that was ever ate.[21]

Jane Austen wrote like this because she knew her sister wanted as much news as possible. For any other reader, though, a little of this goes a long way. E.M. Forster, an admirer of her fiction, found her letters tedious and scrappy, mere 'catalogues of trivialities'.[22]

Forster was further troubled by what he called 'touches of ill breeding'.[23] Jane Austen could be rather graceless in her appraisals of others, for example a young woman seen at a party: 'Miss Langley is like any other short girl with a broad nose & wide mouth, fashionable dress, & exposed bosom.'[24] A notorious instance concerns a miscarriage: 'Mrs Hall of Sherbourn was brought to bed yesterday of a dead child, some weeks before she expected, oweing to a fright. – I suppose she happened unawares to look at her husband.'[25] Such frankness about physical appearance is typical of the period, for while beauty weighed no more heavily in the scales of consideration than it does now, the idea that remarking on its absence is unkind was but little developed. As for Jane Austen's robust, even insouciant comments on illness and death, they are born of her perception of emotional insincerity in others and a determination to avoid it herself.

The letters of Katherine Bisshopp (those reproduced above and those to come) follow the same conversational precept as Jane Austen's, and have the same vivid immediacy. Both women are inveterate, unapologetic gossips. Jane begins a letter to Cassandra by asking 'Which of all my important nothings shall I tell you first?'[26] Katherine, having described a dinner in detail, asks Harriet for an equally elaborate account of another in return. Such gossiping expresses sisterly love, affirming a common perspective and values and the wish to share a naughty pleasure. Like Jane Austen, Katherine has a keen sense of humour. She delights in awkward moments of social interaction and the incongruities that mar formal occasions, and she deploys mock-sensational or mock-earnest registers to heighten the effect of the scenes she sketches. Arguably, her expansive style makes her a more entertaining anecdotalist than the more hurried Jane Austen, though her individual observations have less bite.

Neither saw any more need than other Regency ladies to mince their words. In her letters and her journal, Katherine is just as unmerciful towards her tedious suitors and people she met in Gloucestershire and Oxfordshire in 1808 as Jane Austen is to women she observed at balls and assemblies. Katherine does not shy away from indelicate terms, writing 'snout' for 'nose', 'brat' for 'baby', and 'produce' for 'give birth', and Jane's letters likewise contain robust references to bodily reality. James Edward Austen-Leigh's *Memoir* and Lord Brabourne's edition of letters, which introduced the author as a woman to the Victorians, were therefore obliged to supress such usages which, in just a few decades, had become unthinkable in a respectable woman.

There are, of course, differences between the letter-writers. Katherine is occasionally sentimental, Jane Austen never. In her mature years, Katherine is more willing to convey deep feeling, especially sorrow. Most strikingly, while the novelist is self-aware in her choice of language, the non-novelist unthinkingly uses the slang of the day. Anyone Katherine cares for is a 'poor dear' or a 'dear love', people 'trot' from place to place, they have a 'phiz' rather than a face, and anything unusual is 'not to be described'. She also has a weakness for French phrases, albeit to nothing like the extent of some of her aristocratic contemporaries. Jane Austen makes fun of such modishness, telling her sister to 'get ready the proper selection of adverbs, & due scraps of Italian & French' if she wishes to impress a particular young woman.[27] One of the adverbs she has in mind is 'incessantly',[28] which Katherine uses, though she is fonder of 'excessively', meaning 'very much'. Lady Bisshopp employs 'amazingly' in the same sense, a habit that Henry Tilney mocks in *Northanger Abbey*.[29]

The letters of Katherine Bisshopp and Jane Austen owe their freshness to not being intended for the printed page. The same is true of Katherine's journals: unlike diarists with half an eye on publication, she neither strives for literary effect nor packages herself carefully for posterity; rather she seeks to order her thoughts, relieve her feelings, and aid future retrospection. Both women in their private writings are uninhibited by worries about how their style and opinions will be judged by strangers. They could be spontaneous and candid, and they were.

2

Sorrow and Hope

1812

In February Robert Curzon left Hagley to attend parliament, and in his absence Harriet's confidence again crumbled. Her mother tried to shore it up, telling her that all Staffordshire was singing her praises and that Lord Curzon had called her '*a prodigious* well bred woman'. She also reiterated her own love: 'I think of you all day long, and I trust you give me credit for this, beyond any other human being, for Bob and Kate love you perhaps as well as I do, yet as one is not a woman and the other not a mother. I must think Snugest can follow up all your dear innocent sweet thoughts and fears for your self even beyond either of them.' Even with Robert by her side Harriet sometimes pined for her mother, though she knew this was 'very silly' given her many blessings. Lady Bisshopp reproved her affectionately for lack of spirit, but was glad that her child still sought refuge under her wing and felt better for her encouragement.

Meanwhile Sir Cecil was often away from his family for weeks and months, we know not where, leaving his wife and younger daughter to keep each other company. Katherine's letters to Harriet are vignettes of their life together, reading and playing with their dogs at Parham and going into society in London. By this time, over three years after Harriet had left home, differences in temperament between the sisters stood out as clearly as differences in looks and aptitudes. Naturally there were similarities too: both were gregarious but domestic, chatty but serious-minded, censorious but kind-hearted. Katherine had more independence of judgement and pluck, though she was just as prone to anxiety and self-doubt. There was also an astringency to her character that contrasted with Harriet's soft-edged charm. She was proud, even thin-skinned, hating to be laughed at, and despite a strong attachment to her mother she did not always respond well to her criticism. On the other hand, like Jane Austen, she poked fun at herself as readily as at the foibles of others.

In August Sir Cecil wrote a letter to the prime minister. Katherine made a copy.

SIR CECIL BISSHOPP TO LORD LIVERPOOL
PARHAM, 21 AUGUST 1812
My Lord – The obliging manner in which you attended to my son's application relative to the barony of Zouche induces me to take the liberty of troubling your Lordship on a subject in which myself and family are so greatly interested. I hope your Lordship will not refuse my earnest request to lay my peculiar situation before His Royal [Highness] The Prince Regent, as mine is the only case in which on the petitioning coheir being allowed to assert his claim, and the House of Lords having decided in his favor, the grace of the Crown has not immediately followed the favourable report of the House.

I therefore cannot but flatter myself that through your Lordships kind and powerful recommendation His Royal Highness will be graciously pleased to terminate the abeyance in my favor, and it would be more particularly gratifying to me to owe the obligation to a minister with whose family I have the honor to be connected ...

The barony of Zouche, or De La Zouche, of Haryngworth in Northamptonshire, was created in 1308 for William La Zouche, a successful soldier and military governor of Breton ancestry. The title passed down the generations until the 11th Baron died, without male heir, in 1625. He did, however, leave two daughters, and it was from the elder that Sir Cecil claimed descent through his mother Susannah Hedges, who, he aimed to prove, was her great-great-great-granddaughter. He began his quest to become the 12th Baron in 1799, and soon it was the only matter apart from his yeomanry troop to which he gave any sustained attention. For days at a time he would sit at the elbow of Francis Townsend of the College of Arms, whom he had engaged as his herald. Among the fruits of their labours were a 276-page printed book, much of it in Latin, and a four-foot-long pedigree on linen-backed paper with green trim and wooden batons.

Progress was incredibly slow, with each hurdle cleared revealing more ahead. In 1802 a favourable report by the attorney general opened the way to the privileges committee of the House of Lords, only for a technicality to block it again. Meanwhile another family joined the hunt for the same title and had to be fended off, requiring Mr Townsend to go to Bristol to check burial registers. The privileges committee examined the case in 1807 and found that Sir Cecil had made good his claim, which now only needed royal approval. However the monarch acted on ministerial advice, and the weak governments of the next few years shied away from politically unnecessary elevations. In 1812 the prime minister Spencer Perceval finally agreed to push the matter forward, only to be shot dead shortly afterwards in the lobby of the House of Commons. But all was not lost, for his replacement Lord Liverpool was the stepson of one of Sir Cecil's aunts and his wife was Katherine's godmother.

Lady Bisshopp and her daughters backed the peerage claim, and family legend has it that Katherine, who was something of an amateur genealogist, uncovered an important piece of information to strengthen it. Charles felt differently, and a letter written to a friend a few months before his death explains why. In Plymouth he had fallen in love with a girl of respectable but obscure family, and he knew his parents' eagerness for the barony would make them oppose the match: 'For Godsake, they would say, do not tarnish the descent of your own family at the very moment when it is so material to keep it unsullied.' Charles understood but did not share this attitude: 'I hope that I shall never consider rank as honourable but when supported I find it by merit, and that an honest man will be ever in my opinion the *noblest* work of God.' The romance fizzled out, and this most dutiful of sons did not have to choose whether to take a step that would have vexed his parents.

Once he had become an MP Cecil joined his father in pressing for the peerage, but although as the first son he had more to gain than Charles he too was cool on the subject, and some of his references to it are flippant. He was probably worried about the cost. As well as fees and duties, Sir Cecil had to pay for Mr Townsend's labour and for the time the attorney general and the privileges committee spent on the case. After the extravagances of the 1780s and 1790s the Bisshopps needed to retrench; instead they spent as much as ever. In 1805 Charles was obliged to lend his father £1,000, most of the accrued interest on a legacy from a distant relative, and there were delays in the payment of Cecil's allowance. In the end the family's finances were so ravaged that a crash was inevitable.

Cecil had long felt uneasy about his dwindling prospects and feared he might not be able to maintain even the rank of baronet decently by the time it was his. 'I understand we are reduced,' he wrote to his mother in 1802. 'Pray what is to become of me, I should like to know my fate.' Two years later he told Harriet their father would not stir himself to sort out his affairs: '[He] knows how miserable he makes himself, but little does he think how miserable he makes other people.' After his wife Charlotte's death a portion of what her family had settled on the couple became Cecil's own, but he could not afford to live without his army pay despite giving up Holmbush. He was therefore irritated that instead of reforming the lax management at Parham his mother spoke of needless expense when he took a small house in Conduit Street, Mayfair in late 1811.

In June 1812 the United States of America declared war on Great Britain. The ostensible reason was the British policy of intercepting American mercantile ships trading with France (which had itself blockaded Britain), but the Americans also calculated that the British were so heavily engaged in the struggle against Napoleon that they would be unable to defend Canada from a determined attack. Within weeks the Americans recorded naval victories, but their attempts to invade Canada were halted by a combination of British regulars, Canadian militia and American Indians. In February Cecil had been appointed an inspecting field officer of militia in Canada with the local rank of lieutenant-colonel – quite senior for a man still in his twenties. He had not immediately been sent across the Atlantic, but the outbreak of hostilities in the summer brought his departure forward.

After going to Parham to say goodbye he sailed in August in the frigate HMS *Porcupine*.

CECIL BISSHOPP TO KATHERINE
ENTRANCE TO THE ST LAWRENCE RIVER,
9 OCTOBER 1812

... [Captain Elliot] is about 50 years of age, the oldest man in the ship. The other officers are all very young men, but the first lieut. a Mr Smith, a friend of poor Charles', is a most excellent officer and good sort of young man. He was put into the Porcupine thro' the interest of Mr W[ellesley] Pole, being of the same county, and resembles that family very much. Amongst the other passenger's were two dogs brother and sister, natives of South America that had scarce ever been out of the ship. Sancho is a great favorite and at all times admitted into the cabin, but the Lady Bess was not so fortunate, at last she did not honor us with her company as often. The dog was a great source of amusement during the whole of the voyage as he would jump about and play all sorts of tricks. I played a great deal at chess with Captain Elliot, which we were both of us very fond of, so that we endeavoured to kill time a little in occupying our minds in this way, but many a dreary hour we were obliged to wade thro' during the long voyage we afterwards had, when our books were all read thro' over and over again, and our faculties were no longer able to pour over the chessmen ...

I never saw land from the 18th of August to the 5th of October, on which day we made St Pauls Island in the Gulph of St Lawrence. On the banks of Newfoundland we caught great quantities of cod fish which are even better than the cod you get in England. In the St Lawrence we caught macruel and other fish, on the 3d of October we retook a small schooner laden with sheep and oxen from Prince Edwards Island which had been taken only a few hour's before by a privateer, the American's having taken every person out of her except one old man, and had manned her with five Americans to take into port, but luckily for the poor people to whom she belonged we fell in with her. Prince Edwards Island you will see by the map is just within the Gulph of St Lawrence. There is a great trade from there of cattle to Newfoundland, which is entirely supplied from the opposite coast. This ship was the property of perhaps 50 poor people, farmer's who get back tea sugar and sometimes tins in return for their cattle.

This schooner came very opportunely, as from the length of our voyage we had eat up all our fresh meat except one pig, which had just been ordered to be killed. Captain Elliot thought it better, as the schooner belonged to so many poor people, to take out of her only the quantity of cattle we wanted for the remainder of our voyage, and to give up the ship and property to its original owners. Taking the American prisoners out of her we gave the old man two men from our ship to take her back to Prince Edwards Island, and happy the poor man was. Indeed I think I never shall forget his expression of countenance when he found he had fallen in with a British ship of war and was once more set free ...

On the instructions of Lieutenant-General Sir George Prevost, commander-in-chief in North America, Cecil proceeded to Upper Canada, present-day Southern Ontario, where in addition to his inspecting duties he commanded a small regular and militia force stationed near Fort Erie. In November he played a signal part in repulsing an American attack across the Niagara River, the border between the two countries, in what became known as the Battle of Frenchman's Creek. Their failure to take Fort Erie or win any other ground forced the Americans to suspend their operations for the winter. A general order issued at British army headquarters in Quebec City praised Cecil for the 'most spirited and gallant manner' in which he had defeated a larger force, and a despatch from Major-General Sheaffe, the commander in Upper Canada, noted his 'celerity and decision'.

News of this triumph took months to reach Parham, but already Sir Cecil hoped that his elder son's extensive military service, together with his younger son's death in uniform, would improve his chances of ennoblement. In November he again put his case to Lord Liverpool: 'I am induced ... once more to trespass on your indulgence, and to express my sanguine hopes that through your very powerful recommendation the abeyance of the Zouche peerage will now be terminated in my favor by His Royal Highness The Prince Regent.' The prime minister replied that the regent had no intention of creating any peers at present, but that he would advance Sir Cecil's claim as soon as an opportunity arose.

After passing the spring and early summer in London the Curzons went, as in previous years, to Parham, arriving in time to bid Cecil farewell. At the end of October both families were back in London for Harriet's second lying-in. Because of the illness of a servant in Welbeck Street, Harriet was confined in Lord Curzon's house in Davies Street. This time the birth was easier, and the subsequent complications came from an unexpected quarter.

HARRIET'S JOURNAL

7 November. – I was very ill all day and the next morning. Sunday the 8th I was brought to bed after a labor of seven hours, but thank God I had a good time and a nice little fellow to give my beloved husband. I was very ill afterwards and Dr Pemberton was sent for, and I got better in a few hours. Dear Mama was not with me till it was all over as she was not well, and it was so bad a night I would not send for her but contented myself with dear Fattest,[30] who came to me at 7, an hour before Edward was born. My baby was baptized the third day Edward Cecil by Dr Combe. I nursed him myself and we went on extremely well.

I had been brought to bed about a fortnight when William Dugdale came to see us with so bad a cough that we thought it best to keep him with us a day or two to attend to it. Unfortunately it proved to be the measles which we had not suspected or indeed thought of till the Wednesday, four days after he had been in the house, when Dr Pemberton very kindly called upon Bob to tell him the measles had appeared in the boarding house at Westminster School and recommended him to remove Little Bob if possible. My father was so good to allow him to go to his house in Stratford Place that very evening, but too late for he had already caught the infection.

He was very ill for sixteen days and during all that time we were in the greatest anxiety, for no eruption appearing we were uncertain how to proceed, so much so that when it did come out at the end of that period it was quite a relief. He had the desease severely, and during the whole time his patience and invariable sweetness and good temper endeared him to all who saw him, dear little fellow. I was not permitted to see him for fear of my baby, but Mama and Akerman nursed him with the most unrimitted attention and kindness and my dear Bob went to see him constantly.

The twelve-year-old William Dudgale recovered from his disorder and was taken into the country by his parents. There is more on the measles and the new baby in Katherine's journal, which at her mother's suggestion she resumed on her twenty-first birthday.

KATHERINE'S JOURNAL

1 December. – Dear Harriet gave me a beautiful bracelet of Mamma's hair, with four stones set on the clasp, the first letter of each stone forming together the word Love. The stones are lapislazuli, opal, vermilion, emerald. Under the clasp is Papa's hair. I carried a long letter to the post office I had written to Cecil under cover to Sir George Prevost, at Quebec.

17 December. – Poor dear Little Bob is getting quite well, he has been very ill with the measles. He is with us in Stratford Place, as we were afraid the baby would catch it had he remained in Davies Street, though I have not had it. On this day we went to St Georges Church to have the baby christened. The party consisted of Mamma, Marianne La Housse, Harriet and Mr Curzon and Myself, Mrs Mitchell and the child. We waited about ½ an hour in the vestry for General Grosvenor, who represented Cecil as godfather, but not present. Mamma stood in for Miss Curzon, my father was at Parham. The child's name is Edward Cecil, he is very handsome. Sir Robert Bromley was the other godfather, but not present … We took leave of dear Harriet and Mr Curzon Friday evening, and Saturday morning the 19th we left London and arrived at Parham about five o'clock. Papa had lighted up the hall and old rooms for our reception.

20 December. – I was taken ill with the measles. Mr Martin attended me and was very kind and goodnatured. Dear Harriet and her baby had the measles in London at the same time.

1813

Katherine was unwell for many weeks, but Harriet and baby Edward were soon better and the Curzons returned to Hagley. At the end of January Harriet cut a dash at a local ball, as Robert proudly informed his mother-in-law: 'The Fright was reckoned the prettiest woman at Lord Bagots ball, tho it will be no gratification to you to hear it. Yet I was determined to tell you notwithstanding, her complection has got quite fine and [she] is in rude health.' Not just her health, but her spirits too were far better than after Little Bob's birth two and a half years before.

HARRIET TO KATHERINE AND LADY BISSHOPP
HAGLEY, 13 FEBRUARY 1813

... I am very glad you approved of my dear Bobs going to London and my staying here with the brats. They are both well and Elizabeth has given her godson a beautiful frock today. He is very much grown and is very good humoured and merry, and thank God his nurse goes on as well as I can wish. Little Bob is a very great love, I flatter myself he now knows almost all his letters perfectly and that when we go to London we may begin to read little words. He often enquires after you both and t'other grandpapa as he calls Grumpus.

Charlotte Grimston writes me word she was at the Princes ball and she thinks Princess Charlotte pretty, and says the opposition pay her great court. What do you think of the Princess of Wales publishing her foolish letter, and insisting upon her conduct being again enquired into to be laid before the world, and then dining with such people as Lord and Lady Oxford. En passant the last named lady has so enchanted Lord Byron that he has taken a house in Herefordshire near Eywood ...

The letter referred to here was composed by the Whig politician Henry Brougham for Caroline of Brunswick, Princess of Wales, and addressed to her estranged husband the prince regent. It protested against his humiliating treatment of her and the limited access he granted her to their daughter Charlotte. The 'Regent's Valentine', as people called it, found its way into the columns of the *Morning Post* and aroused widespread sympathy for the spurned princess. However, the Bisshopps and Curzons, keen monarchists all, hated anything that lowered the dignity of the royal house: Robert called the letter 'nuts for the Jacobins'; Lady Bisshopp lamented its contents and the princess's intimacy with the rakish Countess of Oxford; and Katherine could 'only deplore the poor woman's want of judgement in the whole tenor of her conduct'. Jane Austen also criticised her, but was riled by the double standards of a debauched man calling his wronged wife an unfit mother:

I suppose all the World is sitting in Judgement upon the Princess of Wales's Letter. Poor Woman, I shall support her as long as I can, because she *is* a Woman, & because I hate her Husband – but I can hardly forgive her for calling herself 'attached & affectionate' to a Man whom she must detest – & the intimacy said to subsist between her & Lady Oxford is bad. – I do not know what to do about it; – but if I must give up the Princess, I am resolved at least always to think that she would have been respectable, if the Prince had behaved only tolerably by her at first.[31]

Meanwhile Cecil was pleased with life in Canada. The climate suited him and he had the satisfaction of a responsible command, close to the enemy. During the day he inspected the troops under arms and organised parades, attended by a staff adjutant and an aide-de-camp, and in the evening he dined and played whist with eight or ten fellow officers. His military correspondence shows an energetic officer who inspired respect but was lenient when he could afford to be. He won the trust of the Canadian militia, sometimes treated a little cavalierly by the British, and of the American Indians, whose courage and prowess he admired.

He was, however, gloomy about British prospects. There was a severe shortage of men and supplies in Upper Canada and of ships to patrol the Great Lakes, so that despite their poor leadership and discipline it was only a matter of time before the Americans made their numerical superiority tell. 'Nothing can be so bad entre nous as the whole military establishment of the country,' Cecil confided to Robert. Britain was treating Canada as a sideshow to the great conflict in Europe, he said, and yet she was potentially the jewel in the imperial crown, with resources to sustain large-scale settlement, almost limitless potential for agriculture, and a deeply loyal population: 'I am so much *enraged* with [the] government for the little succour that they have sent to this country that I shall not be able to sit still in the House of C[ommons] without abusing them.'

Equally disquieting was the news from home, where the peerage claim was at a standstill and money was tight. Because letters took so long to reach him Cecil was in the dark about his own affairs, and despite his promised tirade in parliament he could not be sure he was still an MP. Nor did he know the current status of his Conduit Street establishment; whether the Townshends, in severe straits because of Lord Townshend's will, were still paying his annuity; or whether his own family's difficulties were not worse than his mother was admitting. 'I must say I have always been happier abroad as there I have no troubles about money, at least very little compared to what I have at home,' he told her pointedly. At least his victory at Fort Erie, if it be properly estimated in Britain, would bestow an ermine robe on his father. '[I hope] by the time you receive this letter there will be a Lord and Lady Zouch,' he wrote to Katherine, 'and that we shall hear no more about this nonsense in future. That will be one plague got over.'

Katherine was now Cecil's principal correspondent, receiving his Canadian letters with the 'greatest possible delight' and replying with jaunty bulletins of news. The young ladies of his acquaintance were disconsolate that he was to miss the Season, she told him, and one had said that London would not be London without him.

KATHERINE TO CECIL BISSHOPP
PARHAM, 14 FEBRUARY 1813
My dearest Jig – An opportunity offers of sending you a letter by the Jubilee. I hope you have received all my letters. All yours are come safe up to the 22d of October, Montreal, which we received in December …

Snugest and Grumpus are very well and desire to be most affectionately remembered to you. We talk of you constantly and look forward to the period of the termination of your *rambling mania* with the most ardent hopes that it is not very far distant. Dearest Harriet is at Hagley with her children, quite well, Bob gone to London for the meeting of Parliament. He returns to Harriet in a week, and they stay with Lord Curzon as long as he is in the country and then make some visits in Staffordshire before we all meet in London in the spring.

If you have received my last you will have heard I have been very ill, as well as the Fright and children with the measles. We are all quite well again, except that I have not quite gained my strength again, which will I hope excuse the illegibility of this beautiful epistle. All our letters have been inclosed to Sir George Prevost, if he communicates with General Sheaffe you may manage to get them.

We went to see Mrs Walker, they are very comfortably settled at Muntham for two years. Mr Walker means to fit up the old house at Michell Grove as soon as he is of age. She is a very pleasing and agreeable [woman] and a great acquisition to the neighbourhood. Every body laments the death of poor Lord Tyrconnel in Russia. The present [lord] is left quite destitute and his poor mother, but they are in hopes to get a pension from government. William Lytelton is to marry Lady Sarah Spencer. She has 20,000, and Lord Lytelton gives them 1,000 a year in addition to what little fortune he has. Lord De La Warr and Lady E. S. is going on I hear, but not yet declared. The approaching Season will probably decide their fates.

There has been a report that Lady Hester Stanhope has been taken prisoner with her two friends Mr Bruce and Mr Leigh by the Bedouin Arabs. She travelled with tents and an immense retinue, which excited the avarice of the Arabs. I dare say you recollect having seen at Portsmouth the beautiful horses she sent over as presents to the Duke of York. If government does not negociate some exchange and she really is a prisoner, her friends will have the pleasure of paying an immense ransom for her liberty, and for her foolish curiosity in rambling all the world over.

Sir William Manners two sons, young men of 15 and 16, have disappeared, and nobody knows what is become of them. A farmer lent them £400 to facilitate their escape from home, two village girls are supposed to be with them. Their poor parents must be disconsolate, but Sir William is very odd, you know he will not let his daughters dance because he fancies its wrong. Nothing can excuse the abominable conduct of the boys ...

Aside from his safety, the Bisshopps' main concern was whether Cecil was serving his interests as well abroad as he might at home. Because of his long absence he had indeed lost Newport and had not been entered for New Shoreham following the dissolution of October 1812, and it seemed far from certain that going to Canada was worth this sacrifice. However, his success at Fort Erie, when they finally learnt of it, blew away some of their doubts.

KATHERINE TO HARRIET
PARHAM, FEBRUARY 1813
My dearest dear Fright – How very delightful it is that the dearest Jig's should have distinguished himself so honorably

dear love, and that it has pleased God to spare him. I have not felt so rejoiced at any event [in] a long time. Dear Snugest and Grumpus are much agitated, and we all feel perfectly overjoyed at knowing even that he was alive and well the 9th of December, as we began to be excessively uneasy at not hearing any account of him. You have of course seen the account of it by a private letter in the Morning Post, which mentions that the troops were *concentrated under the judicious arrangements* of Lt Col. Bisshopp, and that the enemy had the *presumption to send a summons* to Lt Col. B. requiring the surrender of Erie, and that he sent them word, *come* and *take* it. I think one can picture to oneself exactly dear Jig's quite fierce and determined to astonish them, which he appears to have done most effectually, as the American militia seems to be dispersed for the winter.

In short I am so happy that dear Jig *se fait un nom* (I cannot say it in English) as I have never ceased to lament till this moment his having what I foolishly considered banished himself to America, but as he is really *doing* something and distinguishing himself with so much credit one must be extremely thankful he is imploying his time so well, instead of repining at his absence.

Dearest Bob wrote to congratulate us which was very kind and amiable of him. Snugest has just written to thank him, and *hopes* you will excuse her not writing to you, as besides being agitated she is working very hard at your shawl to get it completed by tomorrow evening as Mrs Anderson who is going to London Thursday will give it to Bob to take to you, but I do not think Snugest will accomplish finishing it as there is a great deal to do. It is very beautiful, but I think the other two still more so, I dare say this brown one will become your dear white complection extremely. Many thanks for the riddle, we admire the allusion to the belles jambes very much, tho' we have not yet had time to digest its other merits au reste ... I am much amused with Dr Johnson spelling incorrectly and with the whole of your very agreeable letter my dearest Fright. I am very glad dear little Bob remembers us all sweet love. Adieu my dearest, I cannot write any more as my hand shakes so I should not send you such a scrawl if I could perform another but non posso piu adesso ... [32]

Lady Bisshopp sent Cecil a heartfelt letter about his valiant action and the encomiums it had won, his father wrote separately to congratulate him, and Robert rejoiced that he had 'drubbed the Yankees handsomely'.

Back in England, the arrival of spring meant it was time for the Season. This annual migration to London, already mentioned in passing, took place in March or April, and the return to the country followed in June. While in the metropolis elegant society pursued a round of balls, dinners and parties; it was exhilarating to some, tedious to others, and exhausting to all. A highlight were the balls at the exclusive Almack's Assembly Rooms in St James's on Wednesday evenings.

KATHERINE'S JOURNAL

26 March. – Mamma and I and the maids came to London in the coach, my father intending to follow us in a few days. On the next day dear Harriet and Mr Curzon and the children arrived in London.

30 March. – We went to a small party at Lady Alvanly's and heard Miss Smith read part of King John. We went afterwards to a dance at Mrs Ross's. I was able to dance only two dances with great difficulty, being still very ill and melancholy at the idea of going out in Cecils absence. Partner Mr Crackenthorpe. Sarah Hobart said he would talk me to death.

6 April. – We were at a very pleasant ball at Allmacks, one of the most agreeable evenings I ever passed. I danced with Mr Arthur Eden and Mr Foley. I was present at a number of balls, the pleasantest were Mrs Bethels, Lady Cardigan's, Lord Sidneys and Lady Mildmay's. I was much gratified during my stay in London with seeing the Mint, the Tower, Sir Joshua Reynold's pictures. Those I admired the most were Garrick between Tragedy and Comedy, an Infant Samuel, Miss Bowles, Lady Hamilton etc. etc. I saw them lighted up and the effect was not near so good as by daylight.

26 June. – We went to a breakfast at Fitz Roy Farm given by Lady Buckinghamshire. It is a pretty villa and a most beautiful entertainment, and we danced out of doors on a raised platform. Our party consisted of Papa and Mamma, Lady and Miss Pechell, Harriet and Mr Curzon and Mr Martin. We received letters from Cecil several times during this month. I was much gratified with hearing Mrs Siddons read.

Across the Atlantic, spring brought Cecil the grim satisfaction of observing the decline of British strength that he had predicted. He was also beginning to grow bored of his unvaried routine as he awaited a renewal of hostilities. Instead of the gaieties of the Season, he had to make do with a small number of male companions and could 'only see a female face by going thirty six miles'. Still, he felt he had learnt far more of his profession than he would have done even in Spain and was proud of the trust his superiors placed in him. And the country still enchanted him; it was the most delightful he had ever beheld, he told his father, with an ideal climate and rich vegetation. If only it were governed rationally it could be 'the very garden of the earth'.

In late May Cecil was obliged to pull his forces back from Fort Erie after the Americans took Fort George, on the Canadian side of the Niagara. However, he did so without losses and destroyed everything in his rear to prevent it falling into enemy hands. The attackers pressed on, but the tables were turned a month later when a body of Indians under Cecil's command captured an American detachment. He signed its capitulation and then wrote to his father: 'If you have not your peerage now, as I hope you will have had before, I do not know what I can do that will give it you.' He also said he was tired of the war and would be glad to return to England as soon as he could do so with honour.

The Americans were now penned in at Fort George, allowing the British to carry out raids across the Niagara to the American side. One of these took place in the early morning of 11 July, Cecil leading a combined regular and militia force of 240 against Black Rock, today part of Buffalo. They stormed the small fort and routed its defenders, burned its blockhouse and barracks, destroyed several boats, and took the portable stores as well as eight pieces of artillery. Instead of evacuating, Cecil then decided to remove over a hundred barrels of salt, an item much wanted by the British commissariat, and the delay allowed the Americans to regroup. At the same time a party of Tuscarora Indians, fighting on the American side, came unexpectedly on the scene and opened fire from the surrounding woods. The British retreated hastily but were easy targets as they clambered into their boats; fifteen were killed and twenty wounded. Cecil, leading a small detachment to cover the retreat, was shot in the left thigh. As he was carried to a boat he received further wounds to his left wrist and upper right arm.

The surgeon who attended him after the evacuation at first judged his chances of recovery to be good.

W. HACKET TO SIR CECIL BISSHOPP
VILLAGE OF ST DAVIDS, UPPER CANADA, 20 JULY 1813
... On his arrival at Chipaawa, a post of ours, he wished much for my attendance and desired I might be permitted to remain altogether with him. I found him suffering more mental than bodily pain, expressing to me his great uneasiness that a single soldier should have been hurt, which appeared very much to annoy him. The wound of his wrist I found of little consequence as the ball had penetrated merely the skin and took its course immediately under it and lodged near the elbow. His thigh must have been struck by a spent ball, tho' the bone was fractured the skin was *merely* broken without the wound penetrating further. The right arm suffered most, the bone was much shattered, but no blood vessel of any consequence injured. This was the only wound that excited in my breast any apprehension, but considering his being a very young man with an unbroken constitution, tho' apparently delicate, yet I entertained the most sanguine hopes of being able again to restore him to a profession to which he was much attached and which his commencement promised so much he would adorn, as well as to his friends relatives and country.

But alas! the constitution was not equal to the shock it had received. His wounds looked healthy and well, the symptomatic fever never ran high, pain had subsided, the prospect was cheering and animating. On Wednesday after a good nights rest he was particularly chearful and conversed with me much about home, expressing his regrets at what you Sir would suffer as well as Lady Bishop on his account. [He] wished much I should accompany him home and hoped we would arrive in a very short period after your having heard of his misfortune. The first part of that night he rested well, but about one o'clock in the morn got restless and uneasy which encreased till day break. He then slumbered a little, but afterwards I found a change, an alarming degree of debility attended with low fever exhibited itself. From his restlessness I was obliged to open his bandages, and found every wound appearing as well as it was possible to expect.

Tho' thro' the day he was chearful and collected yet his countenance became bad, and towards the eve [he] began to wander much, talked much of home and still expressed his uneasiness at the loss of the men in this affair, tho' I had hoped both the district order and the visit of General De Rottenburg, who commands here and who with his wonted benevolence kindly came some distance in the early stage of his wounds to see him, had removed all uneasiness from his mind on this subject, and giving directions to his servant Reece for his departure for England, he spoke the whole day. This night (Thursday) he past very badly, and on Friday morn all hope vanished. The loss of the men he still spoke of, and continued to talk as the day before, till about half past six o'clock in the eve he expired without a struggle, nay almost without a groan.

I have been thus minute in every thing concerning this worthy invaluable and much esteemed officer, who fell in the zealous discharge of his duty. I trust it will be a consolatory reflection to his friends that whatever the most humane attention could afford, or friendship supply, was furnished by Col. Clarke of the militia, who shared in his danger and was partner in the enterprise, to whose house he was removed shortly after his arrival on our shore. Mr Barnard, who was his staff adjutant since his arrival in this country, was constant and unremitting in his attentions. In short Sir, so much was he esteemed both by the natives of the province and throughout the army that every individual was anxious to be of service and employed about him. Here I would indeed be wanting in justice were I not to bear testimony to the zealous and affectionate attention of Reece to his wounded master, his attendance was assiduous and constant. Every attention has been paid to his remains, tho' on the day of his burial a forward movement was made towards the enemy, yet General De Rottenburg with most of his staff came to pay the last sad duties to departed worth. He is buried in the church yard of Stamford within a half mile of the Falls of Niagara under an oak tree ...

It was not until early September that news of the engagement at Black Rock reached England. The first newspaper reports indicated Cecil had been seriously but not dangerously wounded, and the same information was contained in a letter his adjutant Lieutenant

Barnard wrote to Robert the day after the raid. Concerned friends wrote to the Bisshopps with their fervent wishes for his recovery, but the following weeks brought a second letter from Barnard and Surgeon Hacket's account, both confirming the reports of his death now also appearing in the press. The family fell into a shocked silence. Letters of condolence arrived one after another, all of them dignified and sensitive testimonials of regard for a man who promised by his energy and valour to rise high in his profession.

Sir Cecil obtained leave from the command of his militia and he, Lady Bisshopp and Katherine stayed quietly in their London house. In December they moved to Parham, and Harriet wrote to her father from Hagley to ask if her mother had become more composed. Perhaps they found solace in a *Morning Post* article that praised Cecil's 'repeated proofs of great skill and bravery' at Black Rock and in the verse commemorations of friends. Sir Cecil made a gift of £100 to his son's servant John Reece, who had done all he could for him after his wounding and brought home his personal effects. A tablet to Cecil's memory was unveiled in Parham Church:

> His pillow, root of sturdy oak,
> His shroud, a soldier's simple cloak,
> His dirge, 'twill sound 'till time's no more,
> Niagra's loud deep solemn roar;
> There Cecil lies; say where the grave,
> More worthy of a Briton brave.

1814

The grief of Harriet and Katherine at Cecil's death was far greater than it had been in the case of Charles, of whom they had seen little since early childhood. That Cecil was an only surviving son, the repository of the Bisshopps' hopes and ambitions, made the blow even harder. There are almost no family letters until well into 1814, and for months the sisters wrote nothing in their journals.

KATHERINE'S JOURNAL

16 April. – It is now nine months since I have looked into this book, and when I reflect on the dreadful anguish and sufferings I have endured in the interval I shrink from the task of recording that miserable period. I have almost lost my sight owing to the chicken pox in the midst of my [*illeg.*] affliction, and the impossibility at the same time of repairing from tears. I have passed the whole winter alone with my father and mother, and I feel that the efforts I have made to appear cheerful and to keep up their spirits has injured my health and made me almost blind. How foolish I have been.

We came to London the beginning of this month April 1814. I went with Harriet and Mr Curzon to Lady Holland's in Piccadilly to see Louis 18th make his entry into London. It was a very fine and interesting sight, the Prince Regent and the Duchess d'Angouleme accompanied Louis 18th in the Regent's coach drawn by the 8 cream coloured horses. The Regent had been to Stanmore to meet the King of France and his suite. I was very ill and low as all our relations were at Lady Hollands, Cardigan's, Aboynes etc. etc. and it was the first time I had seen so many people together since our great misfortune, and I could scarcely refrain from tears whenever I attempted to speak.

On this day (the 20th I believe) we desired to be introduced to Mr George Bisshopp, who was of the party and who by a most unaccountable neglect of the family on all sides we had never happened to meet before. He is very like poor Charles and seemed much gratified with the manner in which we received him.

George Bisshopp, who on Cecil's death became heir to the Bisshopp baronetcy, was the only son of Sir Cecil's paternal uncle Edward. His elderly father died when he was an infant, and the charge of his education fell to his mother's second husband, a Gloucestershire clergyman, who intended him for the church. He was content with his stepfather's scheme, and in September of this year, aged twenty, he was ordained. However, like many young sprigs of divinity in these times, he was more interested in preferment than in the spiritual or pastoral aspects of his calling, and it was in Ireland, that seedbed of Anglican sinecures, that his career would unfold. He was a jovial, gossipy companion, always ready to amuse and be amused. Whether he was also, as his obituarist in the *Gentleman's Magazine* claimed, 'an elegant scholar and a highly accomplished man' is much less certain.

Dejected though they were, Harriet and Katherine could not avoid being caught up in the celebrations of the 1814 Season.

The fall of Paris in March and Napoleon's abdication in April sparked a round of festivities that lasted through the summer, with the Russian tsar, the Prussian king, minor Allied sovereigns, generals and statesmen congregating in London to toast their victory and receive the acclamations of the crowd.

KATHERINE'S JOURNAL
10 June. – My eyes were so much swelled with crying I thought I should not be able to go to Lady Anson's ball. However I was dressed in white and gold and diamonds and I went with Harriet and Mr Curzon. On this night London was illuminated to celebrate the peace, and I carried a heavy heart amidst the general joy and exultation. I no sooner arrived at Lady Anson's than I was prevailed upon to dance much against my inclination with Mr Martin of Worcestershire. It was eleven months since I had heard the sound of a fiddle or anything like gaiety, and affliction and illness had rendered me so very unfit to join in any thing of the kind that I had scarcely resolution enough to bear it.

I felt so overwhelmed and depressed by affliction and sufferings that the society of young people was dreadfully irksome to me. Some came laughing and making a noise, wondering they had not seen me before this year and asking me what I could have been doing so long in the country. Others appeared to pity me so much that though I felt grateful for their commiseration I was quite over come by their display of it. Some looked at me reproachfully as I was dancing and said they were delighted to see me enjoying myself. A few were indeed really kind, and I shall always feel obliged to them for feeling for me. After the first two dances I was too happy to go and sit in a corner out of the way of the noise. I refused to dance any more, and went to supper with George Dashwood, who is always quiet and agreeable and no trouble.

20 June. – Went in the coach with Harriet and Mr Curzon and Papa and George [Bisshopp] to a great fete given by Whites Club at Burlington House to celebrate peace and to amuse the illustrious visitors. It was a most magnificent sight, and seemed very wonderful to be in a room with so many crowned heads. The Emperor of Russia danced with Lady Jersey and walzed a little with Mrs Lyttleton and Miss Rawdon. I walked about with

George the beginning of the evening then with my father, I went
in to the supper room with Mr Duckinfield. Mr Bankes asked me
to dance with him, but Harriet was so nervous and anxious that
she frightened me so I said no instead of yes, though I should have
liked to have danced in the same country dance with the Emperor
of Russia.

I was so low and miserable that the least thing overcame me,
indeed I was scarcely equall to going out at all. My right eye gave
me dreadful pain, and I wanted every kind of encouragement
to bear up in any degree. I had then lost all sense of worldly
amusement and enjoyment, the object in whom all my ambition
was centered, in whom all my views were terminated is now
removed for ever from me. I endeavour cheerfully to submit to
the will of God, and trust he will enable me to bear with patience
and resignation the dreadful blank Cecils death has made in my
existence.

9 July. – I went to Mrs Grenville Howards ball with Harriet,
danced with Mr Cousmaker and Sir Lawrence Palk. Refused to
dance with Bird Lime and another and affronted both.

13 July. – I went to a ball at Lady Carringtons, Lady Cardigan
was my chaperon. Danced with Arthur Eden and Sir Lawrence
Palk and Lord Newbattle, a very pleasant evening. I felt this
evening for the first time this year that it was possible I could
again be amused. I experienced a great deal of kindness from
several people this evening, which I hope I shall never forget.

The ball in Burlington House was attended by Jane Austen's
brother Henry, a banker at this time; this is probably the only time
Katherine was in the same room as member of the Austen family.

The following day Robert left London to accompany his nephew
Penn Curzon and his tutor John Moore on a tour of Northern
France and the Netherlands. Penn was seventeen, and now that
his Eton days were over his mother Lady Howe had been obliged
to pass him into the hands of Lord Curzon, who wished to guide
his approach to man's estate. A tour of Scotland had been the
main activity of 1813, and this year he was to join the stream of
British tourists profiting from the peace to visit the Continent. Lord
Curzon asked Robert to supervise the trip.

Surgeon Hacket arrived in London at this time, and Lady
Bisshopp invited him to Stratford Place to thank him for his

kind services to Cecil. 'He was as much distressed at seeing us as we could be to see him,' wrote Harriet, 'and felt sincerely for our sad affliction and for the irreparable loss we have sustained.' Lady Bisshopp gave him a gold repeater watch intended for Cecil and spoke with him about the idea of erecting a monument over the fallen soldier's grave. They considered different designs, and Mr Hacket promised to execute whichever they fixed on when he was back in Canada. Letters written some years later requesting a good word in the right ear suggest that his help was not entirely altruistic, but it would have been unusual for a man in his circumstances to oblige a well-placed family and not seek any return.

One day in July George Bisshopp stopped Harriet's carriage in the street and told her that Viscount Whitworth, the Lord Lieutenant of Ireland and a distant relative of his, had just got him a good living. This, it later transpired, was Trim in County Meath, worth £600 a year. He also became a chaplain at Dublin Castle, and it was there and at Phoenix Park, the Lord Lieutenant's residence outside the city, that for the next few years he mainly lived.

The highlight of the summer festivities for the general public took place in St James's Park, Green Park and Hyde Park on the first day of August. Fantastical structures were erected, a mock naval battle was fought on the Serpentine, and balloons ascended into the skies. The entertainment continued after nightfall with a theatrical firework display.

HARRIET'S JOURNAL

1 August. – In the evening Kate, my father and I went to Lord Ardens to see the fireworks, after having dined together with dear Snugest. We agreed to go in good time to avoid the croud which had been collected all day and filled all the streets in the morning to see the Naumachia on the Serpentine river in Hydepark. At ½ past 8 we arrived in St James Place, and did not get home till past one. The fireworks were very beautiful and so well managed that no accident happened in the Green Park, which was the part of the exhibition that we saw. They lasted from ten o'clock till considerably after twelve, and begun by a discharge of cannon, I think 101, after which there was a great display of rockets etc. etc. ended by a magnificent and immense Temple of Peace and Concord entirely covered with coloured lamps, and appearing to be built with fire, like a scene in a opera. The multitudes of people in the Green Park, upon whom the light of the fireworks threw an occasional bright gleam, shewing all their countenances and figures in different attitudes of delighted astonishment, the bands of the Guards and other regiments playing in the booths and tents, the fineness of the night and the hurrah's of the populace, rendered the whole a most interesting scene. The party in Lord Ardens house was very numerous, but I did not know who many of them were.

In early August the family, including Harriet and her sons, converged at Parham. One evening Edmund Cartwright, rector of Earnley and later of Parham, came to dine and told an anecdote of Tsar Alexander I and his surprise at a Quaker's characteristic lack of social deference.

HARRIET'S JOURNAL
7 August. – We talked about the Emperor etc. and his having been here [in Sussex]. Mr C. said it was a very curious thing to see all the country people old and young placing themselves on the road where they thought they had the best chance of seeing the royal party pass, and Lord Egremont permitted every body to come into the park to see them arrive at Petworth. But the most interesting and flattering visit that the Emperor of Russia made in this country was on the following day. Having passed through Brighton in his way to Dover on the road between Lewes and Hailsham, at Hellingly he passed a farm house inhabited by Mr Rickman, a very respectable yeoman and a Quaker. Mr R. stood at his door with his family to see the Emperor pass, but did not take off his hat when His Majesty bowed, which struck him so much that he ordered the carriage to be stopped and desired to be acquainted with Mr R. The farmer invited his illustrious friend to come into the house, which the Emperor and his sister who was in the carriage with him agreed to, and they went all over the farm house, into every room, every stable, walked about the whole place, and enquired the use of every thing they saw. Stables, outhouses, dairy etc. etc. were in their turn examined and admired. Mr Rickman asked whether they would condescend to eat any thing he could offer them, they were much pleased with his civility and partook of the homely cheer such a place could afford, and having passed some time there the Emperor wrote Mr Rickmans name

in his pocket book, and assured him he should never forget his attentions and civility.

Earlier in the summer the tsar had been in Hampshire, where people were just a keen to catch a glimpse of him. 'Take care of yourself, & do not be trampled to death in running after the Emperor,' Jane Austen warned Cassandra.[33]

A week later Harriet gave her mother a scare.

HARRIET'S JOURNAL
14 August. – Kate and I went to Sullington in the phaeton to see Mrs Dixon. When we arrived there in getting out of the carriage my grey petticoat caught in the splinter bar and I fell down and in the fall sprained one of my ancles so very much that it was with some difficulty I got into the house. Kate sent home for the post chaise and poor Mrs Dixon was frightened out of her wits. My petticoat being so strong and not giving way I fell with great violence, and besides the sprain got a great bruise on the side of my leg, so that it was a mercy my leg was not broken.

When the carriage returned we drove home, not without great apprehension that poor Mama should hear some accident had happened, but we flattered ourselves she would be reading her book and never know of our having sent for the chaise. Unluckily my father saw the horses changed, but it did not at first strike him till upon a little reflection he began to think it was odd and went into the house to enquire of Mama how it could be. They then both became exceedingly alarmed, and when we arrived down windmill hill we met poor dear Snugest walking as fast as she could to meet us in the greatest agitation at the end of the lawn. Kate and I were extremely vexed to have occasioned such a piece of work, which added to the sufferings I felt with the pain of my leg. We sent for Mr Martin, he examined my leg and finding nothing broke he gave me some goulard, and I was obliged to be carried up and down stairs and kept upon the couch all day, being perfectly unable to move about.

Later in August Robert joined the party, having crossed from the Netherlands and taken leave of Penn and Mr Moore in

London. The day of his arrival was a joyous one for Harriet: 'I was enchanted to see his dear kind face again and felt as if I could never have a care now he is returned.' We may assume he was just as pleased, for in his letters from abroad he had said how he missed the light of her countenance and her sweet voice. He wrote at length but without animation on what he and the others had seen in the way of art and architecture, and with greater interest on inns and agriculture. He was glad to leave Paris, finding their apartment dirty, the city noisy and smelly, and its inhabitants hostile. Brussels was pleasanter, with better food and friendlier people, while Holland had clean towns but dreary countryside. He returned home a confirmed John Bull: 'I am more satisfied than ever with old England and feel it an honor to be an Englishman. Where we are not loved we are respected, never did the national character stand so high.'

In September the Curzons travelled to Hagley and the Bisshopps to London, where their newly discovered relative George Bisshopp was in an alarming condition.

KATHERINE'S JOURNAL

17 September. – Poor G. B. has been dying of a fever. I trust it will please God to spare his life. I should be truly concerned to lose so valuable and affectionate a friend.

30 September. – Lady Warren called here. I heard from poor dear Harriet that Edward has tumbled down and hurt his head, and that there will always be a mark, thank God it is no worse. George has called on us he is recovered. We met Sir Lawrence Palk and his brother at the door. During our stay in London I have walked out once in Kensington Gardens with dear Snugest, and every other day with Ann, generally in Hyde Park, one day down Oxford Street, and yesterday I was foolish enough to indulge my sorrow by walking down Upper Berkeley Street by dear Jigs house ...

I am reading Robertson's History of Scotland aloud, a terrible narrative of iniquity! I must read some other History of Scot. as Robertson does not relate particulars enough concerning the 5 James's, but his language is so very perfect and elegant one cannot help being delighted with it as an amusing book, tho' it does not appear to me to be a satisfactory historical account of Scotland.[34]

In October Katherine and her parents left London to join the
Curzons at Hagley. As usual they travelled in their own vehicles –
a curricle and a chariot, and as usual they saw plenty of sights,
including on this occasion Hatfield House and Woburn Abbey, so
that it took them four days to reach their destination. In parts of
her journal Katherine is like a Regency Pevsner, detailing important
buildings and the treasures they contained.

KATHERINE'S JOURNAL
6 October. – We went to see Woburn Abbey, we were not
admitted into the house. We drove two miles through a very
handsome extensive park, a good approach and fine avenue,
quantities of deer. I can not say I am much delighted with
the little I saw of Woburn, tho' it is a very fine style of place.
The outside of the house is ugly. The three centre windows
are ornamented by broken pediments and all the others are
plain pediments, this has a very odd effect I think. Then there
is not only a row of balustrades over the attic story, but the
space between that and the next story is also interspersed with
little short bits of balustrades. This is no doubt very correct
architecture, but I do not like it. We saw the tennis court 98 feet
in length, and the riding house the same size. A beautiful old
gothick church covered with ivy and belfry detached. We dined
at Newport Pagnell and slept at Northampton. We passed the
Queen's Cross which was erected by Edward 1st to the memory
of his wife Eleanor of Castille. There is a fine old church at
Northampton.

From Northampton they drove through the village of Welford and
saw Naseby field, where Charles I was defeated by the New Model
Army, and Holdenby House, where he was imprisoned. Then they
took a winding course through Leicestershire and Warwickshire
into Staffordshire.

KATHERINE'S JOURNAL
8 October. – We arrived at Hagley a little after four having been
overtaken by dear Bob, who had been buying a dark chestnut
horse at Lichfield. We had the happiness of finding dearest
Harriet and her dear children in good health. Mr and Mrs Palmer
and Miss Byron were staying in the house, Lord Curzon, Lady

Bromley and Miss Curzon and Penn and ourselves formed the rest of the party. In the evening poor Snugest was so overcome and agitated at being in a house of reception for the first time since our great affliction that she was obliged to go to bed almost immediately after dinner.

10 October. – I was to have rode out having promised Penn to ride, but the rest of the party having settled to go to Ingestrie, Harriet said it would be too far for me to ride so I went in the curricle. Ingestrie is an old Elizabethan mansion and very much to be admired for its being perfectly in character in every respect. Lord Talbot has just altered the back to suit the front. The inside of the house is extremely comfortable and furnished to the highest degree of luxury.

11 October. – We could not ride for it rained. I began reading Mansfield Park. We sang in the evening and played at loo, very pleasant.

12 October. – Mr and Mrs Palmer went away. I was sorry, he seems to be very clever and is a very agreeable man, she is a little fidgety woman but very entertaining and goodhumoured.

13 October. – I went to the stables with Harriet and Penn to see the great dog and his shooting dogs. It was a very fine day so dear Bob took me out riding upon the chestnut horse. We galloped upon the training ground. When I came home Penn had returned from shooting and was set off to look for us.

14 October. – We went to Kings Bromley Mr Lane's, about 7 miles off. I rode with Penn and Bob, the others went in open carriages. It is a very ugly place. We were all put into a boat and taken across the water to an island which is made into a flower garden, I enjoyed my ride very much indeed. In the evening we played at loo come il solito.[35] Poor Penn was so low and melancholy at going to Oxford the next morning that he was sulky and would not play, which was inconvenient to me as he has always delt for me and taken all the trouble.

15 October. – I have read Mansfield Park. I think Fanny's love and Miss Crawford's ambition both equally absurd, the other characters are all very nonsensical. I have read Lara, it is very beautiful poetry. What a pity that Lord Byron should still continue to profess such principles!! Miss Byron is very good humoured and agreeable, and has taken a fancy to me for which I am very much obliged to her. She says I am extremely like her niece Mrs Leigh, Lord Byron's sister, and she makes so many apologies for having mentioned the likeness and is so afraid I should be affronted about it that I suppose poor Mrs Leigh, whom I have never seen, is very ugly and disagreeable.

20 October. – One day this week Mr Gisborne and Mr Henry Ryder called at Hagley. I was much gratified by seeing the former, I happened to be reading his 'Duties of Women' when he entered the room.

It is a pity Katherine did not think better of *Mansfield Park*. On the other hand, she joined its author in liking Thomas Gisborne's *Enquiry into the Duties of the Female Sex*. This was one of the 'conduct books', or guides to female behaviour, that were influential at this time. In *Pride and Prejudice* Mr Collins makes himself disagreeable by reading another such text, James Fordyce's *Sermons to Young Women*, to the Bennet sisters. Jane Austen probably found the genre and her fictional clergyman equally pompous, and was reluctant to read Gisborne's book. She did so when Cassandra persuaded her and admitted she was 'pleased with it'.[36]

Katherine's stay at Hagley was a perfect tonic: 'I did not think I could ever have been so happy again as I have been for the last three weeks.' At the end of October the Bisshopps and Curzons moved on to Merevale Hall in Warwickshire, the home of the Dugdales, who have already made several appearances in these pages. Charlotte Dugdale was a full sibling of Robert Curzon, born like him and their sister Elizabeth of Lord Curzon's second wife Dorothy Grosvenor. Her husband Dudgale Stratford Dugdale was MP for Warwickshire. Their son William was the Westminster schoolboy who had given Little Bob the measles two years before. From Merevale there were excursions, including one to Gopsall Hall in Leicestershire, the splendid Georgian seat of Baroness Howe and Penn Curzon, and then the party broke up: Harriet returned to her children at Hagley, Robert went to London for the new session of parliament, and the Bisshopps headed back to Parham.

In the Midlands Katherine had made notes on paintings in various country houses, and under this stimulation she began a catalogue of the portrait collection at Parham. She had already appended remarks to the list of the house's pictures printed for Sir Cecil in 1794 and compiled a smaller catalogue of engraved portraits, which does not survive. Her catalogue of painted portraits took five years to complete. Each page of the folio-sized volume gives information on a particular canvas, written in black, coloured and gilt letters, and illustrated with coats of arms or other images related to the sitter, surrounded by ruled borders entwined with a bright array of horticultural motifs, often with further ornamentation below. No two pages have the same design, and the whole is of a delicate, refined artistry. Bound in finely tooled goatskin boards decorated with the family's armorial bearings, the catalogue is still in the library at Parham today.

This undertaking added interest to Katherine's quiet winter routine.

KATHERINE'S JOURNAL

December. – If it pleases God that I should live I shall perhaps like to look at this journal at some future time to recall past events. I will therefore write down the manner in which we pass our time here. I get up at nine and go and see Mama, I then breakfast alone in the end parlour, and afterwards play on the harp or piano forte till Mama comes down stairs. I then generally write letters for her or my father, or write to dear Harriet. If it is fine weather I walk with Snugest or ride out on horseback about the park, but it generally rains and then I have time to do my catalogue or do something of that sort (one winter I painted some velvet curtains for the saloon). We dine at ½ past four. In the evening I read and work and play on the P. F. Dear Paley is always with me. We never see anybody but the clergyman on Sunday. I am very glad when it is Mr Cartwright.

On Christmas Eve the Treaty of Ghent was signed, bringing the war between Great Britain and the United States to an end. The defeat of France in the spring had enabled Britain to devote more resources to North America and thereby avert the disasters that Cecil had foretold. By the terms of the treaty the belligerents were back where they had been in 1812, with no loss of territory on either side.

1815

The Curzons stayed at Hagley for the rest of the winter: Robert attended to various items of business and Harriet made the local social calls that occupied so much of a gentlewoman's time. The main occasion for conviviality was at Hagley itself.

HARRIET'S JOURNAL
13 February. – This day being Lord Curzon's birthday and also the day on which my dear Bob fortunately for me came into the world, a large party assembled at dinner to celebrate the anniversary. Mr and Mrs Lister came to dinner, the rest remained all night, Mr and Mrs Dugdale who came from Merevale, Lord Talbot and Mr Talbot, Mr and Mrs Lane and Mr Richard Bagot and Mr Inge, fifteen in all set down to two tables. In the evening the gentlemen were very merry and facetious over the loo and whist parties, and we did not go to bed till past twelve, leaving them to finish their festivities with another glass of punch. Notwithstanding the number and noise of the party Lord Curzon was not at all fatigued, but enjoyed himself extremely and was as cheerful and happy as anybody. We had been a little alarmed by his having lately had repeated bleedings at the nose, but thank God he seems none the worse for it, and has accomplished his 86th year in perfect good health and spirits.

Important to Harriet, and evident throughout her journal, was her Christian faith. While her mother and sister were orthodox churchwomen who invoked the Lord's name at conventional moments, Harriet was sincerely devout and had a clear sense of being in communion through prayer with a living God. She studied the works of religious writers and copied lengthy passages from them into her commonplace book. She was sorry when she had to miss her public devotions, and often recorded the topics of the Sunday sermons she heard.

HARRIET'S JOURNAL
22 January. – Went to church, heard a very good and entertaining sermon from Mr Inge upon the Creation.
29 January. – Went to church, Mr Inges sermon on the happiness of the Just in another world, from this text: 'The Righteous shall shine like the sun in the kingdom of their Father.'

5 February. – Went to church, Mr Inges sermon on charity: 'Then abideth faith, hope and charity, these three, but the greatest of these is charity.'

12 February. – Mr Inges sermon on the parable of the Prodigal Son, from St Luke.

19 February. – Mr Inges sermon upon the duties of children to their parents, and from that subject he took occasion to advert to our great duties to the great parent of the universe. Not so good a sermon as usual.

26 February. – Went to church. Mr Inge gave us a very good sermon upon the education of children and particularly insisted upon the propriety of teaching little children very early the first principles of religion, which gave me great satisfaction as it confirmed me in my own opinion.

At Parham Katherine tried to rouse her parents from the desolation caused by Cecil's death, and she was assisted by their neighbours the Howard Molyneux family, who drew them slowly back into sociable habits, and by Lady Warren, who had lost a son in early manhood and learnt to live with her grief. When they moved to London in spring, soon to be joined by the Curzons, Lady Bisshopp still had no wish to go out and instead held small parties at home for friends. Katherine, who as an unmarried young woman was expected to attend larger entertainments, had to do so without her usual chaperone. This upset her sufficiently to cause headaches and disordered nerves: 'No one can imagine what I suffer in being launched out into the wide world without my mother.'

Although young, unmarried British women had more freedom than their Continental counterparts, they were always accompanied to public gatherings by their mothers or by an older female relative or friend. It was a dull task for a middle-aged woman, whose excitement in balls and assemblies was usually long past. Chaperones in Jane Austen's novels are rarely up to their task: Mrs Allen is a well-meaning but ineffectual guide to Catherine Morland in *Northanger Abbey*; Mrs Jennings a warm-hearted but tactless and obtuse protector of the Dashwood sisters in *Sense and Sensibility*; and Mrs Forster an inadequate brake on the reckless Lydia Bennet in *Pride and Prejudice*. Katherine had several chaperones during periods when her mother felt unable to perform the task and, unlike their fictional counterparts, they all took good care of her.

London was astir this spring, but for a quite different reason from the previous year. Napoleon's escape from Elba and triumphant progress to Paris in March had made a mockery of the victory festivities of 1814, and it would take a mighty effort to subdue him again. The social round went on much as usual, however, and Harriet and Katherine attended numerous balls. None of Katherine's regular dancing partners had advanced any further in her favour. Arthur Eden had long been assiduous, as had Mr Foley, but the latter must have displeased her, for she 'concluded finally' with him at the end of May.

This year the highlight of the social calendar was not in London, but at Arundel Castle, the seat of the Duke of Norfolk.

KATHERINE'S JOURNAL

13 June. – I went [from London] to Parham with Harriet and Mr Curzon and the children in the coach that we might be present at the Duke of Norfolk's fete at Arundel on the 15th, that day being the 600th anniversary of the day on which Magna Charta was signed and which the Duke was to celebrate by opening for the first time the baronial hall, which he has been taking great pains to get ready for this memorable occasion.

15 June. – Mr Curzon, Harriet and I went in the coach to Arundel Castle. Harriet and I were dressed in white muslin and lace, rose coloured ribbons, diamond necklaces and earrings, combs etc. etc. On our entrance into the castle gate our names were called out, and we were received with a flourish of trumpets which so astonished our leaders that we were too happy to find ourselves safely deposited in the house. The Duke received in the gallery and we then proceeded into the drawing room, where we found Lady Stafford and Lady Suffolk. After walking about sometime in the magnificent library, dinner was announced and Mr Dalloway called our names over, and we were sent down according to our rank into the baronial hall, where we sat down 76 to a very fine dinner …

After dinner the Duke rose and made us a speech describing the intention of the entertainment. We then drank his health with three cheers. We afterwards proceeded into the ballroom, when we were joined by some of the neighbours and townspeople, the whole party did not exceed two hundred. The ball was opened by the old Duke of Norfolk and Lady Stafford. I danced with Lord Percy, Lord Gower and Mr Tredcroft, Harriet with Mr Howard the heir. We supped in the barons hall.

After it was all over we came home again. The country was in all the splendid beauty of summer, hightened at this moment in a magnificent degree by the beauteous rising sun. I enjoyed the drive home much more than the ball although I thought I liked *that* very much while I was there. How infinitely superior are the beauties of nature to the poor little attempts at grandeur made by foolish trifling mortals. What a contrast!! To hear the birds singing, to view the glories of the creation, after jogging about on a dusty floor to the sound of a squeaking fiddle by the light of a thousand stinking lamps and candles, which only served to make darkness and dulness visible.

After returning to London Katherine heard reports of the Battle of Waterloo, fought on 18 June. It was a great victory but bought at great cost. Among the fallen was William Curzon, a son of Robert's cousin Lord Scarsdale.

KATHERINE'S JOURNAL

22 June. – After several days anxiety, this days Gazette announced the death of dear William Curzon. I was completely overcome, not on account of his fate, for as it has pleased God he should fall it is doubtless for wise and good purposes, and those are not to be pitied who are snatched in innocence from this vale of tears to be spared future suffering, but to his friends his loss is indeed severe, and to me it renews all the anguish of former sorrows. It was decided I should go to Lady Buckinghamshire's breakfast and I went with George and the Pechells. My father came afterwards. I walked about a little with him and with George Pechell. He was so good to enter into my feelings on hearing every one celebrating the victory of Waterloo and not to mind my stupidity and melancholy ...

There was a ball at Lady Robert Fitzgeralds tonight but I could not think of going. I went to poor Harriet and wept with her. All the other Curzons excepting Bob were playing at loo as if nothing had happened. I have read in the Gazette of this melancholy day the names of eleven men killed and wounded with whom I have been well acquainted. This dreadful slaughter on the plains of Belle Alliance will be deeply felt by many agonized wives, mothers and sisters. I returned this night completely overcome and afflicted with the painful occurrences of the anxious day, to which I had long looked forward with impatience, but how often are our expectations disappointed and why do we ever abandon our imaginations to the pleasing visions of hope.

July brought a flurry of correspondence about the Zouche peerage. It was eight years since the privileges committee had approved the claim and since then, only a stroke of the royal pen had been wanting. Sensing that the final obstacles were melting away, Robert became active on his father-in-law's behalf and waited on Lord Liverpool 'continually'. At last the premier exerted himself for his relations, who learnt to their joy that a warrant for the termination of the abeyance had been placed in a box of documents for the regent to sign. On 1 August a notice appeared in the *London Gazette*. It was reprinted the next day in the newspaper of fashionable society.

MORNING POST
2 AUGUST 1815
His Royal Highness the PRINCE REGENT, in the name and on the behalf of his MAJESTY, has been graciously pleased to order a writ to be issued under the Great Seal of the United Kingdom of Great Britain and Ireland, for summoning Sir CECIL BISSHOPP, of Parham Park, in the county of Sussex, Baronet, up to the House of Peers, by the name, style, and title of Baron Zouche, of Haryngworth, he being lineally descended from the eldest of the two daughters of Edward the last Lord Zouche, of Haryngworth, who died without issue male in 1625, and one of the rightful heirs of the said Barony, which was created by writ of summons in the reign of King Edward the Second.

The new Lady Zouche rejoiced. The title was, she told her husband, a reward and consolation for the sacrifice of their brave sons. The feelings of her daughters were more subdued. Katherine's journal expressed no other emotion than relief that a source of anxiety had been removed, but noted that her mother was so delighted she took her to the opera on the day of the announcement. Harriet too had mixed feelings: 'The attainment of my fathers peerage, the object of so many years anxiety and great expense, is also a circumstance of satisfaction, but alas I can but the more keenly feel that they are gone who would most have enjoyed this honor.' Harriet was the most likely successor – as a baroness in her own right, but for this the title would have to be called out of abeyance again. Katherine gained the style 'the Honourable' before her name, which Harriet already had as the wife of a viscount's son.

Later in August the Curzons left their children with Lady Zouche and set off on a tour of Cheshire, Flintshire, Denbighshire, Lancashire, Westmorland and Cumberland. It was a delightful holiday for Harriet – 'such an admirer of scenery and all those sort of things', as she called herself. From the 1780s William Gilpin's illustrated tours of various parts of Great Britain had created a new appreciation for wild, rugged landscapes, and his concept of 'picturesque' beauty gained wide acceptance. In *Sense and Sensibility* Marianne Dashwood's enthusiasm for the picturesque is gently mocked. Likewise in *Pride and Prejudice*, where Elizabeth Bennet is so thrilled at the prospect of a tour to the Lakes that she dismisses her romantic difficulties: 'Adieu to disappointment and spleen. What are men to rocks and mountains?'[37] The Lakes, Gilpin's most prized landscape, were the climax of Harriet's tour, and a page from her journal shows her adopting a style befitting the sublimity of the subject.

HARRIET'S JOURNAL

27 September. – The whole of the road from Ambleside to Keswick 16 miles is one continued chain of the most enchanting mountain scenery, diversified with every variety of prospect in the different shapes in the hills, some covered with wood, others rising boldly above their craggy heads stretching up to the clouds, some again softly swelling a beautiful extent of the finest verdure, occasional valleys cultivated with corn and enclosed with hedges, and Helvellyn, the parent of a thousand streams, falling in inumberable cascades into the lakes and river below. Grasmere is exactly described by Gray. We got out of the carriage at a farm house and walked on a high knoll in a field, where we had a very good view of the lake from nearly the centre. The torrents which had made the road almost impassable yesterday at Wythburn were now reduced to their own channels and crossed the road in every direction, forming beautiful waterfalls as they bounded along.

After her return Harriet heard from her cousin George Bisshopp. He was enjoying life in Ireland, but already hoping for a benefice to add to the living of Trim that he had been given the previous year.

THE REV. GEORGE BISSHOPP TO HARRIET
VICEREGAL LODGE, PHOENIX PARK, 30 NOVEMBER 1815
... You see by the date of this that I am on a visit to Lord Whitworth and the Duchess,[38] who are, and have been ever since my arrival in Dublin, as attentive as I could have wished them to be. With respect to preferment I am still living on promises, which you may say are very meagre diet, and still every one here says I am growing fatter than I was upon my arrival in Dublin. I know not what to think of this seeming paradox. The truth is that Lord Whitworth has had nothing in his gift since my arrival here, and all the old clergymen seem to have taken new leases. Our old gentleman the Dean of Cloyne died about four days ago. He had very good preferments, but no one seems to know whom Lord Whitworth intends to set up in his stead. I wish he would think of me, and I am sure he cannot forget that there is such a being in existence *when I dine with him every day*. If any thing should turn up in my favor you may rely upon hearing from me amongst the first.

You express a hope that I am passing my time pleasantly; in answer to which I can only say that I am becoming acquainted with all the best society here, and that I meet with such hospitality and attentions of every description as far surpass my expectations, although they had been raised to a pretty high pitch previous to my leaving England. Here we live very quietly. The Duchess and Lord Whitworth breakfast together, as he frequently transacts business with his secretaries at that time. The Aid-de-Camp in waiting Mr Slade and I breakfast together. We then follow our own fancies till dinner time, 7 o'clock. Lord Whitworth does not sit long after dinner, though quite long enough, and we then have coffee in the drawing room, converse upon the rebellion etc. etc. Mr Slade then reads aloud. The work now in hand is

Eustace's Tour. When this is done we all retire. Thus have I given your a true and faithful account of my proceedings, and as you requested me *to tell you all about it* you must not complain of the prolixity of my narrative. It has the same fault as Lord Blaney's, too much eating and drinking in it ...

It is barely necessary to read between the lines here to see a case of toadying to put William Collins in *Pride and Prejudice* quite in the shade. Even less blatantly ambitious clergymen often saw their careers in purely worldly terms, and Henry Tilney in *Northanger Abbey* and Philip Elton in *Emma* are representative specimens of the late Georgian age, just before the Victorian revival in ecclesiastical rigour. George Bisshopp's efforts in his own cause were well rewarded. Shortly after writing to Harriet he was made archdeacon of Aghadoe in County Kerry, an outright sinecure relating to a ruined cathedral church with an inactive parish in an extinct town. 'It is a great blessing to have him well provided for,' remarked Katherine.

At Parham Lady Zouche and Katherine enjoyed caring for Little Bob and Edward, known as 'Bunch' or 'Bunny', and were sad to send them back to their parents in November. Then they and Lord Zouche removed to Brighton, and for seven weeks Katherine combined bracing dips in the sea with equally vigorous social activity. At the Royal Pavilion she was introduced to two 'horridly stupid' Austrian archdukes and saw her parents presented to Queen Charlotte under their new name. Then, at a ball at the Old Ship Inn, she was 'delighted with the unexpected appearance of George Pechell'. This is the first suggestion of an attachment warmer than friendship between Katherine and the young naval officer who had been so sympathetic as she sorrowed amidst the Waterloo celebrations earlier in the year.

The Pechells were old friends of the family, and before George and Katherine were born their parents had spent time together in Paris. Like the Bisshopps, the Pechells had a home in Stratford Place and another in Sussex, theirs being at Aldwick, just outside Bognor. Both George and his elder brother Samuel were in the navy, and as their mother was Lady Warren's sister they benefited from the patronage of Sir John Warren just as Cecil and Charles had done. Samuel was a friend of Charles's, and in 1803 he had visited Parham while on leave to give the family recent news of him.

In 1811 the Bisshopps visited the Pechells at Aldwick, and when Cecil died two years later the Pechells were naturally among those who sent a letter of condolence.

Their unusual surname, pronounced 'Peach-ul', was a deformation of the French Péchels. A noble Huguenot family of Montauban, they were dispossessed and arrested following the revocation of the Edict of Nantes in 1685. Samuel de Péchels was transported to the West Indies but escaped and sailed for London, where he joined a Huguenot regiment that fought with William III's army in Ireland. In a few years more he was reunited with his wife and settled in Dublin. Their son Jacob also entered the army, and when the War Office misspelled his surname he accepted the new version. The family's position was cemented by Jacob's son Paul, who married an Essex heiress and had a successful army career, for which he received a baronetcy in 1797. His son Thomas succeeded him in 1800 and added his mother's maiden name to his own in accordance with a stipulation of her will. Henceforward the current baronet was always Brooke-Pechell and other family members Pechell, though the shorter form tended to be used for everyone.

Sir Thomas Brooke-Pechell, 2nd Baronet, of Paglesham in Essex, had an ornamental army career and served for thirty years as a gentleman usher to Queen Charlotte, who granted him a grace-and-favour apartment in Hampton Court Palace. In 1813 he became MP for the Tory pocket borough of Downton in Wiltshire. He was a deeply religious man, and, in an inversion of the intolerance meted out to his ancestors, he opposed the full emancipation of the king's Catholic subjects. His wife Charlotte was a tall, stately woman with a sonorous voice and a formidable manner, who never forgot, or allowed others to forget, that her late father was Sir John Clavering, Commander-in-Chief in India. The Pechells' estate, acquired by their forebears, was in County Kildare, but they spent all their time in England. Of their five children, three survived into adulthood: Samuel, born in 1785; George, born in 1789; and Frances (Fanny), born in 1795.

George was a tall man, slim but well built, with strong, rugged features, and something of a dandy, often getting through two pairs of white trousers in a day. At twenty-six he already had a creditable naval career behind him. He had joined as a midshipman at fourteen and served under Nelson at the blockade of Toulon in 1804. The next few years took him all round European waters and as far as North America and Bengal, and while he never had the opportunity to shine in a major engagement he displayed energy and courage in disrupting enemy trade and capturing enemy vessels.[39] He was promoted lieutenant in 1810 and commander in 1814. His elder brother Samuel, under whom he briefly served, was present at two of the most brilliant frigate actions of the war and in 1815 was made a Companion of the Bath. Their sister Fanny, who became Katherine's friend, was a quiet girl very much under her mother's thumb.

Precisely when George began to fill Katherine's mind is hard to know; references to him in her journal are coy – in part from delicacy of feeling, in part because elaboration was unnecessary for later recollection. There was also great uncertainty about where the attachment would lead.

1816

This year is thinly documented, and much of what there is concerns Penn Curzon, now aged nineteen. No effort or expense was being spared to prepare him for his majority and succession to his grandfather's title, and Robert, acting for Lord Curzon, looked after his finances and general wellbeing and kept an eye on Gopsall. Penn's educational peregrinations round Scotland in 1813 and France and the Netherlands in 1814 were followed by an exploration of the West Country in 1815; but these were mere preliminaries for the Grand Tour of Europe, to begin when he finished at Oxford in the summer of 1816. Robert made an itinerary that would take him through France, Italy, Switzerland, Austria and Germany, once again with his tutor John Moore, with advice on how he might profit from his experiences. As on previous journeys, Moore was to submit details of their expenses.

Following their standard practice, Harriet saw out the winter with the children at Hagley while Robert attended parliament. During the first years of their marriage he not included much politics in his London letters, thinking the subject would bore her; but he came to realise his error and kept her abreast of the shifts and manoeuvres around the great questions of the day. A reliable supporter of the Tory government, he ascribed calls for social or political change to 'the revolutionary reforming demagogues and rabble', a sentiment Harriet shared. Otherwise his letters contain expressions of solicitude for her, news of family and friends, gossip about those in the public eye, and details of his daily round. He still contrived little gallantries, for instance telling her he intended to visit 'one H. A. C., the most charming of her sex, it would not be discreet to mention names'. He signed himself 'R. Curzon', adhering to the common practice of using surnames even for the most intimate exchanges. Unfortunately her letters to him are almost all lost.

For Lord and Lady Zouche and Katherine the return to Parham in January after the winter carnival of Brighton was sobering. The expense of the barony had not ended with its announcement in the *London Gazette*. In fact several hundreds of pounds were wanted for various purposes, not including the cost of a new livery for the butler, coachman and footmen. On 1 February Lord Zouche took his seat in the House of Lords, but he did so as a man only months away from a humiliating exposure of his ruined finances.

KATHERINE'S JOURNAL
8 January. – I left Brighton with great regret, having passed many pleasant hours there and met with much kindness. I rode home, the rest of the family in the carriage. It rained very hard so I went fast and arrived at Parham alone. It looked very damp and cold but I was glad to pay my respects to my ancestors, as I can always fancy they look pleased at seeing me. We remained at Parham longer than we intended on tiresome business. I forget what day in March Mama and I at length determined to follow my father to town. I went with him the next evening to a party at Lady Warrens, poor dear Snugest sat at home with Mr Rhoades. During this spring we had a variety of painful occurrences. My health and spirits almost sunk under our distresses. I however exerted myself so far as to make up a dress and go to the drawing room with Lady Bulkely. The civilities we had received from the royal family at Brighton made Mama wish that I should show myself immediately. I went again in the course of the spring with Harriet. I also went to Buckingham House the day Princess Charlotte was married to see her dressed for the ceremony. Her head was covered with a profusion of

diamonds, and she looked very handsome and very pale. This was the 2d May.[40]

I went several times to Almacks, where I went with my sister. I sat by her all the evening as it is the fashion to dance quadrilles and waltzes neither of which I join in. I went one evening with Lady E. Palk, and one evening with Lady C. Barham. On these occasions, I was obliged to dance country dances. Mr Cust, Lord Kinnaird and Mr Barham were my partners. Mama was particularly desirous that I should dance the quadrilles to my very great annoyance. I hate shewing off and the standers by make so many ill natured observations it is very alarming. I have suffered so much in my mind I have no pleasure in that kind of amusement, and if I had I should not think there was much gaiety in dancing by rule and for admiration.

Here we see Lady Zouche in the guise of the marrying mother. And although Katherine may have been striking an attitude with her frequently professed loathing for balls and parties, it must have been discomfiting to be paraded about for the delectation of men. When the Season ended she and her parents returned to Parham, where they were joined by the Curzons and received a visit from Sir Thomas and Lady Pechell and their daughter Fanny. Lady Zouche had 'St Anthony's fire' in her leg and could not move from the couch, so the burden of entertaining fell on Katherine. It probably felt like a valedictory performance, for she knew the financial underpinnings of the family's lifestyle were giving way. It looked as if Parham might have to be sold, and although this was averted the need to shut up the house and auction its contents was galling enough. What, if anything, could be saved was a thorny question.

KATHERINE'S JOURNAL
November. – We had much painful business all the month of November. My father was in London, dear Snugest and I in the most distressing anxiety. We sent for Mr Blake and he was of great use to us, but our situation was very trying. My father returned and we hoped we should pass the remainder of the winter in peace, but alas, after many struggles to keep up appearances, my dearest mother and myself were compelled to leave poor dear Parham and on the 2d of December (through the

kindness of Mr Rhoades we were enabled by the protection and assistance he afforded us and which we stood so much in need of) to take refuge in Stratford Place. I attempted to make dear Mama as happy as I could, but I found it very difficult to support my own spirits under the continual harassing I was obliged to sustain. I endeavoured to amuse myself with my catalogue, but even that occupation only served to recall a train of melancholy and heart-breaking reflections.

I had a difficult and irksome task in relating our humiliating situation to Lady Liverpool and Miss Brudenell, but I was fortunate in their both expressing themselves with much kindness and affection, particularly the former, as from her such sympathy is quite unexpected. We saw George Bisshopp, he soon returned to Ireland. Helena Robinson came to town in January and it was some comfort to me to have a person so near whom I could find pleasure in conversing with and who would enter warmly into my distresses. To Mary Poulett and George Pechell I never can feel enough obliged for the kind and warm manner with which they both in their different ways did everything in their power to alleviate my sorrows and afford me comfort and consolation. George Pechell came twice to London to see me, and the affectionate sympathy of this dear friend in some measure prevented my sinking in to despondence. I have indeed found a brother in him.

Poor dear Nelson was run over and killed.[41] He has followed the carriage morning, noon and night for so many years and I have so many pleasing associations connected with his dear black head that his death is quite a sorrow for me. I wish great affliction had the effect of making me unmindful of lesser ones, but I think I am grown more susceptible of trifles than I used to be in happier times and before I thought of beginning this journal, which has only proved the record of a succession of misery and anxiety. I am sometimes tempted to discontinue and destroy it, *but I lament so much having kept no account of many happy days I passed from the time I was seventeen until one and twenty* that I will endeavour to persevere in writing this, as perhaps I may at some future time (if it pleases God to spare my life) derive some pleasure in looking over even this deplorable remembrancer of my troubles, and I now resume it after the interval of nearly a years cessation, as I cannot bear to write at the moment of painful anxiety. If I die I shall be much obliged to the first person into whose hands this book may happen to fall to destroy it instantly.

1817

As the auction at Parham was prepared Katherine stayed with her mother in London, relieved that at least the most precious heirlooms would not feature in the catalogue. Lord Zouche wanted to include them, but was prevented by a deed resettling the estate on Cecil's marriage in 1805. The sale took place over four days at the beginning of February; furniture, plate, china, glass, linen, wines, musical instruments, carriages and horses all went under the hammer, and what remained was dispersed later in smaller sales organised on behalf of individual creditors.

These proceedings placed further stress on the relationship between Lord Zouche and his family. He lived apart from them, answered none of their questions, and acted secretively and unpredictably. For a while he refused to let out the park and its farm despite being unable to pay his labourers, who went hungry. It was left to his wife and daughters to safeguard their own interests. Robert assured Harriet that her allowance was guaranteed by her marriage settlement, and that if necessary they could appoint receivers to enforce its payment. The positions of Katherine and Lady Zouche were more precarious, and it was some time before they could be certain that their incomes would continue. Robert discreetly sounded out friends about loans – not required as it turned out – to tide them over until their affairs were in order. Meanwhile Lord Curzon offered to assist Harriet if there was something in the sale she particularly wished to have.

In the spring Katherine was pitched into another Season, and there was nothing affected in her expressions of distaste for its offerings this year. The depredation of Parham was not her only worry, for George Pechell was in love with her and she with him, but her parents would not let them marry. The reasons for this can be guessed. Although the Pechells were their friends, they were not on a par with the Bisshopps even before the acquisition of the Zouche peerage. The Bisshopp baronetcy dated back to 1620, nine years after James I established the title as a hereditary honour, whereas the Pechell baronetcy was only two decades old, one of hundreds awarded in George III's reign. This torrent of fresh titles diluted their individual value, and holders of older titles looked down on them from a great height. Moreover the Pechells' landholdings were in Ireland rather than England; the 'Marine Cottage' at Aldwick, built for Sir Thomas on a seven-acre site in 1802, was a country retreat rather than a family seat; and George was a second son with his own way to make in the world. Set against all this were the Bisshopps' financial woes, but these may have made them more, not less, determined to find a good match for Katherine.

Harriet, who agreed with her parents, told George he must give up hope of obtaining her.

GEORGE PECHELL TO HARRIET
STRATFORD PLACE, LATE MAY 1817

My dear Mrs Curzon – As I can never forget the kindness displayed on your part on my most unfortunate case, so under that impression do I ask you to give me your advice as to my future conduct towards your dear sister. I am willing to be guided by your known good opinion, and if it is your wish *as well as her own* that I should retire from the world I will add to that sacrifice to which I challenge the world to find a parallel.

I have thought that when we meet abroad it is disadvantageous to us both to appear as if a quarrel had taken place. I am myself of [the] opinion that we should be upon friendly terms, as the extraordinary difference that appeared last night only gives the world more reason to talk us over.

It will be my most anxious desire to do all that is honourable by dear Katherine, but it is not to be expected that I can *forget* what has passed, yet in my conversations I will studiously avoid touching upon any subject that may relate to our truly distressing situation.

As perhaps this is the last time of my giving you any concern by raking up unpleasant sensations, so if you think it proper to shew this to Katherine it may be consoling to her to reflect that whatever I do I trust she will consider that I endeavour to act for the best.

I think I need not add that I feel the highest respect *for you and yours* and that you will believe me

Ever yours most sincerely and obliged
George R. Pechell

HARRIET TO GEORGE PECHELL
WELBECK STREET, 31 MAY 1817

Dear George – I am extremely obliged to you for your note and for the kind expressions you employ in mentioning me. It is my opinion that you should leave London for a time, and this I think is advisable on your own account as well as for the sake of my sister. I have no doubt that you are always desirous to act in the most honorable and proper manner on all occasions, as your whole conduct has proved upon this subject. Particularly I am sure you will not hesitate to do any thing that your mutual friends recommend to put an end to further discussion and recover your own peace of mind. It appears to me that you subject yourself to very unpleasant observation by continuing to meet Katherine in general society, where you must be aware your attentions excite notice which we agreed is always better to be avoided, or if you do not speak to each other the reason must be obvious to every body, and I am anxious no more reports should arise. If you find any comfort in talking the matter over with me once more I shall be happy to see you, but I believe I have already made you acquainted with my opinions and can only add that I sincerely regret the difficulties should be so great as to put an end to your hopes and give you such pain.

I trust you will always continue to consider me as one of your most obliged and sincere friends

H. A. C.

I shall not see dear Kate again today, but I certainly will communicate to her your note and my answer.

She did so, and Katherine thanked her for treating George and herself so considerately. Lady Zouche was growing impatient, and told Harriet she hoped the matter was now closed: 'I think your note a very proper one and I hope it will give a total end to this silly business.' Katherine had just had a fit of crying, she said, but would no doubt soon feel better: 'Her own good sense and excellent principles will prevent her allowing this incident to dwell too much on her dear mind.'

It only remained for the lovers to part.

GEORGE PECHELL TO HARRIET
LONDON, EARLY JUNE 1817

My dear Mrs Curzon – The painful task of taking leave of her who has been the sole occupier of my thoughts has this day taken place, and for which kind consideration I stand in the highest degree indebted, as it has shewn with what confidence I have been honoured with, and I beg you will convey to her and Lady d. L. Z. my warmest thanks.

I have resolved to set out for Stapleford[42] (on the receipt of Lady Warren's letter) on Thursday night by the mail, as from what we have all agreed a little absence may benefit those parties for whom I feel the most concern. As for myself, I consider it a lost case, and whether it is one day or one year no change can take place in my sentiments, whatever alteration may ensue in other respects.

I propose remaining till Lady W. returns to town, about the 15th or 20th, when I hope my ever valued friend will have so far recovered her spirits as to meet each other occasionally in that world which has been the occasion of all our misery. I have promised K. not to banish myself from my family, and perhaps the short period from my returning to town to the time of our going into Sussex will not exceed a week, so that I apprehend we shall not (however the separation must be painful to me) meet very often, but it will be I trust upon the terms of an affectionate *sister*, which has been some relief to *that mind* which I do assure you has felt in the most sincere manner a trial which few ever I believe have had the equal to sustain …

For the interest you have taken in my distressing case accept my dear Mrs Curzon the durable tribute of a grateful heart, and that prosperity and happiness may again be centered in that family (in which I had placed my fondest hopes) will be the constant prayer of

> Your most affectionately and ever obliged
> George Richard Pechell

Should you wish to see me before I go at any time I shall be most happy to come to Welbeck Street.

He does not appear to be committing himself to a very strenuous avoidance of Katherine. Nor did she regard the courtship as dead; she would not deceive her mother or Harriet, but expected that in time their opposition would fall away. Nevertheless she was dejected, and after encountering George in the street one day felt 'very melancholy'. She lost weight and looked off-colour, and it was decided that she needed a spell at Hastings. The Curzons took her there and rented a house in The Croft, one of the town's smartest streets. Soon they fell into a relaxing, healthy routine.

HARRIET'S JOURNAL
Early August. – My morning life is to rise about 8, breakfast at 9, then walk down to the sea for a little while. At eleven the childrens lessons till one, their dinner hour, the rest of the morning spent in walking about with my sister and sometimes taking a drive in one of the little donkey carts which are constantly waiting to be hired on the sands at the price of 18 pence per hour. Dinner at 5, after dinner another walk, and tea and my books and music conclude the day, go to bed about ten. On Thursday [7 August] the dear boys bathed for the first time. Bob was delighted, Edward rather frightened. The weather proved too stormy and the sea too rough for them to bathe again the two following days.

16 August. – I bathed in the warm bath for the first time in my life, and was surprised to find it made me rather nervous and giddy ... Today I walked down the hill behind our house for the second time, having only ventured to do so with Bob first the day before, and I was happy to find myself rather improved in courage.

17 August. – Went to church to the upper church, made a variety of good resolutions. Dr Whistler the clergyman, a respectable looking old man, preached upon the Parable of the Publican and the Pharisee going to the temple to pray. Returned home and took a walk with Bob and Kate upon the opposite hill. A beautiful view of the sea, quite rough with one of the high south west winds so common upon this coast, and yet a very fine clear day. Set on the parade, came home and wrote my journal.

KATHERINE'S JOURNAL
18 August. – I was made happy by the arrival of my dearest mother. I had bathed on that day for the first time. I bathed 10 times, the sea is very rough at Hastings, but I enjoyed bathing

very much notwithstanding. Dear Harriet and Bob were so excessively kind to me during the fortnight I was with them that I feel truly grateful for their tender care of me, indeed I believe it saved my life.

28 August. – In the evening to our great astonishment my father sent us word he was in Hastings and would dine with us the next day.

29 August. – We had a delightful walk towards the Priory over some styles, which abound in this country. Papa dined with us, and we all went excepting him to a party at Mrs Manns. I danced kitchen dances to two broken fiddle's and afterwards quadrilles, which the people could not dance.

30 August. – Harriet, Snugest and I set out in Harriets carriage to go to Ashburnham. One of the post horses kicked and was so restive that we were very much frightened and all got out. Papa came out of the inn and set us off in his carriage. The entrance to the park at Ashburnham is very handsome indeed, the house a sort of modern gothic not good looking. We were not admitted to see it which we thought very inhospitable after we had taken the trouble to go twelve miles to see it. However we persisted in going into the church, where we saw the shirt poor King Charles 1st [wore] when he was beheaded, his watch was also there. Lady Ashburnham has lately had the shirt washed to the great regret of the old man who shows it.

Lord Zouche did not remain long at the inn, but the others stayed at their house in The Croft for another two weeks. There was more walking, sea-bathing and churchgoing, as well as excursions to other country houses, to Battle Abbey, and to the Martello towers that dotted the coastline. Then the Curzons went to Walmer Castle in Kent at the invitation of Lord Liverpool, who sometimes resided there in his capacity as Lord Warden of the Cinque Ports. Katherine and Lady Zouche were reunited with them in London, and Katherine and the Curzons continued to Gorhambury, near St Albans in Hertfordshire. Its mistress, the Countess of Verulam, was Lord Liverpool's half-sister and a daughter of one of Lord Zouche's aunts. She was very much a great lady and sometimes a little stern, but had a good heart and a sincere desire to help others. Her husband was a kind man and a generous host, always keen to have as many friends around him as possible. Both were fond of the Curzons, who rarely travelled between London and Hagley without stopping at Gorhambury.

Harriet hoped that these hosts and their guests would carry on the good work begun at Hastings in distracting Katherine from sad thoughts. As she and George were not engaged they were not allowed to correspond, and her mother and sister hoped she would forget him. She did not, but learned to appear content. The stymied courtship had caused no coolness in the family, but the days of uninhibited frankness were over.

KATHERINE TO LADY ZOUCHE
GORHAMBURY, 21 SEPTEMBER 1817
My dearest Snugest – We are both very much obliged to you for your kind little note ... I am just come from church where we have all been. Eliza Hervey arrived yesterday morning and is staying here, Lady Essex brought her and went on herself to Cashiobury[43] after having passed the whole morning here, which dérangé'd our plans as we were just setting off to go and see Ashridge. Lady Dering and Mrs Cholmondeley Dering also came and made a long visit. Mr and Mrs George Byng dined here and brought the two Miss Townshends tweedle dum and dee with them. They were all very agreeable. I wore my lilac ribbons and the Fright made me put on the amethysts in addition. We make singing in the evening, but not in your way, for Lady Verulam plays Italian bravura's, in which we all take parts and of course ill. There is only one fire, in the library, which I sit quite close to, and the piano forte being in the drawingroom it is very cold and forlorn going in to sing and coming back again. The china closet is made into a book room, and contains all the new novels, plays and trash which cannot be admitted into the library ...

I am sorry my dearest Snugest I frightened you about my cold. It is nothing at all, I am only very susceptible of the cold weather as the climate is so different to Hastings, but I am getting accustomed to it now and I wrap myself up very warm ... I wish you could see the drawingroom curtains here my dear Snugest they are quite beautiful, the blue damask looks so very cheerful. Bob desires me to give you his love, Fright means to write a little bit ...

Katherine liked Gorhambury despite its poor heating, and after three weeks with her parents in London she returned alone for another fortnight. Each day she and Lady Verulam walked out to meet the men as they returned from hunting, and Katherine was astonished to see the quantities of game spread out on the steps of the house in the evenings.

KATHERINE TO LADY ZOUCHE
GORHAMBURY, OCTOBER 1817

… We had a grand concert yesterday, Lord and Lady Bridgewater, Lord Essex and a Col. Benington besides ourselves. In the evening Lady Bridgewater and Lord Essex and Charlotte[44] sang, and I tried to *bear a bob* when I was wanted, but I am persecuted with my old enemy the cough, which comes on whenever I attempt to speak or sing and is very tiresome. After the singing we played at commerce and I won the pool, according to custom 20 shillings. This morning Lord and Lady Bridgewater are gone. At 12 o'clock Prince Esterhazy[45] arrived, they all made him go out shooting instantly poor man. They are to have a great battue for him to day and we have just seen the party set off *in carriages* to the place where the game is to be found. I understand this is the way foreigners always expect to chassez au fusil, which rather surprised me …

I can do without my smelling bottle, but perhaps you will be so good to send my brown tassels if you think it worth while by Lady Liverpool if she should come here this week, as I rather think I heard she was expected. I am come without my Common Prayer Book. I do not recollect where I laid it when I returned from church last Sunday, but if you or Ann should see it perhaps you would wrap it up and give it to Lady Liverpool, but do not tell her what it is as I shall hear endless jokes about it, and now I am far away from you I am fallen in to my old feel, je n'aime pas qu'on me ris au nez …

Katherine's hosts took her to a ball at nearby Hatfield House, the seat of the Marquess of Salisbury, and then she returned to London. There she wrote an account of the ball for Harriet, now at Hagley, and followed it with some distressing news just arrived from Claremont House, Surrey, the home of Princess Charlotte and her consort Prince Leopold.

KATHERINE TO HARRIET
STRATFORD PLACE, 5 NOVEMBER 1817
... We had a very pleasant dinner and evening at Hatfield. My dress answered perfectly and looked beautiful, dear Charlotte was so goodnatured to be quite anxious about it. She came in to my dressing room and looked at my head, before proceeding upon the rest of the toilette, the whole of which was completed entirely to her satisfaction.

We had some little degree of manoeuvring to leave Lady Liverpool at home, however she agreed to dine alone and we four set off in the coach. Our four dressing rooms were en suite which was extremely comfortable, they were what are called Lady Salisbury's summer apartments. As soon as we were attired we made our appearance in King James' room, where Lady S. received us surrounded by men, Mr Giles etc. The effect of that beautiful room and the gallery lighted up is quite magnificent.

We were 15 at dinner. I sat between Cecil Jenkinson and Mr Montgomerie of Inadrille fame, whom you of course know by sight. The rest of the party consisted of Sir Joseph, Lady and Miss Banks, Gerald Wellesley, Lady Westmeath and some men. Lord Salisbury and Lord Westmeath are absent. After dinner several people came in and sat down to three card tables, having admired my dress which Lady Salisbury showed off and explained. We sat very formal for some time, and I was thinking how dull it was when Lady S. jumped up from her whist and desired me to go and dance. So I walked down the gallery with my partner, and finding myself followed by three misses and men I had not seen before who rose out of the furniture, we performed a quadrille. I never was more frightened, for the natives stood all in a hord just opposite to me. Sir Joseph Banks was wheeled in in his chair to see, and Lord and Lady Verulam came out of the card room to look as they said after their child. Wasn't it very kind of them?

After I had performed this I set every body a going at an English country dance, and then danced quadrilles alternately with C. Jenkinson and Mr Montgomerie, in which Charlotte joined. She attempted waltzing, but it did not take. When the cards were over we concluded with the coquet, which was the greatest fun in the world. Lady Salisbury danced it to perfection, I wish you had seen her do it with Lord V. I enjoyed it very much and danced my shoes into holes. At twelve o'clock we returned home safe in spite of a most impenetrable fog, and I left dear Gorhambury with great regret.

Poor Princess Charlotte has been a most terrible long time in labour. I hope it will be over before I close this, that you may be duly informed of the event …

I must wish you a good night, my dearest Fright, as I am very sleepy. I fear this is all scarcely legible. I will resume tomorrow. Ever your most affectionate

Katherine Bisshopp

Thursday morning
The dreadful news of poor Princess Charlotte's death has just reached London. They do not own it yet at Camelford House, no official account of the court having as yet been received by the Queen etc. It is very shocking Sir Richard Croft could not save the poor child even. It was a boy, which adds to the national calamity. I saw Lady Ashbrook yesterday. She said Princess Charlotte was so feverish she had not been allowed to taste meat or wine for a considerable time …

At twenty-one Charlotte was the people's idol, adored for her artless manner, her wholesome good looks, and the quiet felicity of her marriage. Her pregnancy, on which the succession appeared to depend, became a subject of intense public interest, only heightened when it went two weeks beyond its expected term. Fifty hours of labour yielded a stillborn boy on the evening of 5 November, and in a few hours more the princess died of postpartum bleeding. There was an outpouring of grief; two ladies of the Curzons' acquaintance miscarried and a third suffered convulsions. Questions about the *accoucheur* Sir Richard Croft turned into accusations and jibes, and although he had done nothing that departed from standard obstetric practice, his reputation was ruined. Three months later he shot himself.

After just a few days at Stratford Place Katherine was despatched to Hagley with a maid and a footman, continuing the policy of occupying her as much as possible and keeping her from London and the possibility of meeting George. On her journey north she stayed at Sulby Hall, Northamptonshire, the home of Viscount Barnard, who had married her friend Mary Poulett's elder sister Sophia. Sulby's problem was its intermittent connection with the postal system. Since letters were the only means of remote communication, any disruption in their conveyance excited all manner of fears.

KATHERINE TO LADY ZOUCHE
SULBY HALL, 17 NOVEMBER 1817
My dearest Snugest – I have this morning received two more letters from you including Brom, Eliz. and Thorpe. I am only quite shocked at my apparent ingratitude in not being able to acknowledge all the time and thought you bestowed upon me last week. I would not lose such a very kind and entertaining letter as that which has at length reached me upon any account. Sophia means I believe to make a great fuss at the post office as mistake's often occur, and as she truly says if you had wished to call me suddenly home it would have been a very great distress. I flatter myself I bore the thing rather heroically, as I never was before so far away from every body I belong to …

All you say of Sir R. C. and the Princess is very interesting. I think (as dear Grandmama used to say) the man ought to be kicked. I hope the Frights black slip you mention arrived in time. How could she think of being at the trouble of sending for it, as a few yards of silk bought at Rugely and run up would do as well. I feel quite anxious it should get safe as the crape would be very odd without, but I shall see her tomorrow dear love …

I hear to day the medical people say Princess Charlotte was not formed ever to bring a living child into this world, but surely this only makes the case worse, as they ought to have made more efforts to insure her safety the day before she actually died. The Hanburys do not talk much on the subject, which Sophia is surprised at, as she says when Mrs Poulett was dying they could talk of nothing else, but all the particulars …

In fact conversation at Sulby was quite light-hearted, and included an anecdote that Katherine told her mother after arriving at Hagley.

KATHERINE TO LADY ZOUCHE
HAGLEY, 23 NOVEMBER 1817
… I must tell you my dear Snugest a story I heared there as all Northamptonshire vary with it. Lady Jersey upon going abroad last year happened to say to some people who were setting round

her, what shall I do with my youngest boy. Lady Althorpe who is *not* her particular friend but very fond of children said, do leave it with me. The business was settled in a moment and the child sent to Lady Althorpe, who kept it for months and guarded it with the most unremitting attention. Now Lady Jersey is come home she has sent for the child, and also sent *a gown* to Lady Althorpe with her best thanks. The same message and present was sent at the same time to the head nurse. Lady Althorpe is furious and thinks herself quizzed, every body abuses Lady Jerseys insolence …

At Hagley Katherine was warmly received, and Lord Curzon told her she must do as she liked in every way. Everyone there was well and in good spirits. Harriet had grown plump and looked good in her mourning for Princess Charlotte, and Edward had been 'breeched', the change that boys underwent when the frocks all small children wore were discarded in favour of trousers: 'He is really now what Nature intended him to be, a very handsome boy,' wrote Katherine. He and Little Bob were delighted with the books she had brought them and enjoyed trying out their newly acquired French. Robert and Harriet took her to stay with the Dugdales at Merevale and Penn Curzon showed her round the house and gardens at Gopsall. The high point of her six-week stay was a party to celebrate Penn's majority. Lord Curzon, aged eighty-eight, was delighted to have lived long enough to witness it.

The paroxysm of public grief and finger-pointing that followed Princess Charlotte's death slowly subsided, and Harriet took a measured view of what had happened.

HARRIET'S JOURNAL
I took some pains at the time and since to obtain information of the particulars of her illness and death, but all the accounts I received were so uncertain and often contradictory that I could not feel any thing I heard could be depended upon sufficiently to record. The system of low living which she adopted and which was Sir Richard Crofts usual practice seems to have been ill suited to her constitution, as it has always been believed contrary to the constitution of all the royal family. It was therefore very unlucky in this instance that it was so

rigidly adhered to that she had eat no meat nor drunk wine for 3 months and consequently suffered a long and tedious labour, and she was never strong. The melancholy death of Dr Crofts some months after gave rise to many foolish conjectures, which had certainly no foundation, for till he shot himself he was universally respected and consulted and allowed to be one of the first men in this branch of his profession.

Princess Charlottes resignation, her patience, and still more the regular, quiet, and exemplary life she had led since her marriage made her beloved by all ranks of people, and in their grief for her unexpected death every body seemed to forget she had ever erred, and attributed her failings to her youth and her improvement to her experience. I could not help feeling that she died at a fortunate moment, for she probably never would have been so deeply regretted.

Correspondences with Persuasion

A few months before Princess Charlotte, on 18 July 1817, Jane Austen died in Winchester at the age of forty-one. She and her sister had moved into rooms in College Street in May so that a local doctor could treat her for a nameless illness, but the case was hopeless and the end soon came. Jane Austen's death went almost unnoticed outside her family, but her brother Henry arranged for her to be buried in Winchester Cathedral, where the inscription on her marble gravestone celebrates her qualities of character and mind.

In December of the same year, *Persuasion* and *Northanger Abbey* were published together in four volumes, with a short biographical notice by Henry Austen. As usual with books appearing towards the end of a year, the next was indicated on the title page. *Northanger Abbey* was an old manuscript, but *Persuasion* was Jane Austen's last complete novel, begun in August 1815 and finished in August 1816. It was set in the very recent past, the months from the summer of 1814 until February 1815, in other words the period before the Hundred Days in which the United Kingdom prematurely celebrated victory over the Emperor Napoleon.

The significance of *Persuasion* to our subject is that it intensifies the reflection of the real world of the Bisshopps in the imagined world of Jane Austen. We have already seen parallels with the other novels in aspects of social and cultural life and in the circumstances and outlooks of individual people. *Persuasion* presents an extension of this, no less than the story of a heroine that matches, to a remarkable degree, the situation and experiences of the central figure of our narrative. The configuration of people around Anne Elliot and Katherine Bisshopp, the problems attending their courtships, and the natures, habits and sentiments of the two women themselves all correspond.

Anne Elliot only gradually comes into focus in *Persuasion*. The first three chapters are devoted to her father Sir Walter Elliot, Baronet, of Kellynch Hall in Somerset. The novel opens with him reading his family's entry in the baronetage 'with an interest which never failed'.[46] It is, for him, 'the book of books',[47] and perusing it is his favourite occupation and readiest consolation. As his title dates from the reign of Charles II he feels disdain for 'the almost endless creations of the last century',[48] a view probably shared by Sir Cecil Bisshopp, whose title is even older. And if Sir Walter has no extinct peerage to chase, he instead runs after his aristocratic connections the Dowager Viscountess Dalrymple and her daughter the Hon. Miss Carteret. The nullity of these ladies, aside from the handles to their names, makes Sir Walter's eagerness to cultivate and parade their acquaintance seem nakedly snobbish. With both baronets, the lack of a son to succeed them only adds to the futility of their obsession with rank.

A man of high pedigree must live in high style. Sir Walter's sumptuous wardrobe and household expenditure and his sojourns in London are, like Sir Cecil's paintings and other artefacts, his gifts of game, and the fortune he spends claiming the Zouche barony, not just luxuries, but statements of personal consequence. Such men are too lordly to pay close attention to the management of their estates, and so they neglect the source of their wealth. Sir Walter leaves everything in the hands of his legal agent Mr Shepherd and sees his tenants and cottagers purely as adjuncts of his own grandeur. Sir Cecil does not even reply to letters from his agent Robert Hurst about problems with his landholdings and is served with a subpoena because he fails to meet his obligations under a timber contract.

The natural result of such neglect is mounting financial trouble. As with Parham and Sir Cecil, 'the Kellynch property was good, but not equal to Sir Walter's apprehension of the state required in its possessor'.[49] Sir Walter ignores his tradesmen's bills and half-heartedly contemplates a few minor economies, but his approach to his difficulties is to dither. Sir Cecil is both secretive and inactive, much to the vexation of his son Cecil. With absolute power over money matters, and a refusal to exercise the responsibility that comes with it, the baronets place a burden on their wives and fail in their duty to their children. At last they are forced to take the drastic step of quitting their estates, Sir Walter to move to Bath while Kellynch is let to Admiral Croft, and Sir Cecil to reside in London while the contents of Parham are sold and the house left empty.[50]

From the fourth chapter of *Persuasion* the dominant character is its heroine, who has far more in common with Katherine Bisshopp than an unsatisfactory father. In social background they are as close as can be, growing up in large country houses as daughters of baronets with inherited acres. Like Katherine, Anne Elliot has an 'elegant and cultivated mind'.[51] She is a keen reader and discusses important literary works of the day with Captain Benwick, to whom she recommends a selection of memoirs, collections of letters and works by moralists to help him cope with a bereavement. Anne and Katherine are all too familiar with lowness of spirits themselves, and have recourse to reading for consolation and distraction as well as mental improvement. Perhaps Anne finds solace in making a duplicate of the catalogue of pictures at Kellynch, as Katherine does in making a new one of the painted portraits at Parham.

In accomplishments they are much alike. Anne is musical, a better player on the pianoforte than the Miss Musgroves even if their performances win more parental acclaim, and when she leaves Kellynch books and music are the main possessions she has to sort through. She shares Katherine's relatively unusual ability to read Italian, and at a concert in Bath she translates at sight some Italian lyrics for her cousin William Elliot. Both women show touches of romanticism, admiring Lord Byron and thrilling to the beauties of nature. Katherine contrasts the tawdry splendour of a ball at Arundel Castle with the glories of creation and the dawn chorus on the way home, while Anne enjoys 'the

last smiles of the year upon the tawny leaves and withered hedges'
during the walk to Winthrop and calls to mind some poetical
evocations of autumn.[52]

Katherine's journal and letters reveal a lively awareness
of the feelings and motives of people around her, sometimes
approaching Anne's almost superhuman powers of penetration.
They are good-natured observers, but capable of wry and critical
judgements, as when Anne notes that Captain Wentworth is
basking a little in the adulation of the Musgrove sisters. In flashes
Anne has Katherine's sense of humour. She is amused by the
driving style of Admiral and Mrs Croft, with him holding the
reins and her giving them a tug when he threatens to veer off
course. She can also smile at herself: 'What wild imaginations one
forms, where dear self is concerned! How sure to be mistaken!'
she remarks after her assumptions about something William Elliot
has said of her are corrected.[53]

The pain their fathers' shallow pride of status causes to Anne and
Katherine is aggravated by their own more rational attachment to
the dignity of their families. Anne's 'desolate tranquillity' on giving
up Kellynch is a stronger emotion than any of the other Elliots
feel,[54] and Katherine almost makes herself ill with the humiliation
of abandoning Parham. Yet they remain resolute and try to keep
up appearances. Katherine makes financial and other arrangements
while her father is away in London and carries out the painful task
of informing acquaintances of their situation, while Anne speaks
with the head gardener and pays leave-taking visits to the poor
of the parish. Later we learn of her charitable work, as we will
of Katherine's, the proper discharge of a responsibility that social
privilege imposes.

It is partly because of their sense of family honour that Anne
and Katherine heartily wish they could respect their fathers. The
Bisshopp women try to prop up Sir Cecil's public respectability
for all their private irritation with him, and on his death a few
years hence Katherine formulates some positive words about him
for posterity, though afterwards she recoils from the memory of
the ordeals his financial entanglements caused her. For her part,
Anne is mortified to read William Elliot's description of Sir Walter
as a fool whose company is unbearable, but her own desire to
esteem him is impeded by 'a great deal of quiet observation,
and a knowledge, which she often wished less, of her father's

character'.[55] The fathers are fortunate not to know what their daughters think of them.

Given the correspondences between them, it is natural that Anne and Katherine should fall in love with similar men. All the same, the extent of their similarity is striking. George Pechell's circumstances and character will appear more fully in due course, but a comparison with those of Frederick Wentworth can be outlined. They are younger brothers of gentry stock, needing to earn their own keep. They have entered the navy out of inclination and served with merit, Pechell having several more years at sea ahead of him. Wentworth is introduced to the reader as 'a remarkably fine young man, with a great deal of intelligence, spirit and brilliancy',[56] a description that applies equally to Pechell. Wentworth is so handsome that even the fastidious Sir Walter is 'very much struck by his personal claims',[57] while Pechell's good looks are clear from his portraits. They are naval men in the true Jane Austen style: manly in their bearing, sure of their abilities, and eager for success.

In their dealings with others they are independent-minded, honest and forthright, but without coarseness of manner. Pechell makes his first substantial appearance in Katherine's journal at an outdoor breakfast party in June 1815, where he is sympathetic to her grief over her brother Cecil's death even as everyone else is celebrating the victory at Waterloo. With pardonable self-delusion, she feels she has found a new brother in him. Wentworth shows the same delicacy when, overcoming his distaste at the memory of the worthless Dick Musgrove, he tries to soothe Mrs Musgrove's reheated sorrow about his death some years earlier: '[He] entered into conversation with her, in a low voice, about her son, doing it with so much sympathy and natural grace, as shewed the kindest consideration for all that was real and unabsurd in the parent's feelings.'[58]

Another point in common is musicality, though neither man gives any sign of being a performer. Wentworth is 'very fond of music'[59] and well able to discuss the merits of the Bath concert with Anne. Katherine's journal for 1818 records that George was 'very much vexed' when she sold her harp, a step presumably taken because of her family's financial woes, and he is meant when she writes five years later that she has shown her new guitar to a good judge. Finally, neither man is averse to romantic expression, appealing to that strain in the women they love. Pechell's letters of 1817 powerfully convey his anguish at the dashing of his hopes with Katherine, and at the same time his refusal to believe that all is lost. Likewise the soulful letter Wentworth writes to Anne at the White Hart in Bath: 'You pierce my soul. I am half agony, half hope. Tell me not that I am too late, that such precious feelings are gone for ever.'[60]

For the female protagonist, the most important person apart from the man she loves is her mother. In Anne's case the maternal role belongs to her godmother Lady Russell, her own mother having died when she was fourteen. Lady Russell is a childless widow, 'a sensible, deserving woman' who is 'of steady age and character', with 'excellent judgment' and 'strict integrity'.[61] She is 'a benevolent, charitable, good woman, and capable of strong attachments; most correct in her conduct, strict in her notions of decorum, and with manners that were held a standard of good-breeding'.[62] On Lady Elliot's death, after seventeen years of suffering at Sir Walter's side but before the narrative begins, Lady Russell took over responsibility for Anne, watching over her with pride and solicitude, with 'almost a mother's love, and mother's rights'.[63] Anne returns her feelings, and readily defers to the woman who seems so well suited to guide her across the threshold to adulthood.

The qualities ascribed to Lady Russell mirror those of Katherine's mother Lady Bisshopp, afterwards Lady Zouche. Another resemblance lies in Lady Russell being a highly cultivated woman, a keen reader who likes to pass on books that have stimulated her. Furthermore, her intimacy with the late Lady Elliot, so strong that she settled in Kellynch village just to be near her, recalls Lady Bisshopp's sentimental friendships with Lady Stawell, Lady Bromley and Lady Warren. This female solidarity, deepened by the experience of difficult husbands, extends to a concern for one another's children. Lady Warren keeps young Cecil in order in St Petersburg and looks after Charles 'in a motherly way' in Plymouth, while Lady Russell takes almost complete charge of Anne from the hopelessly self-absorbed Sir Walter.[64]

The commendations with which the narrator introduces Lady Russell are justified by the good sense, affability and kindness she shows when she appears as a speaking person. In particular, her constant concern for Anne's welfare and her charitable attitude to Anne's impoverished friend Mrs Smith count strongly in her favour. However, she has a weakness, namely 'prejudices on the side of ancestry' and 'a value for rank and consequence' that sometimes impair her judgement.[65] Lady Bisshopp has the same weakness, and exults on becoming Lady Zouche despite the ruinous cost of this feudal bauble. With too much regard for birth, the ladies have arguably too little for talent, and this brings us to the closest parallel of all between the stories of Anne Elliot and Katherine Bisshopp: the broken engagement.

Of the real-life tale much is still to be told, but even what we know so far seems a retelling of the fictional one. A naval officer who has distinguished himself in European and other waters comes ashore and meets the second daughter of a baronet:

> They were gradually acquainted, and when acquainted, rapidly and deeply in love. It would be difficult to say which had seen highest perfection in the other, or which had been the happiest; she, in receiving his declarations and proposals, or he in having them accepted.
>
>   A short period of exquisite felicity followed, and but a short one.[66]

Her father is not in favour of the match, but with the passivity of a weak character, and in any case his influence has waned. It is the maternal figure whose views really matter. She feels that her charge's 'claims of birth, beauty, and mind' entitle her to more than 'a young man, who had nothing but himself to recommend him, and no hopes of attaining affluence, but in the chances of a most uncertain profession'. His bride would, she predicts, be 'sunk by him into a state of most wearing, anxious, youth-killing dependence'.[67] Thus she resolves to prevent the union.

Anne's response is the same as Katherine's:

> Such opposition, as these feelings [in Lady Russell] produced, was more than Anne could combat. Young and gentle as she was, it might yet have been possible to withstand her father's ill-will, though unsoftened by one kind word or look on the part of her sister; – but Lady Russell, whom she had always loved and relied on, could not, with such steadiness

of opinion, and such tenderness of manner, be continually advising her in vain. She was persuaded to believe the engagement a wrong thing.[68]

The lovers part, compliant but unhappy, and as a consequence of her stifled romance the young woman finds that the relationship of absolute candour with her guide is at an end: 'They knew not each other's opinion, either its constancy or its change.'[69] Nonetheless she continues to look to her for love and counsel, and thinks 'with heightened gratitude of the extraordinary blessing of having one such truly sympathising friend'.[70]

In both cases, the question of social status plays a part in the maternal rejection of the young man's suit. Just as the Bisshopps consider the Pechells a few notches beneath them, so Lady Russell, who is as proud on the Elliots' behalf as Sir Walter himself, probably agrees with him that the Wentworths are 'quite unconnected'.[71] Her main objection is that Anne's wooer will be unable to support her in the style to which her background and personal merits entitle her. And there is something more – Wentworth's breezy self-confidence appeals to Anne, but not to Lady Russell: 'His sanguine temper, and fearlessness of mind, operated very differently on her. She saw in it but an aggravation of the evil. It only added a dangerous character to himself.' It is this, as much as his current financial position, that makes her determine that keeping up the engagement would be 'indiscreet, improper, hardly capable of success, and not deserving it'.[72] George Pechell is quite as sure of himself, and Lady Bisshopp, as we shall see, likes this trait as little as Lady Russell.

The older woman owes her powers of persuasion as much to her innate moral authority as to her parental role. Lady Bisshopp has the strongest personality in her family, and Lady Russell is equally formidable, as Henrietta Musgrove testifies:

> I have always heard of Lady Russell, as a woman of the greatest influence with every body! I always look upon her as able to persuade a person to any thing! I am afraid of her, as I have told you before, quite afraid of her, because she is so very clever; but I respect her amazingly.[73]

People with such force of character are used to being right, and used to having their own way. There is something possessive, slightly high-handed in Lady Bisshopp's treatment of Katherine's love affair with George Pechell. Lady Russell's opposition to Anne's engagement has the same peremptory quality, and we learn that 'her heart revelled in angry pleasure, in pleased contempt' when events appear to vindicate her stance.[74]

Whether these ladies exert their influence for better or for worse is something to consider once Katherine's story is further developed. We shall also have more likenesses between members of Katherine's family and Anne's family to describe.

3

Anxiously Waiting

1818

Katherine's visit to Hagley seemed to fulfil its purpose of taking her mind off George Pechell. Harriet reported to Lady Zouche that she looked well and not too thin, and Lord Curzon found her '*vastly* handsome' and 'as bright as the sun'. At the beginning of January she joined her mother in London. This year Robert Curzon remained at Hagley through the winter, which he and Harriet passed in visiting and being visited. In early spring there was a rare disagreement between them on the question of a school for Little Bob.

HARRIET'S JOURNAL

10 March. – Arrived in town where we remained some time. It was now our great anxiety to fix upon a school to send dear Little Bob to. Mr C. had already nearly determined upon one kept by a Mr Price at High Wycombe, which made me very unhappy as there was a story about a boy having been ill used there, but as the child was still there Mr C. thought this circumstance no objection, and on the other hand Mr Estcourt, who had had several of his boys there, strongly recommended the school, and B. persuaded me to submit, tho' I was also very sorry [for] the distance from London. However on the 17th of March Bob and I went to Wycombe to see the local. It is a very nice house close to the church in the town, being the parsonage, but a very pretty garden and nice field for the boys to play in on the side hill to the south behind the house. I liked Mrs Prices manner and appearance very much, but I thought Mr P. a very

disagreeable man. Perhaps I was prejudiced. It was settled Little
Bob should go there immediately after Easter, Easter Sunday
being the next Sunday, but an illness in which he was delirious
one night put it off and he did not leave me till the 16th of April,
Thursday very early morning, when his father took him to school
and I parted with my dear little fellow with many earnest prayers
that the blessing of God might continue with him.

The Curzons spent the spring in and around London and went
to High Wycombe to see Little Bob, who seemed to be settling in
well. In June Robert travelled to Clitheroe to be returned for the
seat he had held for over twenty years. As we have seen, even with
no serious challenger, elections were costly and he must have been
glad that the bill for £258 was settled by his father. Nationally,
Lord Liverpool's Tories were victorious, though with a reduced
majority.

In Stratford Place Katherine's spirits were wilting again. Perhaps
to her surprise, certainly to her deep disappointment, her parents
had remained firm against George despite her steady attachment
to him and utter indifference to other men. Her honesty, family
pride and love for her mother made a surreptitious marriage
unthinkable, and George respected her too much to suggest one.
Since the peace with France he had been at home on half-pay, but
in the hope of forgetting his misery he decided to go to sea again.
He was appointed to the command of HMS *Bellette*, an 18-gun
sloop bound for the Halifax Station to enforce the stipulations of
the Treaty of Ghent regarding fisheries and customs duties. This
would mean a long absence. As the Season ground on, the lovers
snatched a final few moments together.

KATHERINE'S JOURNAL
July. – This spring has passed with a few pleasant moments and
much anxiety of mind. I went 5 times to Almacks before Easter
with Mrs Fremantle and Lady Henley and constantly to the
French play. I have not enjoyed myself much owing to various
reasons ... I hope we shall stay here all the summer. This house
is dear to my tenderest retrospect, and the associations with it,
tho' some of them are as painful as some others are delightful,
make me feel altogether that it is the most agreeable place to my
feelings I can possibly be in.

14 July. – George Pechell arrived just as we returned home from [*illeg.*]. In the evening we all took a little walk, Mr and Mrs Fremantle drank tea with us. It was a very fine night, I went out for a few minutes before we all went to bed, as the window was wide open. I never shall forget those moments.

15 July. – I parted with the beloved friend who has been for three years and a half, including four springs in London, the greatest comfort and consolation to me in all the sorrows and distresses I have had the misfortune to undergo. It is possible we may never meet again, and even if we do it is more than probable we shall not be in the same situation, and it is almost certain in a different frame of mind. I feel quite overwhelmed with sorrow, but dear Snugest is so good as to say I behave admirably. I will endeavour to bear up and not give way to the affliction I can not help feeling, and I trust Providence will support us and watch over us both, and protect the amiable and benevolent being who is now separated from me perhaps for ever.

Katherine was crushed, but stayed outwardly composed during a busy summer of engagements. Two of these were interesting enough to distract her from her misery, for they brought her into contact with a new royal duchess. As a consequence of Princess Charlotte's death at least one of the regent's middle-aged brothers had to produce an heir to ensure the succession. Accordingly the Dukes of Clarence, Kent and Cambridge all wed German princesses, and as Clarence was the eldest it was in him and his wife Adelaide of Saxe-Meiningen, twenty-seven years his junior, that hopes for the future of the royal house were primarily vouchsafed. In July Katherine and Lady Zouche were presented to the new duchess at Windsor Castle, and Katherine found her a quiet but friendly woman with 'very white hair and pale complexion and a slight airy figure'. She was far more dignified than her boisterous husband, who good-naturedly showed the visitors round the castle and explained the pictures in his execrable French. This good first impression was soon confirmed.

KATHERINE'S JOURNAL
1 August. – I got up to go with dear Snugest to a party at Lady Warrens, as I was determined to exert myself to the utmost of my power, but I had the greatest difficulty in going, I was so

excessively ill. The Duke and Dutchess of Clarence dined with Sir J. and Lady Warren, Harriet was introduced to her R. H. She was extremely civil to us all, and said she should have known Harriet from her likeness to me, having seen me first at Windsor. She said, 'C'est tout à fait charmant de voir une mere et deux filles qui se ressemblent tout.' She also said of us, 'C'est tout comme chez nous, la cadette est la plus grande,' the Duchess of Saxe Weimar being taller than herself. The D. of Clarence sat down by me and asked me several questions about Mr Curzon. It was a pleasant party, and an interesting evening as the D. and Duchess of Clarence left England the following Monday. I was not the worse for the feat I performed, tho I am far from well.

The Welbeck Street and Stratford Place establishments were a good deal together during the summer, and in August the Curzons set off for Weymouth. Before getting there they intended to pass a week at Cranbury Park, Hampshire, as the guests of Lady Holland, one of Lord Zouche's paternal aunts and the widow of the successful portrait painter Sir Nathaniel Holland. The Curzons' journey from London took the whole of a hot, dusty day. One of the horses threw up a stone that hit Robert in the eye, and another collapsed near Winchester and had to be hauled up again. The travellers reached their destination in a drooping state.

HARRIET TO LADY ZOUCHE
CRANBURY PARK, 7 AUGUST 1818
... We arrived at Cranbury thank God about half past nine, and you cannot think what a contrast I felt it was to see Lady Holland in white gloves and clean brilliant sattin ribbons and white muslin. She received us very graciously and was very glad to see the children, poor little loves they had luckily fallen asleep the last few miles which did them an infinity of good, and they drank tea and went to bed, and I soon made my excuses and went to bed too. Little Bob slept in a little bed in my dressing room ...
    I was just going to sleep when Little Bob screamed and called out. I jumped out of bed to him and found him in such a fit of nerves that neither Bob nor I could pacify him for some time, and we took him into our own bed to console him poor love. He was so over tired he could not rest. I found it was such close quarters I got into his bed and at last went to sleep like you my dear

Snugest, and left the two Bobs together. Little Bob waked again in the night but Papa Bob quieted him and he is very well today ...

HARRIET TO LADY ZOUCHE
CRANBURY PARK, 11 AUGUST 1818

My dearest Snugest – Lady Holland has persuaded us to stay over tomorrow to go to see the cathedral at Winchester, so we go away Thursday, and I hope get to Weymouth Friday. We are to go to the hotel for we have not yet got a house, and I think it will be as well to fix for ourselves. I was so ill I could not have gone before, and Lady H. has been very good to us and seems to like Bob most prodigiously. Last night she asked me to play on the piano forte and I also sung, with which she was very much pleased and Bob too, and he was very much amused by her manner and Mrs Boscawens manner of approving of my singing, for not knowing anything about the matter they complimented me as one would encourage anybody. Bob liked his expedition yesterday very much, and saw Lady Hollands other place as well as Nettley Abbey and Castle.

My dear Snugest I began this yesterday. Lady H. takes us to Winchester today. Dr Nott I find lives there and she intends to ask him to dine here today to meet us. I am quite well and took a long walk about this place, which is very pretty indeed and larger than I expected, and more of a park. I fell asleep when I came home, and was fresh again to sing and play in the evening ...

They continued to Weymouth, where they resided in a hotel until their house in Melcombe Regis was ready. The two neighbouring resorts, considered a single town by this time, had been made popular by George III, a frequent sojourner and enthusiastic sea-bather. The Curzons saw the sights, visited the theatre, walked on the esplanade, went to church, and drank tea with acquaintances staying in the town. The boys did not enjoy bathing, but their parents were sure it was good for them and took them to the beach every second day. In October they progressed slowly back to Welbeck Street.

With Parham still shut up, Lady Zouche and Katherine spent the autumn in London, sometimes going out or inviting a small circle of friends but mainly biding at home together. Katherine tried to present a smiling face to the world, but was easily disheartened:

'I find even in the most trifling occurrence I have always something to regret. I suppose it pleases God to suffer this in order to wean us sufficiently from this world.' At the end of November Stratford Place was burgled.

KATHERINE TO HARRIET
STRATFORD PLACE, 2 DECEMBER 1818
My dearest Harriet – I am afraid you expected to hear from me yesterday but we are all in such a bustle and agitation that I could not, and indeed I am not much better today. We had the house robbed and though this is a common occurrence that I believe takes place every day in every street, yet we are as much frightened and annoyed as if such a thing had never been heard of. I think it was extremely lucky we were not all murdered. The thieves made off with the silver forks and spoons in use, about two dozen altogether, and the two tea pots, and stand and tea things etc. Since the house has been repairing the few little things in use are taken into the kitchen, which is locked up as soon as the tea is over and the fire can be put out. This was all done regularly as usual, but there appears to have been an unlucky interval between the time that Jonathan carried the tea things down there, and went back to lock up the room, for he was obliged to go out, and asked Frankland and Thorpe to answer our bell, and the maids happened to go upstairs. The thief was undoubtedly concealed in the house and watched his opportunity, as the doors were all so fastened that nobody could come in, though it is easy to get out unperceived.

The next morning when the kitchen was unlocked they saw the things had disappeared. The distress and despair of poor Jonathan is beyond every thing you ever saw. Thursby has been ill in bed for several days with a bandage. Grumpus went to Parham on Saturday with Benwell and the postilion, so we were absolutely without any body to take care of us. The thief must have known all this, and all our ways of going on, and must have been one of the workmen that mended our house. We have luckily plenty of forks and spoons out of Jig's plate chest to go on with, but Snugest and I are most particularly vexed and annoyed about the tea pot and stand, as I certainly expected to have outlived it, and it is now probably melted down. We have had people from Marlborough St and every step has been taken.

Poor dear Snugest is so cast down and annoyed with this fright altogether that I could write ten thousand pages about it, but it is no use my worrying you dearest Fright …

Shortly after this unpleasant occurrence came some good news: 'Sir Thomas Pechell passed the evening with us and told us that George had been sent from Halifax to Bermuda with a little freight and is now returned to Halifax, which is a great comfort as the yellow fever is at Bermuda.' The *Bellette* had been patrolling the coastlines of Nova Scotia and New Brunswick with success, fulfilling the promise of 'a good station for prize money' on the handbill issued to entice seamen to sail under George's command. It is not clear how recent Sir Thomas's information was, but it is interesting to see that he remained on good enough terms with Lady Zouche to come to her house with it. Lady Pechell, who lived mainly at Hampton Court Palace, was also civil. Possibly they accepted that a lack of money on both sides made their son's marriage to Katherine inadvisable. Nor did they discourage Katherine's friendship with their daughter Fanny, and it was sometimes through her that she heard of George.

In late November, after two years of self-inflicted banishment, Lord Zouche moved back to Parham, which he now felt sufficiently solvent to inhabit; his wife and daughter followed a month later. The family's domain did not extend far beyond the house, for the park and farm were still let out. The interior was clean, but so empty of furniture and ornaments that it looked dismal. The garden was in a deplorable state, the lawns like a churchyard and the borders choked with weeds, and Katherine resolved to help the gardener Moody to restore order. Lady Zouche steeled herself to face their neighbours at church, and Katherine found that Dr Penfold, the vicar of Steyning, had sent her a horse to ride and undertaken to stable it nearby if this could not be done at Parham. Unfortunately the ladies' pleasure in returning to 'this beautiful dear old place', as Katherine called it, was marred by a 'terrible storming' from Lord Zouche during their first evening together.

1819

In early January, while her husband was in London, Harriet miscarried at Hagley.

KATHERINE TO HARRIET
PARHAM, JANUARY 1819

My dearest Harriet – You will more easily imagine than I can describe what we felt at hearing you had been so ill. Thank God the brandy saved you, and I will try not to mind about the poor dear brat. It was terrible you should suffer so much pain, but now I trust in God it is all over and you are getting right again. Pray my dearest love do not write and worry yourself, and if you wish to see us, you know either dear Snugest or I would fly to you upon the slightest hint, indeed I hope you would have made Tucker mention it if you had liked to have either or both of us. We have received accounts of you from Bob, Brom and Tucker and I am in the greatest distress to think how ill you have been, and I feel very much overcome at the idea that we might have lost you that I am scarcely able to write. Pray my dearest Fright try and keep yourself as quiet as possible for fear of any return of that terrible weakness. I wish I had been with you to nurse you, poor dear love, I would have set as quiet as possible and if you like to have me now only say so. God bless you my dearest Harriet, I will not fatigue you with a long letter but believe that I am always thinking of you and that I am

Ever your most affectionate
Kitten

Harriet recovered from her miscarriage, but her general health was not good. Women of the higher classes were often unwell at this time or thought themselves so, and Harriet, Katherine, and Lady Zouche were typical in calling themselves 'ill' or even 'very ill' when they had a headache or a common cold. They fretted over every little indisposition of their own and one another's, and the idea of quietly bearing up against minor ailments would not have occurred to them. However, for some years Harriet had exhibited more serious symptoms, including nausea, faintness and nervous attacks, and in particular spasms in her joints and back. Until 1819 these episodes passed quickly, but thenceforward they became chronic. Her case is hard to diagnose, and 'rheumatism', the word she applied to it, encompasses too much to be considered useful by modern medical science. Whatever the correct term for her condition, it made her an invalid for much of her life: often she needed crutches to walk and was unable to go up or down stairs.

It is understood today, but was not then, that symptoms like Harriet's can be caused or exacerbated by depression and anxiety. She was certainly prone to both, especially when her husband was absent. It seems that her health faltered under the pressures of everyday life, and that when she was ill she appreciated being cosseted and relieved of her responsibilities. Lady Zouche feared the Curzons would find her sickliness tiresome, but was reassured by Lady Bromley, who said that 'anybody must be a brute [that] could be unkind to her'. She was never querulous or demanding, but resigned and helpless, and the more delicate she became, the more solicitous they grew. Robert's concern never wavered, and her equally apprehensive mother and sister could hardly have desired a more understanding husband for her. This is not to say that Harriet simulated illness in order to garner affection, but that bad health, when it came, brought its compensations.

While his wife languished at Hagley, Robert was in London for parliament and various business matters, including helping his in-laws to straighten out their finances. There was some uncertainty about the payment of Harriet's allowance, and creditors were threatening to seize Rackham Common, a part of the Parham estate not far from the house. Once she was able to leave her bed Harriet joined him and her own family came from Sussex, where they had spent their first winter for three years. Katherine devoted a lot of time to nursing Harriet, and in her journal she expressed the earnest hope that she was of use in comforting her sister and in alleviating their mother's fears. The patient was now under the direction of the regent's physician Sir William Knighton, 'an agreeable insinuating sort of a man' in Katherine's view. Harriet's first impressions of him we do not know, for she had just closed up her journal, but soon she put her entire trust in him.

The autumn Katherine and Lady Zouche divided between London and Parham.

KATHERINE TO HARRIET
PARHAM, 10 SEPTEMBER 1819
I longed to say ten thousand things my dearest Harriet when I left you, but did not dare trust myself to take even an affectionate leave of you. You are incessantly in my thoughts my dearest love. How often I shall wish myself in the chair by your bedside between this and Tuesday, and how happy I shall be to find myself there again.

I send the amethysts, which I hope will not worry you, and the great seal as you was talking about the crest. It can stand on your chimney until I return to you. I extracted dear Bob out of the dining room to wish him good night before I went. I do not like to ask you to write me two words with your pencil, for fear you should not be disposed or able, but you know how very happy it would make me if you could possibly do so, but if you do not pray do not be unhappy for I shall endeavour to bear my absence from you as well and as patiently as I can until Tuesday. God bless you my dearest, and think and believe how much I am your most affectionate,

K. B.

KATHERINE'S JOURNAL
22 October. – Mama and I suddenly went to Parham, having heard a report that the elms in Popes Lane were about to be cut. We felt great regret at leaving poor dear Harriet, but we could not avoid making the exertion to save the beautiful trees. We had the satisfaction of arriving by day light and of finding there was not much mischief done as Papa had been so good to stop the people who were cutting when he received our letters in the morning.

23 October. – We walked all about dear Parham. We met Capt. [Samuel] Pechell walking through the park. We shewed him the gallery and walked on with him to the keepers house. He told us his brother had taken two prizes off Halifax.

25 October. – We returned to London and found dear Harriet better. Thank God I have felt more happy these last three days than I have been for a very great length of time.

23 November. – Poor dear Harriet all this time continues in the same melancholy state. I went on this day with my father and mother to the House of Lords to see the Regent open the Parliament. Lord Shaftesbury took us upstairs into his room to see the procession, which is a very fine sight.

16 December. – I accompanied my mother to an entertainment given by the Spanish Ambassador the Duke of San Carlos to celebrate the nuptials of the King of Spain. I was rather frightened at going through the croud as an immense concourse of people were assembled in Portland Place, and it was thought the mob were rather disposed to be troublesome. However we were fortunate in getting into the house without any difficulty.

The Regent was present at the ball, and stayed [to] supper as well as the Duke and Duchess of Clarence. The Duke and Duchess of Kent retired early. They asked me to go and see the little Princess Alexandrina Victoria the next morning. It was a fine entertainment and rather amusing, but I thought the hour would never arrive when I was to go home to bed.

Presumably Katherine did not fail to visit the Kents the next day and get her first glimpse of their daughter, who had been born in May. The following summer the duchess invited her again for the same purpose. At this time Victoria had only a slim chance of ascending the throne, to which she was fifth in the line of succession, but this slowly changed as her uncles died one by one without having produced legitimate children. Katherine would have many opportunities to observe the little princess as she grew up under her mother's careful control.

1820

After a brief visit to London Robert spent the early months of this year making calls and trying to improve the efficiency of the Hagley farm, among other things by ending the provision of free beer for labourers. Harriet was at Parham, being nursed by her mother and sister. As well as rheumatic pains she had, Katherine noted, 'caught cold in her poor dear ears'. In March Lord Curzon died in his ninety-second year, having remained active and alert almost to the end. Robert, aged forty-six, was now master of Hagley. Meanwhile it became clear that Harriet's unease at the severe regime at Mr and Mrs Price's school in High Wycombe had been well founded, and after less than two years Little Bob was transferred to Mr and Mrs Ruddock's school in Wimbledon, which was run on milder principles. Presently Edward joined him there.

For Katherine 1820 opened cheerlessly. Her family's blighted finances, Harriet's ill health and the perils of George's naval operations all crowded her mind. She herself had an inflammation of the chest wall, but recovered quite speedily and by May was with the Curzons in Welbeck Street. The Season was under way, and Katherine knew her mother wanted her to make the most of her powers of attraction. She therefore crammed her letters with details of her social round, though sometimes she could not refrain from hinting that she was bored with it all.

In June she attended a royal reception or 'drawing room', one of the first since the regent's accession as George IV in January. The public was gripped by the spectacle of the new king's estranged wife jostling to take her place as queen consort and his determination to rebuff her. Despite her brazen conduct for many years Caroline enjoyed strong, often unruly support among the people as a figurehead for the cause of social and parliamentary reform.

KATHERINE TO LADY ZOUCHE
WELBECK STREET, JUNE 1820

My dearest Snugest – I will begin by telling you about the drawing room. My dress answered perfectly and looked extremely well, I put on some of your dark rouge and am only afraid it looked *like a fury* as Miss Long used to say. I called for Lady Bulkeley and Mary Eden, and after the usual shoving and pushing we were launched in to the room where the King stood. I gave my card to one of the men who stood there, but Lord Winchester desired to present me and held my left hand while the King kissed me and asked me how I did by my name, but I walked off as quick as I could as there was a general cry of go on. Princess Augusta and the Duchess of Glos'ter spoke to me. Mary Poulett stood behind the royal family, so we did not speak. We all agreed it was a very empty stupid vulgar drawingroom. I saw Grumpus, who seemed rather glad to see me, he looks very thin I wish he would go into the country ...

All the people who have happened to have their windows broken or been in any way insulted by the Q[ueen]'s mob were taken nervous and stayed away. I had fully made up my mind to have a handful of mud thrown at my beautiful silk, but I was lucky in bringing it home just as it went out. I wore the amethyst earings, necklace and broach and square cross Mr Kitchen lent me, *no diamonds* but my own comb ...

I don't know how to answer you about Harriets being better. She seems to consider herself as getting well, and yet she has all the same complaints and pains and weakness that she had before. She is quite happy that she has got rid of every medico but Sir William, and she is convinced he will cure her. She appears to me to be still more susceptible of noise than she ever was before. It makes me so nervous when any body makes a noise for fear it should affect her that my whole day is a perpetual state of apprehension on her account poor dear love. She says herself nobody knows what she suffers in this respect ...

Katherine's sense of the comic comes across in her sketch of an encounter with Prince Leopold, Princess Charlotte's widower and the future king of the Belgians.

KATHERINE TO LADY ZOUCHE
WELBECK STREET, JUNE 1820
My dearest Snugest – I will begin by giving you an account of yesterday evening. I went to Lady Bulkeley's, the ladies were just come up from dinner. The Duchess of Leeds admired the antiques and took the pattern of the *oyster* flounce which you quizzed, but it looks very brilliant and white. Lady Ashbroke played off very much to the two duchesses, I was thinking how happy her poor mother would have been to see her. We all gossiped two hours, then the Duchess of Leeds went away, after which towards 12 o'clock entered Prince Leopold, the Duke of Wellington, Lord Cathcart, Lord Harrington and Ashbroke, Col. Addisbroke.

Prince Leopold sat down in a chair between Lady Bulkeley and me, and immediately began telling her that he was only come upstairs to tell her that he was going that minute to the Annual Ball at Fishmonger's Hall. He then turned round and said to me, 'I had the pleasure of seeing Miss Bis*shoppe* last winter at Kensing*tone*. How is Ladie De La Zouche and your father.' I answered *fully* as you say my dear Snugest. He then said he supposed I was sharing the gaieties of the London Season. I told him that my friends were always so good to wish me to come to them, but my present object was my sister Mrs Curzon, with whom I was staying, and that she was confined to her room. I wished to give a general idea that I was always included in everything, that he may ask me if he gives a party. He answered, 'I am very glad you are come to town but very sorry indeed for your *motiff*!' *With that*, as the vulgar people say, he got up and bowed off, taking with him the Duke of Wellington etc. etc. without staying for their tea and coffee. I don't think he was in the room half so long as it will take you to read thus far ...

Katherine did not find living with the Curzons altogether easy. Nonetheless, and despite having her gums lanced and leeches placed in her mouth, she kept up a buoyant tone in the letters she sent to Parham.

KATHERINE TO LADY ZOUCHE
WELBECK STREET, JUNE 1820
… About Bob giving 9 and 6d for the plate … there appears to me to be such quantities that it seems absurd on either side to take the trouble of quarrelling about it or being shabby. I am quite ashamed of the fuss they all make. Eliz. keeps saying she is sure she shall be suffocated in Berkeley Square, having been accustomed to a large house. I consider this as the hight of insolence and impertinence and it gives me as you say uncharitable feel's, for I am perfectly comfortable in my garrett with my maid, tho' I come out of Parham, which is a much larger and better house than Eliz. Curzon can boast of ever having called her home. So you see my dearest Snugest we are all *very fierce* …

I went with Lady Bulkeley Sunday to see the national monument to Princess Charlotte. It is in this street, a most frightful figure of herself going up to heaven, a great fat woman with very little drapery, and two stiff angels with great wings all large as life going after her, one with the child. Then at the feet of all this is Princess Charlotte over again dying or dead. So the fat woman ascending is meant to represent her *spiritual existence* taking flight …

KATHERINE TO LADY ZOUCHE
WELBECK STREET, JUNE 1820
My dearest Snugest – I am very much obliged to you for the £10, which I have received quite safe in your kind letter. Dear Harriet was very unwell yesterday and exhausted with the pain she went through. Sir William gave her some laudenum and she got quite well in the evening. I went to her when I came home at night and she seemed quite cheerful, but she is rather low and languid today. I only give you this circumstantial account that you may really be happy when I tell you she is well. We were much disappointed at her being ill yesterday for she had been boasting that she had felt better altogether the three preceding days than for a very long time before …

Lady Barnard and Augusta have settled to dine here Monday, which rather puzzles me for it is Lady Salisbury's, and if I go

I must leave Sophia as she likes gossiping till twelve at night and I suppose I shall be sent for at ten by my chaperon, whoever it is. I happened to over hear Mrs Fremantle make an arrangement which fills her coach, so I thought it best not to ask her and Lady John Thynne whom I have seen has no carriage, so I have thought of Mrs Stewart the primate, who I think very likely will be very glad to have me, but perhaps it will end in my sitting here with Sophia, which is less trouble and more amusing. But you may depend upon my doing my best ...

In July Katherine returned to Sussex and found her mother in 'great distress of mind', presumably because of money troubles. Then it was back to London to accompany Harriet on a curious voyage. Sir William Knighton had ordered her to Clifton, a stylish spa resort by the River Avon, west of Bristol. Being rattled around in a carriage would have been too much for Harriet's back, so another mode of conveyance was chosen.

KATHERINE'S JOURNAL

18 July. – I got up at four o'clock and went downstairs in to the drawing room, where I found Sir William Knighton ready to accompany us on the hazardous voyage by water to Clifton, which we have undertaken on dearest Harriets account. She was carried on her bed to Whitehall Stairs, where we embarked in one of the city barges. We passed four nights and five days on the water.

22 July. – We arrived at Clifton and landed at the dock. Harriet was carried a mile and a half to our house on the top of the hill. I walked by her side. We have been here three weeks and I have not recovered the painful impression of our melancholy entré in to this windy dreary place. Sir William Knighton came from London to see us and talk over Harriets case with Dr Carrick.

31 July. – Mama brought the children.

5 August. – Mama and I went to see Kings Weston, found nobody at home. It is a handsome clean looking place built by Sir Robert Southwell, architect Sir J. Vanburgh. It contains a very numerous collection of portraits, chiefly of the Southwells, which makes it particularly interesting to us. There is a beautiful view of the Severn.

13 August. – I went with Bob and the children to Bristol Cathedral.

16 August. – We went to Stoke Giffard to see the D[owager] Duchess of Beaufort and Lady Frances Somerset. They were very good natured and lent us some books. It is a pretty place, built by Berkeley Lord Bortetourt seventy years ago.

21 August. – I have been much amused by seeing the 12th Regiment Lancers embark at the Bristol Docks for Waterford. There were 380 horses to be swang in to the packets, and while I stood by the water side with Bob, Thorpe and the children I saw about 40 of these poor dear beautiful horses seized round their bodies, pulled up into the air, drawn into the ship, and then let down in to the lower part of the vessel. They were terribly frightened and struggled extremely, some of them squeaked like pigs. It was a very curious sight.

The party saw more of Bristol and the notable houses around it, which according to the code of hospitality among the higher classes they were freely shown, in one case despite arriving just as the family were eating dessert. Katherine was particularly impressed by Leigh Court, a Palladian mansion recently built for a Bristol banker, which had a Velasquez, a Leonardo, two Claudes and a Raphael, as well as an antelope in the park. Despite her evident pleasure in these outings she adopted a virtuous pose in her journal: 'It is very melancholy to leave poor Harriet at home in her bed whenever I go out. I should infinitely prefer staying at home with her.' Robert left the party to deposit his sons at school and then returned, and in October Lady Zouche set off for Parham while her daughters and Robert journeyed slowly along rivers and canals back to London.

Harriet was concerned about the effect of her ill health on those around her.

HARRIET TO LADY ZOUCHE
WELBECK STREET, NOVEMBER 1820
... I am sure [the] principal if not the most distress I feel about my illness is the imposing anxiety upon you and being the source of every kind of trouble to those I love the best. But you have taught me to feel and it is certainly the greatest consolation to consider that it is the will of God, who knows what is best for us, and no doubt in his infinite mercy will support us through all our trials

to obtain I trust that happiness in another world which will not pass away, and where your pure spirit will reap its reward. When I reflect upon all I have endured, I am happy to reflect upon the many chearful hours I have passed in my bed, even in pain, and I am sure I have found a comfort in the reliance you always taught me to place in a kind providence which I cannot easily describe …

There is a certain complacency in this reasoning, but it was not discouraged by Lady Zouche, who assured Harriet that physical suffering would purify her soul. Meanwhile Katherine vaunted her devotion to the invalid. It is as if Harriet's predicament met the needs of both sisters, one for protective solicitude and the other for a legitimate object of love. Their friends would have seen nothing amiss, however, as such emotional straining on the subject of illness was normal at this time.

The year ended with the wrenching loss of Stratford Place. The lease was due to run until 1823, but a shortage of money forced Lord Zouche to give it up early. From this date his family's London abode was the Curzons' home, a hotel or a lodging house. At least Katherine could rejoice in the news of how well George, whom she had not seen for two and a half years, was acquitting himself at the Halifax Station. During 1820 his operations there were interrupted when he was appointed to the command of HMS *Tamar*, which had wandered north from Jamaica having lost her captain and much of her crew. He was then employed by the government of independent Haiti to intercept pirate ships falsely sailing under a Haitian flag, and he captured a large brigantine with a crew of ninety-eight and forged commissions from several South American states. He also saw the Spanish colony of Santo Domingo, on which he wrote a pamphlet entitled *A Visit to the Capital and Chief Ports of the Isle of St Domingo*. After six months he went north again to resume his command of the *Bellette* and add to his tally of prizes.

1821

Harriet's immobility kept the Curzons in London for the whole winter. In March there was more illness in the family, and Katherine did not know which way to turn: 'Little Bob came home with the whooping cough, dearest Harriet is much worse. Mama is so ill I must go home to her. I am sadly perplexed, but there can I hope be no doubt that of the two invalids I ought to go to my mother.'

When she reached Parham she found Lady Zouche better, and in a few weeks Little Bob's whooping cough subsided. Harriet remained much the same.

In March the newspapers informed the British public of another blow to the royal house: Princess Elizabeth, the four-month-old daughter of the Duke and Duchess of Clarence, had died of convulsions caused by entanglement of the bowels. Lady Warren was with the couple and tried to console the duke, who cried like a child, and she was very overcome herself when she spoke to Katherine the next day. Katherine was shocked and upset too, and told her mother the baby's nurse was widely blamed. She reflected that the recently widowed Duchess of Kent, who was staying with the Clarences, must be experiencing 'a most perplexing contrariety of feelings', for if Princess Elizabeth had lived she – and not her own daughter Victoria – would one day be queen. The Duchess of Clarence had already lost two children, one before and one shortly after birth, and in the following year she miscarried of twins. There were rumours of further pregnancies, but the couple remained childless.

Katherine's amusements during the spring included a French play, a performance by a ventriloquist, and a concert at Marlborough House, the residence of Prince Leopold. In the summer she had a few restful weeks at Parham: 'The country looks beautiful, and the calmness of this dear old mansion is always to me the restorer of health and spirits.' Then she and her parents went back to London for George IV's coronation, which the Zouche peerage entitled them to attend, and settled in a lodging house in Welbeck Street.

KATHERINE'S JOURNAL
19 July. – I got up at half past one, and began dressing for the coronation. Papa's hairdresser came at two and at four I had the pleasure of seeing him dressed in his robes. Soon after four we got into the carriage, my father, Mama and myself, and a little before seven we were set down by the platform erected upon this occasion from the House of Lord's to Westminster Abbey. My father went into the hall and we were anxious to secure places in the Abbey. We met the Queen upon the platform returning from her unsuccessful attempt to enter the Abbey. She wore green and silver and was attended by Lady Anne Hamilton and Lady Hood, and looked very quiet.

We were fortunate in obtaining very good places in the organ loft over the altar in the Peeresses Box. We saw the whole of this awful ceremony in the Abbey as well as it could be seen, as being over the altar we sat immediately opposite the King while he was crowned in his chair of state. We proceeded to the hall where we saw the King dine, and the Champion enter on horseback, also the Duke of Wellington, Lord Anglesea and Lord Howard of Effingham. It was upon the whole a prodigious fine sight and the fatigue not so severe as what we were prepared to endure. The King slept the preceeding night at the Speaker's, he arrived at nine o'clock and brought his jewels in his own pocket, not liking to trust any body with articles of such great value ...

The whole concern of the coronation was over by 8 o'clock, and many got their carriages directly. We were not so fortunate and I laid down upon the floor and with many others slept until 12 o'clock. I accompanied Lady Warren to a morning concert in Westminster Abbey, where we heard some very fine music.

During the summer Sir William Knighton decided that Harriet needed to breathe the sea air of Worthing. The problem was getting her there, but he knew of a solution. While keeping up his medical practice he had, by the adroit performance of various delicate commissions, become George IV's right-hand man, and he now asked if Harriet might avail herself of the royal sleeping carriage. 'I cannot tell you how strongly and how graciously His Majesty expressed himself towards you and Mrs Curzon on this occasion,' he wrote to Robert, enclosing a note from the king's private secretary Sir Benjamin Bloomfield placing the vehicle at their disposal. A date was arranged and Robert wrote to Bloomfield to say that he and his wife were 'deeply sensible of His Majestys condescension'. It was a gratifying exchange for all parties, and from this time Harriet travelled recumbent in her sovereign's carriage whenever she pleased.

Nonetheless her departure for Worthing was a worrisome moment, and Katherine ran some way after the carriage to make sure that all was well. Before long she joined Harriet in Worthing, and from there she travelled with her parents to Bognor to wait on the Duchess of Kent, whom they invited to Parham.

Above left: Harriet, Lady Bisshopp *née* Southwell. Portrait by Angelica Kauffman. By descent in the family of the sitter.

Above right: Sir Cecil Bisshopp, later Baron Zouche of Haryngworth. Portrait by Angelica Kauffman. By descent in the family of the sitter.

Parham Park, Sussex. Engraving by Archelaus Cruse after John Preston Neale.

Katherine and Cecil Bisshopp. Pastel by Anna Tonelli. Property of Parham Park Ltd, Parham House, West Sussex. Photography by Elizabeth Zeschin and Hugh Gilbert.

Sir Cecil Bisshopp exercising his yeomanry troop. Oil on canvas by John Rising. Property of Parham Park Ltd, Parham House, West Sussex. Photography by Elizabeth Zeschin and Hugh Gilbert.

Above left: Cecil Bisshopp. Engraving by James Godby after François Huet-Villiers.

Above right: Lady Charlotte Bisshopp *née* Townshend. Oil on canvas. Property of Parham Park Ltd, Parham House, West Sussex. Photography by Elizabeth Zeschin and Hugh Gilbert.

Above left: Charles Bisshopp. Miniature. Property of FitzRoy and Marigold Somerset.

Above right: Cecil Bisshopp's grave. Illustration in Benson J. Lossing, *The Pictorial Field-Book of the War of 1812* (New York: Harper, 1868), p. 628.

Harriet Bisshopp.
Miniature by Andrew
Dunn. Property of
FitzRoy and Marigold
Somerset.

Captain Wentworth
giving Anne Elliot
a letter. From an
illustrated edition of
Persuasion. Courtesy
of Helen Amy.

Katherine Bisshopp. Crayon sketch. Castle Goring MSS/PD/100, West Sussex Record Office, Chichester.

Katherine Bisshopp, Robert Curzon, Harriet Curzon *née* Bisshopp and Assheton Viscount Curzon. Oil on canvas. Property of Parham Park Ltd, Parham House, West Sussex. Photography by Elizabeth Zeschin and Hugh Gilbert.

Hagley Hall, Staffordshire. Engraving by Samuel Lacey after John Preston Neale.

Above left: Robert Curzon. Oil on canvas by Richard Pentreath. By descent in the family of the sitter.

Above right: Harriet Curzon. Oil on canvas by Richard Pentreath. By descent in the family of the sitter.

Gorhambury, Hertfordshire. Engraving by W. Warwick after John Preston Neale.

Above left: George Richard Pechell, Royal Navy, MP. Lithograph by Edward Morton after Thomas Charles Wageman. © National Maritime Museum, Greenwich, London.

Above right: Katherine Bisshopp. Crayon sketch. Castle Goring MSS/PD/101, West Sussex Record Office, Chichester.

Hampton Court Palace, Middlesex. Aquatint by Edward Duncan after Henry Bryan Ziegler, in Hermann von Pückler-Muskau, 'Erinnerungsbilder', vol. 1. Property of the Erbengemeinschaft der Grafen Pückler on permanent loan to the Stiftung Fürst-Pückler-Museum Park und Schloss Branitz.

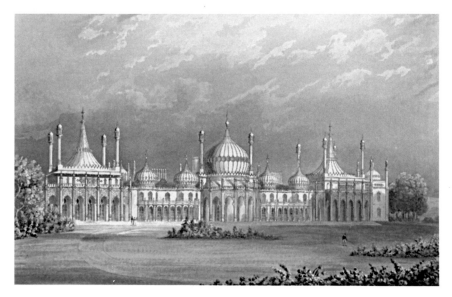

Royal Pavilion, Brighton. Aquatint from John Nash, *The Royal Pavilion at Brighton* (London: Ackermann, 1826). Royal Pavilion & Museums, Brighton & Hove.

Trial of the R.Y.S. Brig *Water Witch*. Engraving by C. Rosenberg after William John Huggins.

William, Henrietta and Adelaide Pechell. Watercolour by Mrs Mannin. Property of FitzRoy and Marigold Somerset.

Above left: Robert Curzon II. Oil on canvas. By descent in the family of the sitter.

Above right: Emily Curzon *née* Wilmot-Horton with her daughter Darea. Oil on canvas by Alexander Glasgow. Property of Parham Park Ltd, Parham House, West Sussex. Photography by Elizabeth Zeschin and Hugh Gilbert.

Above left: Edward Curzon. Photograph of a sketch. Parham Archive 1/5/6/9/28, West Sussex Record Office, Chichester.

Above right: Amelia Curzon *née* Daniell. Photograph of a portrait. Parham Archive 1/5/6/25, West Sussex Record Office, Chichester.

Town Hall, Brighton. Engraving by S. Hall after T. George. Royal Pavilion & Museums, Brighton & Hove.

Above left: Sir George Brooke-Pechell. Engraving of a portrait, reproduced in Anon., *A Bundle of Sticks* (Winchester: Warren, 1914), opp. p. 53.

Above right: William Pechell. Drawing of a statue by Matthew Noble in the *Illustrated London News* of 19 February 1859, reproduced in Anon., *A Bundle of Sticks* (Winchester: Warren, 1914), opp. p. 54.

Above left: Henrietta Burrell *née* Pechell. Photograph. Castle Goring MSS 76, Album 1, p. 38, West Sussex Record Office, Chichester.

Above right: Percy Burrell. Photograph. Castle Goring MSS 77, Album 2, p. 28, West Sussex Record Office, Chichester.

Above left: Adelaide Somerset *née* Pechell, dressed as Margaret of Anjou. Photograph. Castle Goring MSS 78, Album 3, p. 36, West Sussex Record Office, Chichester.

Above right: Alfred Somerset. Photograph. Castle Goring MSS 87, West Sussex Record Office, Chichester.

Harriet Anne Curzon, Baroness Zouche with her granddaughter Darea
Curzon. Photograph. Castle Goring MSS 76, Album 1, p. 38, West Sussex
Record Office, Chichester.

Robert Curzon II, Robin Curzon, Adelaide Somerset and Katherine, Lady Brooke-Pechell. Photograph. Castle Goring MSS 77, Album 2, p. 40, West Sussex Record Office, Chichester.

Parish Church of St Margaret's, Angmering. Lithograph by George Childs, printed by C. Moody.

Castle Goring. Photograph of the northern aspect. Castle Goring MSS 78, Album 3, p. 21, West Sussex Record Office, Chichester.

KATHERINE'S JOURNAL

18 September. – This was the day fixed for the Duchess of Kent to come and see Parham, and we prepared a luncheon for her in the great parlour. The party who met Her Royal Highness consisted of Lady and Miss Pechell, Lord Edward O'Brien, Lady King, Mr and Mrs King, Mr Cartwright, Sir Thomas Webbe, Lady Newburgh besides Sir John and Lady Warren. The Duchess of Kent arrived about three o'clock accompanied by her daughter the Princess Feodor, La Baronne de Speith, and General Wetherell, making with our three selves 18 people. We all received the royal party at the door, and after walking into the hall and saloon we went into the gallery and afterwards into the great parlour, where 14 sat down to the dinner table, and I sat at a little table in the bow window with Mrs King, Fanny Pechell and General Whetherell.

After eating, the Duchess of Kent, Princess Feodor, Lady Newburgh and Mama went in the coach about the park, during which we walked in the pleasure grounds. When they returned the Duchess walked round the garden with us. We then went in to tea, after which Her R.H. returned to Bognor, Lady King went home, and the rest of the party slept at Parham. The next morning after breakfast they all went home, and we drove over to Worthing to see dear Harriet. Nothing could go off better than the Duchess of Kents visit to Parham. She was all good nature and admiration of the dear old house and park. Of the latter she spoke in very high praise and she sent an artist the next morning to take sketches of the different points she admired the most.

There was a pleasing addition to the stitched coronet that had adorned a dining room chair since Princess Charlotte's visit of 1808 in the form of autographs of the duchess and of Princess Feodora, her daughter by her first husband, in the Parham guestbook.

In the same month Robert took his boys back to school from London after their summer holidays. Edward returned to Mr and Mrs Ruddock's in Wimbledon and Little Bob, now eleven, started at Charterhouse.

ROBERT CURZON TO HARRIET
WELBECK STREET, 20 SEPTEMBER 1821

Dearest Harriet – I was quite pleased yesterday to see your hand writing so steady and good. It augurs, I hope, that you are doing well with the dear loves to take care of you. I did not return from Wimbledon time enough for the post. I got to the Charter House with Little Bob soon after one. He kept up surprisingly but his heart was in his mouth all the way, constantly asking whether we were near or half way or a quarter of the way ... When we arrived the boys were at dinner. Little Bob on being asked whether he would have any said no thank you and stuck close to me poor fellow. After I had gone over the House with him and settled his room I went into the dining room, which is a new one built in the yard, lofty, spacious, light and airy. Rob, finding I was going away, no longer declined eating ... The bed rooms are sweet, clean and airy, beds have all white counterpanes and no curtains. I felt much for him at being turned amongst 450 boys he had never seen before. I assured him and have little doubt but that it will be so that in three weeks he would like the Charter House better than Mrs Ruddocks. Most boys in a short time prefer a public to a private school ...

In November Harriet was conveyed from Worthing to a house Robert had taken in Brighton, again in the king's sleeping carriage, and Katherine moved in with them. In Brighton Katherine was unsettled by memories of time spent with George, as she noted in typically oblique style in her journal: 'This place makes me very melancholy as I cannot help regretting the absence of those who constituted my chief amusement and delight when I was last here, but this is only silly and selfish and I will try to think only of endeavouring to alleviate dear Harriets sufferings.' George was on his way home and she knew she might hear of his arrival at any moment. In the middle of December she left Brighton in a state of hope and trepidation: 'I passed the next ten days at Parham listening to the dreadful gales and storms. On Tuesday Xmas Day we received the sacrament, and on Thursday December 27th I had the happiness of hearing that the Bellette was safely arrived at Portsmouth.'

1822

Following his Caribbean interlude George had spent another fruitful year enforcing the terms of the Treaty of Ghent. By the time she was paid off, the *Bellette* had taken about twenty prizes, exceeding the thirteen that Jane Austen's brother Charles had earned plying the same seas twenty years earlier. George's share enriched him considerably, and by now his advancement to the rank of post-captain, which meant a future promotion to admiral even if he never went to sea again, was almost inevitable. For some reason he and Katherine did not meet for five weeks after his return, and she passed January 'in a most distressing state of agitation and agony'. Then, on 4 February: 'I had the happiness of again beholding the beloved friend from whom I have been separated above three years and a half.' Time, she learned, had altered his feelings as little as hers. Now aged thirty-two and thirty, they hoped her parents' opposition to their union would crumble before his improved circumstances and her faithful attachment. To their great consternation it did not.

In mid-March the king's sleeping carriage took Harriet from Brighton to Welbeck Street, and for much of the next two months the sisters lived there together. Lady Zouche, without a London home of her own, remained at Parham. Her husband, however, was staying somewhere in the capital while he attended the House of Lords. 'I am glad you saw your father,' Lady Zouche replied to a letter from Harriet, 'and that he talked of Little Bob, altho' he did not take the trouble to talk to him. I am convinced it is a great satisfaction to him to see him, and the dear Bobbin takes G[rumpus's] odd way so well, and so respectfully and properly, it is quite charming.' Lord Zouche rarely wrote letters, and his family heard nothing of him for long stretches. Nor did they write much to him, and he had known nothing of their sojourn at Clifton in 1820. Sometimes his daughters encountered him in a public place, shook hands with him, and conversed like mere acquaintances.

Almost estranged as they were, Lord and Lady Zouche remained as one on the subject of George. Katherine had little respect for her father's opinion, but remained under her mother's sway and tried hard to believe that she knew best.

KATHERINE TO LADY ZOUCHE
WELBECK STREET, 30 MAY 1822
... Bob got a ticket for Almacks last night, it was extremely empty ... I saw G. P. He seems unsettled and unhappy *but quite to have made up his mind about me*, therefore my dearest Snugest make yourself quite easy upon this subject. Grumpus and I met him this morning alone in the garden at Rose Bank, he talked

of going to sea or abroad. He has called here four times before I came. Harriet of course could not let him in in her state, so that I hope you will be quite comfortable. Pray tell me that you will and that you will trust me and depend upon me, and every thing will I am sure be as you wish. He is not in town but they are all at H[ampton] Court, and none of them come to town this year, so there is no fear of my being watched about in the morning or evening. I am afraid you will be bored with this subject, but you know how very near my heart it is, and it will I trust be a satisfaction to you to know that I am what *you* call taking care of myself ... Pray write me a little comfort in return for my assurances that I really am in the right way.

Your ever most affectionate
Katherine Bisshopp

KATHERINE TO LADY ZOUCHE
WELBECK STREET, 1 JUNE 1822

My dearest Snugest – It is impossible for me to express how very much I feel your kindness in writing me such an affectionate letter, for which indeed I am most truly grateful, and for all your goodness to me. Grumpus was very properly civil to George and I thought did not seem to know or care which brother it was, but yesterday he told me he should be happy to take a drive with me for fresh air any day *only not to meet the Captain,*[75] which vexed me because he seemed to think I had made an *asignation*. I however answered him upon the subject with great *hauteur*, which perhaps was not quite right, but it certainly had the good effect of satisfying him most completely upon the subject, for he was very kind to me, shook hands with me and talked about Rose. If he should say any thing to you, perhaps you will say that I cannot possibly answer for who I may happen to meet any where, and that there are many others who have preferred me that he knows nothing of. But probably the subject may not occur again as he seemed quite easy yesterday.

All this I should not have thought worth while to mention, but I only answer your question. G. P. is not in town, only drives to London occasionally and goes to Almacks if they send him a ticket and no where else in general. I have little chance of getting there again as it is a matter of such very great interest and favour both for men and women, as they admit 100 people less than usual this year, but I shall take my chance as there is plenty of room in the world for us all.

I went to Lady Wemyss assembly with Brom last night, nothing but Scotch people and magnificent furniture. I then went on to Mrs Barnard's ball, where I was plagued with the Indefatigable because I happened to be good natured and civil to him the night before. I am afraid of hurting his feelings because he is so selfish and weakminded he would not mind going in to a *little fit* or any thing for his own gratification, without any consideration for me. I looked very well in the blue flowers, which only roused A. Eden, Mr Foley and all the old bores. In short I came away quite bothered, and envied all the Lady Fortescues and Lady Murray Grevilles who sat round the room in all the respectability of being neglected ...

A day later Katherine had 'a conversation with a beloved friend which was consolatory tho' very short', but they did not contemplate the drastic step of acting against her parents' wishes. Instead George waited for his promotion, which given his distinguished service was long in coming. The situation was tense, and nerves occasionally frayed.

KATHERINE TO LADY ZOUCHE
WELBECK STREET, 5 JUNE 1822
... In answer to your dear little note my dearest Snugest I can only lament how little you really know and appreciate my dear Georges honest and honourable feelings. He is the last man in the world that would attempt to engage me in any promises for the future. He thinks only of my comfort and happiness, and there is nothing he would not do in any way to promote it. At all events my dear Snugest if you *will not* know him you *may* trust *me*, and though he has never urged me to wait for him it may be a satisfaction to you to know that he said these words to me *You have never allowed me to look forward*. I was very glad to hear I had been *so good*, considering how very much I should prefer him to any other man I ever saw. But pray be easy, it is indeed all over, and I hope you will not deny me the only consolation now left me, that of seeing you easy and satisfied with me. I can say no more nor do anything further ...

Shortly afterwards Katherine attended a 'beautiful entertainment' at Carlton House. Happy or sad, she always cherished contact with members of the royal family, whose commonest civilities she took as marks of remarkable generosity and grace. At Carlton House the king, his sister Princess Augusta and the Duchess of Kent all spoke to her, and the next day she met the first two again.

KATHERINE TO LADY ZOUCHE
WELBECK STREET, 15 JUNE 1822

... I got through the drawing room most delightfully yesterday. The King called me by name and asked me how my sister did. Princess Augusta asked me after you. Lady Verulam was very agreeable, we came and went away and saw very few people, but it was altogether the pleasantest drawing room I was ever at at Buckingham House, for we were not pushed about and it was very comfortable. My dress answered perfectly well. The black flowers on the sleeves looked quite black enough, and I put the jet upon my waist and the long black necklace with the tassels all over my back and shoulders and across the front, and diamond necklace and earings ...

Poor dear Harriet suffers very much from the variation of the weather, but she is on the whole much better. You will like to know that G. P. is now at Calais. He will not stay abroad long, but he cannot bear to meet me upon a footing of indifference at present. Do not worry yourself to answer this, it does not signify. I only meant to state the fact of his not being in town ...

She was hurt that her mother no longer fully trusted her about George. It is unlikely that they met covertly, but vows of love must have been exchanged during brief moments alone and Lady Zouche feared a secret engagement. 'Snugest very angry', Katherine wrote in her journal at the end of June. She tried to reassure her, carried on going to balls, concerts and dinners, and wrote lively letters that are belied by her journal, which describes these entertainments as 'stupid and dreary'.

There was no one to whom she could open her heart. Despite their closeness Harriet was not her confidante because she too opposed the match. Moreover, Harriet had a lifelong tendency to shy away from contentious questions. She passed over the love affair in letters to their mother, instead detailing Katherine's social activities and commenting favourably on her appearance. Nor was she simply shielding Lady Zouche, for the topic is also absent from her correspondence with Robert, who left for Staffordshire in July. This repeats the pattern of 1817, when despite Harriet's exchange with George her other letters and her journal have nothing to say of him or his relations with Katherine.

At Parham Lord Zouche's loosening grip on his affairs necessitated the undignified step of appointing John and William Rose as receivers to protect his heirs. The total annual rent of tenants in Oxfordshire was about £3,400 and in Sussex about £5,800, but only two thirds of the latter amount was actually being received, and probably a smaller fraction of the former. Robert made sure Harriet's allowance was paid, but Katherine had to act for herself and twice visited a master in chancery to clarify her position. In the autumn she and her mother lived quietly at Parham or went to see Harriet, who was again 'recruiting' at Worthing and Brighton. Katherine feared she was getting weaker, but Harriet met her difficulties with equanimity. 'I am fully sensible of my many blessings,' she told her mother, 'and if, as you say, my soul profits by the sufferings of my body it is a happiness to me to have been so afflicted.' In her next letter she at last touched on her sister's predicament, stung by Lady Zouche's suspicion that she might be softening towards George.

HARRIET TO LADY ZOUCHE
BRIGHTON, NOVEMBER-DECEMBER 1822
My dearest Snugest – I write to you in a separate cover having sent another to Kate, and I am desirous this should be *for you*. I am truly grieved to see you uncomfortable under any circumstances and can readily enter into all you feel now about our dear Kate. I promise you very easily not to encourage her in thinking you or I could ever agree to her throwing herself away in a bad match in this or any other case, and as you are so good as to say you love and *esteem* me I rather feel mortified that you should think it necessary to caution me upon that subject ... I am soon agitated in my present infirm state, but I cannot consider that as reason to prevent my having the consolation still left me of being at least a comfort to you in sharing and soothing your afflictions and alleviating by my duty and affection all the bitter trials with which it pleases God to try the *pure gold* which he prepares for himself ...

With her mother and sister so firmly against her choice, Katherine's chances of winning through seemed small. It therefore came as very welcome news that George was at last promoted to post rank. He was back on half-pay and would never go to sea again.

1823

This was an uneventful year, best summarised with a selection from Katherine's journal. She and George were now permitted to meet and even – in a relaxation of normal etiquette – to correspond.

KATHERINE'S JOURNAL

January. – We went to the Pavillion during our stay at Brighton. The first evening was a very small party, the 2d was a very large one for the Duke and Duchess of Clarence ... On the 22d of January Mama and I went to London about my teeth for two days, came back in the snow, the most severe weather I ever experienced.

1 March. – I went to pass a few days with my sister at Brighton.

11 March. – My sister too ill to go to London. Sir William Knighton came to see her.

12 March. – We had the melancholy satisfaction of seeing poor dear Harriet put into the King's sleeping carriage as she was well enough to go to London. Mama and I returned to Parham and we had the comfort of hearing the next morning that my dear sister had performed her journey very prosperously and with less pain and fatigue than before.

25 March. – My mother gave me a letter which caused me great surprise and agitation.

27 March. – The two Mr Roses came. Fanny and George Pechell rode from Aldwicke. I had not seen either of them for many months, and had a long conversation with Fanny relating to her intended marriage. I was shocked to see her brother looking so ill and altered.

29 March. – My father set out on a journey into Oxfordshire in order to arrange his concerns and attempt to let his farms, there being three out of cultivation or occupation. We are extremely anxious he should go to settle this.

3 April. – How very tiresome it is to write a journal. The best way is only to keep to dates, which it is sometimes useful to refer too.

25 April. – I went to London to see dearest Harriet who is very ill. I have had the consolation of passing four days with her and returned to Parham to Mama on Wednesday April 30th.

1 May. – I received a letter which occasioned me much distress and agitation.

6 May. – A very bad account of dear Harriet. I was very much overcome and my mother gave me some orange flower water. The accounts of poor dear Harriet continued so indifferent that that on Sunday the 11th of May after church we went to town to Lady Bulkeleys in Stanhope Street. Harriet was very ill all this week, my father and Mama determined on hiring a small house near her. I underwent much needless agitation this week.

16 May. – We removed to No. 50 Welbeck Street, on Saturday [17th]. I went in the carriage about the piano forte and Moses was thrown off the Box in Albemarle Street. The wheel went over his head and I was obliged to leave Jonathan with him and walk home to my great annoyance, but luckily I met with Mr Milbanke in the mob and he brought me to Welbeck Street and another gentleman. I was much frightened.

18 May. – The whole of this week we passed in the greatest anguish of mind and anxiety on Harriets account. On Friday the 23d we had the inexpressible happiness of Dr Baillies opinion that her case was entirely unattended with danger.

30 June. – Shewed my new guittar to a good judge and went to a concert at Lady Boroughs. One day this month I went to the Cambrian Ball with the Barhams, and I passed several pleasant evenings with them. I went to a horridly dull water party in a steam boat and a stupid assembly at Lady Verulams to meet the Duchess of Gloucester and a concert at P[rince] Leopolds.

9 July. – We returned to Parham.

17 July. – Dined at Aldingbourne, all ladies very dull.

25 July. – I went to London to attend my sister on her journey into Staffordshire.

30 July. – My poor sister was put into the Kings carriage. I accompanied her, Mr Curzon followed in his barouche with Mr Higham the apothecary and the maids, and we travelled as far as Daventry, which is 60 Miles from London. I dreaded the bustle and confusion of an inn for her, but she got through it better than I expected.

31 July. – We proceeded on our journey. Harriet suffered most dreadfully going through Coventry, the rattling of the Stones was so great. She was also much overcome between Lichfield and Hagley, she cried and screamed and I was much frightened. We reached Hagley about ½ past four. It was a touching sight to see poor Mr Curzon carry her in to her new home. She seems to feel the dreadful privation of not being able to walk more here than ever, it is indeed a severe trial for her. I passed ten days with her and was most happy to return home as Mama wished me much to come back to her at Parham.

11 August. – I set out upon my return home with Thorpe in the Kings carriage. I went with Thorpe to Daventry. I might have gone further, but I felt so miserable at being alone at an inn, which I never was before in my life, and I felt very désolée and miserable. One's trials are not so difficult to be got through in fact as they appear to be in contemplation, so the next morning I wondered what I had been in such a fuss about.

14 August. – I proceeded to Welbeck Street and Friday 15th I reached dear Parham.

20 August. – G. came to see us. My father and mother and I went in the coach to a cricket match at Mr Kemp's, Dale Park. We dined a party of 30 in the portico. It is a beautiful place.

13 September. – Mama and I went to Brighton and walked on the Chain Pier.

16 September. – Lady Henry Howard and Miss Howard came at four o'clock and returned at night. George Pechell, Lady Mr and Mrs King were also of the party. The Miss Petres came and went before dinner. We have driven over to Bignor one day this month to see all Mr Hawkins's curiosities. The things I admired the most were two filligree crabs, in gold and silver, an amber cup, agate cups and saucers, a miniature of Sir Algernon Sydney by Vandyke, a miniature of the King when very young etc. etc.

20 September. – We dined at Lady Henry Howards, and Miss Petres and George Pechell, a very pleasant party. My father said coming home in the carriage what an agreeable little party it was, which he seldom or never says of any party.

In October Katherine and her mother went to Hagley for the rest of the year; Lord Zouche remained at Parham. It is unlikely that his attempt to bring order to his Oxfordshire estates had yielded much, for his mind was beginning to give way. Hints of this from others are so discreet as to be ambiguous, but a letter he wrote to Harriet in November provides clear and poignant evidence. At least he could persuade himself that he was running his estate. 'I am *content*,' he concluded his letter, 'having an old man *cook* at Parham, and my presence is *very* very much *wanted*, but have great promises of much alteration and better supplies.'

1824

Katherine spent the first half of January at Gorhambury, where the company included Prince Leopold, who had come to shoot. At a grand dinner in his honour she felt rather outshone by her hostess: 'Charlotte looked beautiful in red velvet and pearls, I very thin in a new white silk and antiques.' Not being much of a drinker, the prince cut short the customary postprandial segregation of the sexes (for other men an opportunity for copious libations) and rejoined the ladies for conversation and shilling whist. The evening, like so many at Gorhambury, was rounded off with music, this time difficult ensembles from Rossini's operas. 'I wish you was here to help sing,' Katherine wrote to Harriet.

It was a long while since Harriet's musicianship had been appreciated outside her intimate circle. For four years she had been ill, mostly bedridden, and latterly, in addition to rheumatism, her ears and eyes had troubled her. Lady Zouche counselled her not to write if it gave her any discomfort, although receiving her letters was always a great treat, and she assured her that sympathy with her plight would never wane: 'I am sure your patience and exertion under your protracted sufferings, not only for yourself, but for the welfare and amusement of all around you, must endear you to every one, and I really do not [think] there is a human being hard hearted and stupid enough not to feel obliged and cheered by your sweet smiles and agreeable conversation.'

While Katherine was at Gorhambury and Harriet at Hagley, their parents were in the Curzons' London home. Lord Zouche was taken with a fit of house hunting, and when Lady Zouche told him the places he liked were too expensive he blamed her for ruining their chances of finding something. Then he suggested a drive to Dorking to visit his brother Hugh, whose wife seems to have exercised some tact in bringing the two men together. They were seventy and sixty-eight years old, and had seen little of each other since childhood. This was their last meeting.

LADY ZOUCHE TO HARRIET
PARHAM, 10 JANUARY 1824

... On Wednesday about three o'clock he said to me, Mrs Hugh will give Evelyn's Memoirs to the library at Parham if I will call for it at Dorking, have you any objection to go with me. I said, none at all, as I have always told you, but you had better write to your brother, so he wrote to Hugh that he should be glad of the book, that Lady De La Zouche and himself were to pass by the next day, Katherine having staid at Gorhambury, and that we would call *at two o'clock*. This letter being sent to the post, and another to order our horses to meet us at Horsham, it might have been supposed we were to go, but to my horror and astonishment, *if as you say* one can be astonished at any thing, he said in the evening it was quite impossible for him to go for a day or two. I replied nothing should make me stay, and accordingly about eleven the next day, I sent Jonathan to the hotel for his bags with notice that I was in the carriage ...

Well, at a quarter before one, after many delays, we actually set off, and arrived at Dorking at *half past three*. I expected Hugh would say he was in a fit, but the door flew open and in we went ... The poor little Viper[76] was in tears and much agitated. She pressed my hand, and from her whole manner and deportment you would have thought it had been her dear friend restored to her. I shook hands with her, then with him, and then sat down by her. We had some sotto voce conversation, while the brother's roared in a loud voice at each other. Grumpus asked for something to eat, found fault with the servant, and in short behaved just as he does in an ill humour with Thursby. Hugh ditto. All this quite astonished me, as it is very different from former days when they used to be very civil to each other ...

I said something about the horses being taken off, she said pray let them settle it, and don't speak, I never dare mention horses to men, and my agonies lest *they should quarrel* is indescribable, so pray don't speak. She enquired after you and your illness, I said I hoped Mr B. and she would see both their nieces when they came to town, and that I should request Mr Curzon to be so good to call on them. Hugh observed that Welbeck Street was a fusty place to live in. He looks shockingly drawn in the face, but active, as he kept walking about and ringing the bell. He seems in a great measure to have lost his recollection, for on going away, I told him his niece Katherine would wait upon him when we again came that way, and he said, Lord I thought you told me she was in London going to all the balls and dinners ...

Meanwhile it was dawning on Katherine's family that if she could not marry George she would not marry at all. After returning to Parham from Gorhambury she saw him several times and encouraged him to tackle her mother again.

KATHERINE'S JOURNAL

19 January. – We went to a fancy ball at Mrs Walkers, which was very empty. I had however the happiness of G. P.'s company next to me at supper.

22 January. – I went to Lady Henry Howards, where we had a very pleasant ball indeed. I have not felt so much amused at any ball for years.

29 January. – A ball at Petworth, very magnificent, the supper in the tennis court which would I think have looked better in the house. I danced with Mr Gratwicke, Lord Thomas Hay, George Pechell, and at supper sat between Mr Pocock and Mr King.

3 February. – Mr and Miss Howards and Mr Cartwright and George Pechell came to luncheon and went away again.

11 March. – After many unsuccessful efforts to obtain some quiet animal to ride upon, I was so lucky as to see a dear kind friend who settled to lend me a poney. I hope to derive some benefit from this exercise as I feel very ill. I am trying to read and understand the Bible, and find it very difficult to remember. Miss Hawkins has lent me some maps, and with the help of Calmets Dictionary of the Bible I hope not to read without profit.

1 April. – We called at Lady H. Howards, a stupid fussy morning. I am infinitely better for riding the dear poney.

4 May. – George Pechell brought me his beautiful book. I rode out and he came part of the way with me. The end of this week my father went to town for a month and my mother and I remained alone at Parham.

6 *June*. – George Pechell called and followed us into church. Afterwards he had a long conversation with my mother which fixed my future fate.

For nine years they had been in love; now, at last, Katherine and George were to be married. Soon after this momentous day her parents took Katherine to London so that she could be with Harriet, who had moved there in April, and show herself during the latter part of the Season. No one outside the family was to know her news, and she kept up the pursuits of an unattached young woman. She enjoyed the social whirl more than usual, mainly because George was in London too. In mid-July they all returned to Sussex. One day she and George wandered alone through Parham Park and rested by a stone bench placed there in memory of her sister-in-law Charlotte. 'I passed some of the happiest moments of my life' is all she needed to record.

In August Hugh Bisshopp died. His last requests were that he be buried at Parham, his childhood home, and that the remains of his only son, who had predeceased him, join him there. Under Katherine's gaze Lord Zouche wept as his brother's coffin was lowered into the family vault, but neither she nor anyone else knew what thoughts and emotions filled his confused brain. When Hugh's will was opened it was found that he had left everything to his wife, not just for her lifetime but absolutely, so that she was at liberty to ignore her nieces in her own will. Knowing her so little, they had no idea what to expect of her or even what other attachments she might have. Harriet pronounced the will 'very unkind', though in the circumstances it seems perfectly natural.

In September Katherine said goodbye to George, who spent the next two months with a friend on a long-planned tour of Germany and Switzerland. In early November she began a two-month stay at Hagley, where she cared for Harriet while Robert visited neighbours and relatives. One day he took his sons to visit Penn Curzon at Gopsall. On Lord Curzon's death in 1820 Penn had succeeded to his title, but when he was raised to an earldom a year later he used his mother's surname Howe for the new creation. At twenty-three he had married a daughter of the Earl of Cardigan, and four of their ten children had already been born. He loved all children, and as an Oxford undergraduate he had once collected Little Bob from school and then written to Robert that he did not wish to part with so agreeable a companion. And now, with the open-hearted charm that would so appeal to Queen Adelaide, whose chamberlain he became, he sought to cheer the invalid at Hagley.

LORD HOWE TO HARRIET
GOPSALL, 24 DECEMBER 1824

I cannot resist the pleasure of writing you one line, my dear Harriet, to express the great pleasure I had in seeing your little boys at Gopsall. I can assure you very sincerely they have won *all* our hearts, and we have been agreeing that we never remember to have seen more perfectly wellbred nice looking lads with manners much above their years. They seem also to have that most delightful talent of being always occupied and taking to their books whenever they had nothing better to do. In short I must sum up my praises by saying I shall be perfectly pleased can I see my children turn out like them ...

At the close of the year Lady Zouche fell on the stone terrace at Parham. She soon recovered, but her family could not fail to notice that she was no longer sturdy. She walked with a stick, and ailments she would formerly have thrown off quickly now lingered, while her lifelong love of hot weather turned into a fear of the cold and a reduced ability to cope with it. In temperament too she was altered: the self-confident, forthright manner of her early and middle years had given way to a fretfulness and irritability. Minor problems with servants ruffled her, she worried if letters were slow to arrive, and sometimes she took their contents the wrong way. 'I am sometimes puzzled what to say,' Katherine told her, 'for you have so much time to ponder, you probably attach more consequence to any trifle I may happen to mention en passant than it deserves.' Even Harriet sometimes had to clarify things she had written.

1825

For the Curzons this year began like many another: Harriet stayed at Hagley while Robert took their sons to school and then attended parliament. The great political question of the day was the removal of remaining forms of discrimination against Roman Catholics. This had been more or less promised, but not delivered, at the time of the Act of Union between Great Britain and Ireland in 1800, and had acquired greater urgency with the founding of the Catholic Association by Daniel O'Connell in 1823. The House of Lords was opposed, as were the king and many Tory MPs. Robert felt the same distaste for the measure as others in his party, but perceived that it might be unwise to block it for ever: 'I rather think it would be better, if properly modified, to allow it to pass the Lords as the most likely means to keep the country in a state of peace and quiet.'

In mid-January Katherine, back at Parham, met George for the first time since his Continental journey: 'I saw an old dear friend, upon whose arrival Mamma sent me to hunt about the house for her black silk bag, which as I was already very cold and unwell did not improve my looks, and vexed me.' It is unlikely he noticed her red nose or bleary eyes, for his mind was on the practicalities of their future together. If they were to marry he had to provide her with a home, and to this end he was negotiating with Sir Timothy Shelley, the father of the poet Shelley, for a lease on Castle Goring, just north west of Worthing and north of the seaside village of Goring. In some ways his choice was a natural one, for the house was grand enough to satisfy the most demanding parents-in-law and offered fine views of woodland to the west and the coastal plain and sea to the south. However, these advantages were offset by the fact that the property was, in the words of a court of chancery report of 1819, 'in an unfinished and uninhabitable state'.

Castle Goring is a testament to the architectural exuberance of the age. The north front, of flint and coarsely dressed sandstone, is in a Gothic castellated style, while the south front is Palladian, all pale yellow brick and white stonework. The interior, some of it done later, is mainly classical, but with Gothic interventions, the rooms arranged around a spiral staircase covered with a glass dome. The architect was John Biagio Rebecca, who had a large practice in London and Worthing, and the commission came from Bysshe Shelley, Sir Timothy's father, who knew the baronetcy he aspired to would be granted more readily if he had a suitably impressive seat. Building started in the 1790s and continued fitfully until 1810, by which time it had served its primary purpose of facilitating his elevation to the dignity of Sir Bysshe Shelley, 1st Baronet of Castle Goring. Otherwise it was a disaster, with technical and other problems causing endless delays and ballooning costs.

When Sir Timothy succeeded to his father's title and estates in 1815, the outside of the house and parts of the inside were complete. Nonetheless, having seen a good portion of his inheritance vanish in a cloud of builders' dust, the second baronet would have nothing further to do with it and continued to reside at Field Place near Horsham. Castle Goring remained empty and neglected until a prospective lessee appeared in the form of a retired naval officer about to be married. The agreement he signed in 1825 was a fourteen-year 'repairing lease', by which he undertook to carry out the remedial work and interior decoration needed to make the property habitable and in return paid only the very small annual rent of £20.

To fit up the house George engaged Jeremiah Hemmingway, the Surveyor of Chichester, ignoring his grumbles that 'the whole fabric has been one improvident expenditure'. Broken windows, collapsed floors and sodden plasterwork were probably among the defects Hemmingway had to rectify, but the most serious problem was the inadequate water supply. George thought of applying to Rebecca on this point, but Sir Timothy discouraged him: 'Beware the Great Architect, Rebecca,' he warned in one letter; 'I always told him he was building a castle in the air,' he recalled in another. George liked a challenge, and during the summer months of 1825 he oversaw the work from Parham and Aldwick. He got Sir Timothy's permission for the removal of some trees to create paths and a carriage drive, while Hemmingway ordered fire grates and new glass panes. Some difficulties would be resolved later, but George wanted essential repairs completed before he was married.

Katherine was busy too. Weddings were less elaborate than they subsequently became, but with a house to furnish, presents to choose and thank for, and legal and financial agreements still pending there was plenty to occupy her mind before the ceremony, planned for October. Her parents' circumstances had changed greatly since Harriet's marriage, and she could not expect to be given a house in London; even putting together a respectable allowance proved difficult. Moreover as any settlement would affect the future of the Zouche estate, it required the assent not just of her parents but also of the Curzons. The managing trustee was to be George Bisshopp, who came over from Ireland to perform that function.

KATHERINE TO HARRIET
PARHAM, 31 JULY 1825

My dearest Harriet – I thank you and Bob very much for your letters, and I beg you to give Bob my best love and tell him it is needless for me to trouble him with a separate letter as this is to him. I could not possibly think any delay in my concerns was occasioned by you or ever will be. I only made use of that expression because it was written down for me to write to Bob. Rose goes to London we hope tomorrow to see Lowe.

I am delighted you have been out in your little carriage and that you have seen the kitchen garden again, though it must have been very fatiguing for you dear love.

George Bisshopp arrived yesterday at four instead of one as he said, so dear Snugest was in a great fuss for those three hours of suspense and thought he had broke his neck in Mr Walkers coach. George and I did all we could to comfort her. He brought a quantity of patterns of papers for her to choose, and we have fixed on a very pretty blue stripe for the two square rooms. The centre room is to remain as it is, being only an ugly coffee colour and not dirty.

At length George Bisshopp arrived, and we all sat down to dinner with the two Roses and Mr H. Dixon. I thought the Roses very much de trop, but dear Snugest said it was such a comfort to have plenty of people, but it was very hard work doing it all over again at a nine o'clock supper, and I went to bed quite exhausted and could not sleep. However we were all down at breakfast by ten o'clock on hard talking duty as dear Snugest keep's us tight to it in the fear of Grumpus being cross, while he is in fact the happiest and easiest person of the whole company and seems to enjoy himself very much ...

The Archdeacon of Aghadoe was now a married man with children, but according to Katherine his boyish drollery had not worn off.

KATHERINE TO HARRIET
PARHAM, EARLY AUGUST 1825

My dearest Harriet – Snugest desired me to say she hopes you considered the letter to Little Bob as to your own self and that you will excuse her writing to you today. We are all excessively tired with our exertion. We sent off my George to drive with the Duke and Duchess of Cambridge at Lord Arran's yesterday, as dear Snugest said royalty must take place of every thing, and I too was very glad he should go away as I am frightened to death for fear he should wear out the high favour he is in with my father ...

We took George Bisshopp to see Arundel Castle, with which he was much delighted, and we had a luncheon at Mr Cartwright's. Afterwards we went to the church at Arundel which is to be repaired. My father asked Mr Cartwright if he could give him a print of Castle Goring, and after a great trouble he found a beautiful one, intended for the History of Sussex. My father was so delighted with it that though it was five o'clock he said we must go to it that minute in our way home, so away we went and you may suppose how nervous I felt. However it all turned out very well. We walked all over the house, and my father seemed much interested in all the particulars, only he says we must make the regular entrance to the south front, as the other side is so gloomy he thought it like going into a vault ...

I was much fretted all the way in the coach by George Bisshopps vulgar sort of astonishment at our attempting to live at Castle Goring. He made jokes all the way home, and said he supposed I should kill my own beef and mutton, and put up a flag over the castle when I was at home, and not condescend to call upon any body in a small house, and all that sort of thing, which he thought extremely witty but worried me as it might have indisposed my father with the whole concern, and I thought it was odd that he should not have the tact to see how nervous I was at my father looking at it for the first time ... However I am quite in charity with him this morning, as he means to be very kind to me, and it is only le ton de la bonne compagnie that is wanting and which it is impossible to give him ...

Only think of the Duchess of Dorset dying poor thing. George Bisshopp is in great despair as she might have given him a living to hold with Angmering. We have promised him to intercede with Lord De La Warr, which I hope will do as well. I suppose she over exerted herself poor thing to support Lord Whitworth's loss, and died of apoplexy this hot weather ...

Lady Zouche gave Harriet her own account of this day, remarking that her husband had been 'very tame' throughout. She herself was putting a brave face on the forthcoming nuptials, still convinced that Katherine could have done better: 'My spirits are unequal to dispute on any subject, and I only wish, as you rightly say, to let Kate chuse to be happy in her own way.' Harriet felt the same, and in his innocence Little Bob, hearing his mother speak on the subject, wrote his aunt a note to tell her he hoped she was not unhappy. The Pechells were not rejoicing either; having remained civil to Katherine's family during the years that George had wooed her, they were too proud to toast his success.

KATHERINE TO HARRIET
PARHAM, AUGUST 1825

My dearest Harriet – I am very sorry you have got into a way of not sleeping, which is very bad for you, but I hope upon the whole you really are much better. I long to see you upon your crutches ...

Lady Warren[77] is the only one of George's relations that has written to him with that sort of kindness he expected I should have been greeted with. He is angry his mother has not written me a single word. He says it is so different to my family, who have treated him with so much good nature and civility, Lady V[erulam] inviting us to Gorhambury, and Mrs Bisshopp of Dorking so kind. Lord and Lady Maynard have asked us to their home in Essex, to say nothing of you, dearest Do, and my father and mother doing all they can to help him. He is much annoyed. I have assured him it shall not make the slightest difference in my conduct to them as I shall always treat them with the greatest civility, but he is not pacified with this and he is much annoyed as he really loves them and he thought they would be so enchanted and delighted with him for obtaining me as well as with me for prevailing upon you all to accept of him.

However no signor. We are however very happy notwithstanding all these worries. He is gone to Castle Goring this morning, it is now full of workmen. My father has sent Rose to one of the tenants to tell them to help George about some gravel, and he is gone himself to Steyning and will order something about the clock at C. Goring George has asked him to do ...

About Jonathan, he is certainly to go from here. George told me last winter he wished I could bring Jonathan with me as he would know my ways. I said I had *no ways* and there it ended.

I suspect he wishes to go with me but has not yet offered himself. I fear he will look a quiz in our blue, like a convolvulus with the pink face in the middle ...

KATHERINE TO HARRIET
WELBECK STREET, 19 AUGUST 1825
My dearest Harriet – We arrived here last night after a fatiguing journey, and dear Snugest and I feel quite tired today and delighted to repose in your chateau ...

We set off on Wednesday morning [17th] to Goring in the coach, Snugest and I, and I begged her to let us take Stevenson as I thought she would be useful in telling me about the batterie de cuisine, as George is for doing everything in a magnificent way. I ought to have told you that we have long looked forward to meeting at Castle Goring, for though we have frequently been there separately we have never till then had the pleasure of being there together ... I walked all about with George. The Shrubbery as he calls the five acres is quite beautiful and plenty of bushes and shade, so that one may walk about without being seen. Snugest sat in the drawingroom and worked and said it was quite beautiful and she could set there for ever ...

We had some cold meat in the centre room. I felt quite overcome with being there, but George, who is the funniest lover I ever saw, always brings me a little porter in a pint bottle when he comes in the gig, which he makes me drink about one o'clock to keep up my spirits, so the moment I turned pale out came the little dose well frothed, to the infinite amusement of Rose and Stevenson who are both much captivated with him ...

He puts me so in mind of Bob when he talks of his house, and made dear Snugest understand how well the floors are laid and how beautifully the doors turn upon their hinges and so forth. The brick work he says is not so well executed as the carpentering. The stables and coach house are to be done by contract for 110£. I was rather annoyed at so many men seeing us walk about. The whole house is full of workmen, and Snugest made acquaintance with a carpenter, which amused her very much ...

We arrived here [in London] about ten o'clock, and your Crabb desired me to come into the parlour directly to choose some china Lady Bromley had just left for me. I chose what I thought the prettiest, and luckily it happened to be two guineas less than several of the other patterns. I sent off a note to Brom directly and send her answer in another cover. The whole is about 21£ and very kind of Bob's three sisters to think of me. The ice pails will make very pretty ornaments in the stands between the windows, and the centre piece I shall always keep on the table by way of tray. Mrs Bisshopp showed me the dinner service. It is Barbraux, the same as yours at Parham, only it happens to be Derby, which is less liable to be broken and is fortunate for us as George means to use every thing every day. He does not like having best things to lock up in a dusty cupboard.

He wished to have had grass up to the door on the south front, but Snugest and Grumpus will drive up there as they say the gothic is so triste. So he is going to put a square carpet of gravel *for them*, as he does not like the marks of the wheels upon grass, but he does not intend to allow any body else to come that way as he says we shall never be quiet and comfortable if we let all Worthing in to the south.

I think I have given you quite a dose today of our arrangements. We shall I believe stay here about a week. George is coming to look after us in a few days and to decide about the carriage ... Mrs Walker has offered us Mitchelgrove for the honeymoon as it is so retired. George took it upon himself to say that Miss Bisshopp hated retirement, so I suppose he has made up his mind to my being very riotous, and not quiet and good as I have been at Parham ...

In September Katherine again went to London with Lady Zouche, this time to choose her bridal dress, while George continued to make Castle Goring ready to receive her. Then, suddenly, the bustle of preparation ceased. There would be no wedding, or not yet. The Curzons had been feeling uneasy about the marriage settlement, and after a few vague hints followed by weeks of drift they came into the open with their reservations. The future division of Lord Zouche's estate between the sisters, their liability for mortgages he had raised on it, and whether Katherine's moiety reverted to the Curzons if she had no children were all outstanding points. Until they were resolved no new date for the wedding could be fixed.

1826

In the first half of this year Lady Zouche and Harriet corresponded about Little Bob, books they had read, and a girls' school Harriet had helped set up. They said nothing on the subject of Katherine's marriage settlement, and it was absent too from the letters exchanged by Harriet and Robert, which were mainly concerned with the large house they had acquired in Upper Brook Street, Mayfair, to replace their smaller one in Welbeck Street. They decided to redecorate it, and when Lord Zouche came to see it in February he found the inside 'entirely pulled to pieces'. Robert supervised the work, which took over a year, while Harriet lay in bed at Hagley comparing the wallpaper samples he sent her and mulling over his descriptions of 'crimson silk damask curtains', 'woollen stuffs called cashmeres now much used for furniture', 'patterns of Brussels carpeting for the drawing room', and 'chintz patterns with handsome borders'.

In April Mrs Hugh Bisshopp died. Her will contained a generous bequest for Katherine: a London house with fifteen years left on its lease.

KATHERINE TO HARRIET
PARHAM, 26 APRIL 1826

My dearest Harriet – I am sure you and Bob will be delighted to hear that Mrs Bisshopp has given me her house in Hertford Street and every thing in it. I have just received a letter from Mr Brisley to that effect, and I am to pay the duty and the rent and taxes so I suppose it will cost me several hundreds to get possession. I think it had better be lett to repay me these expenses unless Snugest and Grumpus like to go there for the Season. I hope I shall find something that you will like to have as a remembrance of her. I am going to write to the old servants to beg they will stay there as long as ever they like and make themselves comfortable. The poor footman I am much interested for as he lost his wife in a most shocking way the other day by the overturn of the stage coach.

I am very much obliged to Mrs Bisshopp. I thought she would leave me a pair of candlesticks or an inkstand or something, knowing as she did that I was filling an empty house, but I never could have supposed that she would have left me so very desirable a thing as a house in town, for I really do think it just possible that I shall be able to afford to stay an occasional month there some time or another, though I think it had better be let at first, and this year at all events. It is so very delightful being so near Brook St that if I ever do go there I can walk to see you ...

It so happens that George is gone to Aldwick to see his father who is in bed with a blister upon his knee, and he will not be returned until after the post is gone. Snugest recommends me not to write or do any thing in any way till I have consulted him, but besides that I know he will approve of everything I do there does not appear to me to be any difficulty in telling Mr Brisley to lock up every thing till he hears again and to tell the servants that they shall not be turned out because the house is mine.

Poor Lady King has been in the greatest affliction and anxiety about Mrs Bisshopp, but upon Snugest sending word she was dead, she has sent word 'her compliments, and *she will be here presently* ... ' I hope I shall find some cup and saucer for her if Mrs Bisshopp has left her nothing, for I am so tired of hearing about Lady Evelyns and Lady Batterbys unkindness.

I am very much obliged to you for your agreeable letter today. I have taken dear Snugests advice and not written to Mr Brisley today, so I have contented myself with writing to the maid to beg that she and the man and the under maids will stay where they are and make themselves happy and take care of the little dog Countess that one always tumbled over.

Adieu my dearest Harriet give my love to Bob and believe me,
Your ever most affectionate,
Katherine Bisshopp

KATHERINE TO HARRIET
PARHAM, 27 APRIL 1826
My dearest Harriet – I wish I had been the black kitten you made much of yesterday. Lady and Mrs King called here yesterday after I had written to you. Lady K. looked very melancholy and in mourning for her friend, but she said she was sure of *a clock* this time and I could hardly keep my countenance.

George arrived before dinner yesterday. He seemed surprised I had not answered Mr Brisleys letter, so we wrote instantly to desire he would take the necessary steps previous to giving the house up to me, which *steps* are to make an inventory and let me know what is to pay, I fear several hundreds. My father goodnaturedly congratulated me and talked to George all the evening about the value of the plate, but I believe all those things are at Dorking. As she only went to London for advice it was not likely she should move all the knives and forks.

I told my father I hoped he would take any thing he liked as a remembrance of Mrs Hugh. He said, 'We have plenty of things here and don't want any thing.' I think his manner about it has been very kind, but dear Snugest is vexed you and I have not got the estate and all the things at Dorking, and is hardly glad enough at what it has pleased God to *throw* us in by chance at last ...

Her letters remained sprightly, but the endless postponement of her marriage was bringing Katherine close to a nervous collapse. She opened her journal, which she had dejectedly put away the previous autumn, and poured out her woe.

KATHERINE'S JOURNAL

May. – I open this book at the end of ten months ... and find myself still at Parham unmarried, still enduring the same anxieties and miseries as the preceeding eleven years, still expecting that every succeeding week would bring my fate to a crisis, and what is more odd than all, still alive, and though with spirits broken down and subdued, and health impaired and materially injured by anxieties, still laughing and talking and going on with life, and feeling after all that my predominant wish each returning day is that it may be my last, and that God will be pleased to release me from a turbulent and painful existence. I ought to be more thankful for the opportunity that is graciously granted me of correcting my numerous imperfections and faults, and instead of repining to be cheerful and submit patiently to my fate, but the sight of this odious book, where so many painful events are recorded, is enough to alarm me for the future, when I reflect upon the past and above all upon the sufferings of the last dreadful winter. My dear mother was nearly burnt to death last October, George by extinguishing the flames saved her life. How can I be thankful enough for so great a blessing.

9 June. – George Pechell left me to go and see his father who was ill, with the intention of returning the 11th, our marriage day being fixed for the 12th.

10 June. – I received such a bad account of Sir Thomas Pechell so feelingly described by his son that I thought it incumbent upon me to beg our marriage might be deferred.

13 June. – My father and mother went to London to a house in Hertford Street Mrs Bisshopp has been so good as to leave me. I am left quite alone at Parham. The comparative silence of this dear old house, usually the scene of bustle and confusion, is very striking. I will however be thankful for the quiet that is granted me, and which perhaps will save me a fever, after all the exertions of body and mind I have made this last few days. My father and mother returned in a fortnight during which I was quite alone. Sir Thomas Pechell died on the 17th or 18th. George came back to Parham and we settled to be married in six weeks.

Sir Thomas died with his affairs in good order. After making provision for his wife he left the house at Aldwick and the Irish property to his elder son Samuel, who was currently serving in the Mediterranean. In view of George's intention to marry, the £3,000 he was due to inherit had been paid to him the previous September, but the will contained a bond for a further £2,000, and this, together with rent from Hertford Street, made a welcome addition to the couple's prospective income. By this time, the terms of the marriage settlement were at last agreed. Documents were produced, signatures appended. George and Katherine's eleven-year wait was at an end.

KATHERINE TO HARRIET
PARHAM, JULY 1826
… Rose and Kinderly arrived yesterday. We had a late dinner and in the evening my father signed the 300£ a year for me. He appeared quite satisfied, he came into the room while Snugest and I happened to be alone and he said Captain Pechell settles 700£ a year jointure upon K., which besides her own money will be a sufficient provision in case of accidents, and there is 5,000£ tied up for her besides. We have therefore not been obliged to take advantage of Sams offer of saying he would make up the difference if a thousand was positively required on the man's side, so it is all very lucky and Grumpus understands it all. This morning he got up to breakfast but he gave me the opportunity of signing the deeds for the resettlement of the

estate, which I did not wish to bother him about, and I was so afraid he would not go out of the room and that all would be obliged to be explained to him. However nothing could turn out better, and I have had the comfort of securing my estate to my own family after and only hope you will not cut me out when the Robin comes of age ...

The wedding took place on the morning of 1 August 1826, a Tuesday, at Parham Church. Katherine wore a muslin gown trimmed with lace over a white satin slip, a laced tippet of several layers, a veil pinned to her black hair, pearl earrings, a cross necklace and pearl bracelets. Her hair was dressed under the direction of her friend Mary Poulett, now Lady Charles Somerset. She looked '*very very* handsome', said Lady Zouche, who had settled on a lilac pelisse with a laced scarf for herself. Friends and neighbours crowded the little church up to the altar steps, but because of Sir Thomas's death the wedding party afterwards was a small, private affair. Neither Harriet nor Robert was present, so on the next day Katherine wrote an account for them. She did so from Castle Goring, for she and George had chosen to begin married life in their own home rather than honeymoon elsewhere.

KATHERINE TO HARRIET
CASTLE GORING, 2 AUGUST 1826
My dearest Harriet – I fear you wondered I could pass yesterday without writing to you to thank you for your kind little green note, which reached me while Mary Somerset and her maid were doing up my hair, and making me look a fright according to the present fashion.

We staid [to] dinner at Parham as Snugest seemed to wish it and we got here at five. I feel rather overcome with all I went through yesterday, but of all the people in the world to comfort one you will be surprised when I tell you that I don't know what I should have done without Mr Vernon. He quite took care of me as if I had been his own child. I was very much put out by the extreme agitation of Mr Cartwright. He could scarcely read the ceremony he was so afflicted and overcome. He made me say the words all wrong and then made an [*illeg.*] to Tredcroft and said he felt so interested about me he wished any body else would have performed the ceremony. Then came Fanny all the colours of the rainbow and made a tragedy of it. Why could she not come in white muslin and broad hems? Dear Mary was indeed a comfort. I feel quite at home here, the house looks beautiful and the field to the south grown quite green since I was here to see Lady P[echell] five weeks ago. I am in my black today.

This is an unconnected sort of epistle as George keeps talking to me. I was going to tell you that after the ceremony, instead of letting George take me away, Cartwright gave us a look that we were to stand still, and he had his pen and ink upon the altar and wrote a long story in the register. I thought I should have died of that last five minutes, for the church was extremely crowded and I know all the people were looking on. Then I had to go up [to] the altar and sign my name. When I came out we were pelted with corn and flowers, and the same thing over again upon our arrival here. God bless you my dearest Harriet and excuse this hasty epistle, for I hardly know what I am about. Pray give my best to Bob and your dear boys and believe me ever your most affectionate

Katherine Pechell

I hope there is some cake on its road to you.

For the next few months Katherine's journal contains no personal reflections, but its jaunty tone tells its own story. 'George says she *shall* be a happy wife if he can make her so,' a friend told Harriet, and so she was. The newly-weds threw themselves into a frenzy of socialising, as if eager, after the long secrecy of their courtship, to appear before the world together. When not entertaining at home they bowled along the notoriously bad Sussex roads to attend dinners, balls and hunting parties. They saw the regatta at Cowes in its first year and sailed in the yacht belonging to George Vernon, later Lord Vernon, who had been kind on Katherine's wedding day and whose wife Frances was the Warrens' daughter. 'I was delighted to find myself a good sailor,' wrote Katherine, whose inexperience on the water soon seemed a distant memory. The high point of the autumn was Princess Augusta's visit; she came to Castle Goring from Bognor, ate lunch, and was 'pleased with every thing'.

While Katherine was busy with her new life Harriet was marooned at Hagley. Because of her immobility she had for several years only seen her sons during school holidays. For some reason Edward, now rising fourteen, had been sent to Harrow rather than Charterhouse, which his brother had recently left to be tutored at home prior to going to Oxford. Neither boy did well at school, but Little Bob exhibited a facility with language that later brought him distinction as a writer. Physically they were very dissimilar. Little Bob had been a plain child, and, measuring only five foot three inches at the age of sixteen, he was going to be a short man. 'He is such a love, one cannot but wish there was more of him,' wrote Lady Zouche, who told him he would grow faster if he did not sit still so much. Edward, on the other hand, was already quite tall, with a graceful figure and almost feminine good looks.

Despite their mother's bad health, and the limited time they spent with each other, the boys had an agreeable childhood. Robert visited them at school if they were unwell and had them at weekends during his stays in London, where he showed them the Exeter Change menagerie and other places of interest. In the holidays he took them on social calls, which he reported to Harriet with details of their funny sayings and doings. He was proud of them, but appraised their qualities without foolish partiality. Where he erred, especially as his sons passed from boyhood to youth, was in being too indulgent, and his admonishments for laziness and other faults carried little conviction.

Further Correspondences

In returning to the comparison between *Persuasion* and the story of the Bisshopps after an interval of nine years, our main theme will be the parting and final reunion of the lovers. However, there are also further parallels to draw between the two supporting casts. Sir Walter Elliot and Sir Cecil Bisshopp (Lord Zouche), Anne Elliot and Katherine Bisshopp, Frederick Wentworth and George Pechell, and Lady Russell and Lady Bisshopp (Lady Zouche) have already been placed side by side, and now we turn to the two final pairings: Katherine's sister Harriet and Anne's sister Mary; and their husbands Robert Curzon and Charles Musgrove.

Mary Musgrove is an invalid, and she is introduced as such to the reader of *Persuasion*:

> Mary, often a little unwell, and always thinking a great deal of her own complaints, and always in the habit of claiming Anne when any thing was the matter, was indisposed; and foreseeing that she should not have a day's health all the autumn, entreated, or rather required her, for it was hardly an entreaty, to come to Uppercross Cottage, and bear her company as long as she should want her.[78]

Anne arrives to find her sister lying on a sofa. Her ailment is not specified, but it is exacerbated by her husband's absence:

> Being alone, her being unwell and out of spirits, was almost a matter of course. [...] While well, and happy, and properly attended to, she had great good humour and excellent spirits; but any indisposition sunk her completely.[79]

Mary feels better now that Anne is by her, and soon she is able to sit up.

Like Harriet Curzon, Mary appears to be prey to bodily illness and anxiety, with symptoms ascribable to either or both. They are more likely to be ill if their husbands are not with them, and often call their sisters to their bedsides when they are suffering. Mary complains openly when Charles leaves her alone, while Harriet expresses her sadness at Robert's absences indirectly; it is hard to say which feels her solitude more keenly. On a strict view, their frequent demands for attention, whether passively or actively voiced, may be deemed selfish, especially as they both make the most of their ailments. At some level they understand that being ill confers an identity, increases importance and harvests affection. It is also reasonable to wonder whether an excess of leisure may have contributed to their valetudinarian tendencies.

Jane Austen has little patience with such people, as is clear from several fictional portraits and many barbed remarks in her letters. She describes one acquaintance as 'the sort of woman who gives me the idea of being determined never to be well – & who likes her spasms & nervousness & the consequence they give her, better than anything else'.[80] Even her beloved mother is not spared when Jane suspects her of malingering. Nor would she have sympathised with Harriet's wish that she could have Robert and Lady Zouche to cheer her together: 'As to pitying a young woman merely because she cannot live in two places at the same time, & at once enjoy the comforts of being married & single, I shall not attempt it.'[81] If Jane Austen can seem severe with those who accentuate their ill health, and unaware of psychosomatic disorders, she certainly faced her own final illness, which cut her down in the prime of life, with courage and resolve.

Another point Mary and Harriet have in common with each other, and with their parents and guardians, is a high regard for status and lineage. Mary has 'a considerable share of the Elliot self-importance',[82] which is a regular source of irritation to the less grand family she has married into, while Harriet fully agrees with her mother that George Pechell will not do for Katherine and tries to steer him away from her.

Mary's husband Charles is a straightforward country gentleman, easy-going and kind-hearted, strongly attached to his family and the family home. He has ordinary abilities and lives 'without benefit from books, or any thing else', but is 'civil and agreeable' and enjoys excellent spirits. Best of all, he has the equable temper required to cope with the burden of his wife's invalidism.[83] In all this he resembles Robert Curzon, as he does in his major weakness: a lack of focus in the face of financial difficulty. Charles feels 'the want of more money' and has 'a strong inclination for a handsome present from his father'.[84] Robert fails to keep an eye on his expenses, allows himself to be put upon, and relies on gifts from Lord Curzon. Our acquaintance with Charles ends while he is a young man, before the effects of this laxness are felt; in Robert's case these effects will become apparent with the passage of time.

Like the Curzons, the Musgroves have two sons. The faults of the Curzons as parents are gradually coming into view, while those of the Musgroves are evident from the outset. In her first scene Mary Musgrove calls her sons Charles and Walter noisy and unmanageable,[85] which they certainly are, not least because their parents disagree on how to bring them up. Their feeble response to Charles's dislocated collarbone illustrates their deficiencies, while Walter's clambering onto Anne's back and defying all admonitions to get off again shows how unruly the boys are. What becomes of children who have lost respect for their parents? The adolescence and adulthood of the younger Curzons will indicate what the future might hold for Charles and Walter Musgrove.

Meanwhile, Katherine's story has reached the point where her fictional counterpart's ends. She has waited three years more even than Anne's eight before marrying the man she loves. Like George Pechell, Frederick Wentworth felt a strong urge, after the failure of his first proposal, to overcome his chagrin by returning to active service: 'It was a great object with me, at that time, to be at sea, – a very great object. I wanted to be doing something.'[86] Left behind with her family, Anne meets and attracts other men, but finds no one who can compare with Wentworth, and her maternal adviser watches uneasily as years go by without her darling showing any inclination to bestow her hand elsewhere. During the Bath chapters Anne reflects that even without wedlock her bond with Wentworth is eternal, for which the narrator gently mocks her:

> Prettier musings of high-wrought love and eternal constancy, could never have passed along the streets of Bath, than Anne was sporting with from Camden-place to Westgate-buildings. It was almost enough to spread purification and perfume all the way.[87]

Lady Zouche must find Katherine's undying devotion to George Pechell equally improbable and exorbitant. There is no doubt that several other men court her, but with growing concern Lady Zouche, like Lady Russell, perceives that time effects no change in favour of a second attachment. During these years the young woman's preoccupation with her beloved is revealed in the way she thinks of him without needing to name him. Katherine's journal has several such oblique references, and we see the same thing in Anne's reaction to the news that Wentworth's sister and brother-in-law are to live at Kellynch: '[She] left the room, to seek the comfort of cool air for her flushed cheeks; and as she walked along a favourite grove, said, with a gentle sigh, "a few months more, and *he*, perhaps, may be walking here."'[88]

In both cases we lack the man's perspective during his long absence, but it is clear he too is unable to find anyone to extinguish the memory of his first love. She is his ideal, as he is hers. At least he can be active, numbing his heartache by commanding ships, travelling far and wide, and taking prizes, drawing satisfaction from his responsibility and successes. Meanwhile she is stuck at home with nothing much to do, hopeless, frustrated, close to despair. Anne contrasts the fates of men and women with broken hearts in the scene with Captain Harville at the White Hart:

> We live at home, quiet, confined, and our feelings prey upon us. You are forced on exertion. You have always a profession, pursuits, business of some sort or other, to take you back into the world immediately, and continual occupation and change soon weaken impressions.[89]

The restrictions placed on gentry women by their financial dependency and the narrowness of their horizons are a central question in Jane Austen's fiction. So is the more general curtailment of freedom in highly structured, close-knit societies, and the isolation this can produce, especially in cases of private emotional turmoil. Anne feels solitary even in company, whether at the musical party at Uppercross Hall or on the walk to Winthrop, just as Katherine is lonely amid the wearisome whirl of the Season. Each has an invalid sister who cannot be her confidante, and a mother figure whose thwarting of her romance causes a subtle estrangement. As time goes by Katherine feels less and less sure of agreeing with Lady Zouche, and differences between Anne and Lady Russell emerge during their joint visits to the Crofts at Kellynch and the Musgroves at Uppercross, as well as in their avoidance of mentioning Wentworth to each other.

Rather than succumb to despair, the women seek worthwhile tasks and objects of affection. If their sisters are ill they go to them as a matter of course. When Mary calls her to Uppercross Cottage, Anne is 'glad to be thought of some use, glad to have any thing marked out as a duty'.[90] Katherine does not always find the Curzons easy to live with, and Anne has reservations about the Musgroves' ways, but each tries to fit in as best she can, Anne acknowledging that 'every little social commonwealth should dictate its own matters of discourse'.[91] Later Anne reflects that she is 'of the first utility' with Mary's family, as indeed she is,[92] while Katherine's desire to feel useful to her sister and mother is unmistakeable. This joins the other means, already touched on, by which the women divert their minds from sad thoughts: serious reading and amused observation of life around them.

All the while they follow their lovers' progress at sea. Katherine relies on newspapers and bulletins from the Pechell family; Anne uses newspapers and the navy lists, and it is her familiarity with these sources that allows her to give her father details of Admiral Croft's career. The achievements of Wentworth and Pechell are comparable. Both have two long periods at sea, sometimes at great distances from home. Among other regions they serve in the Caribbean, Wentworth distinguishing himself in an action off Santo Domingo, Pechell visiting the island and writing a slim volume about it. Details of Wentworth's career are sketchy, but the statement that 'his genius and ardour had seemed to foresee and to command his prosperous path' also applies to Pechell, who likewise 'by successive captures' has made 'a handsome fortune'.[93] They end their naval careers as captains, with the prospect of being promoted to the rank of admiral later on.

The only direct evidence of the feelings aroused in the two men by disappointment in love are Pechell's letters to Harriet of 1817 and Wentworth's remarks to Anne at the close of *Persuasion*. For the women there is more. Katherine's wretchedness is expressed in her journal, for example in her horror of London balls and disgust with the journal itself. Anne's thoughts remain her own, but her loss of bloom and her subdued, self-effacing presence show the blight of sorrow. When thrown together with their lovers at a social gathering the women are powerfully agitated. Katherine makes demure but unmistakeable reference to such moments, and with Anne they prompt a fluttering in the narrator's prose, as when she sees Wentworth for the first time in eight years:

> Her eye half met Captain Wentworth's; a bow, a curtsey passed; she heard his voice – he talked to Mary, said all that was right; said something to the Miss Musgroves, enough to mark an easy footing: the room seemed full – full of persons and voices – but a few minutes ended it.[94]

The same sensations are conveyed by the same means when Wentworth helps Anne into the Crofts' carriage after the walk to Winthrop or prises Walter Musgrove from her back, a scene the novelist Maria Edgeworth found so vivid that she could feel him doing the same for her.[95]

Strong as these feelings are, etiquette requires that they be suppressed. At times Katherine seems to drown in emotion, but she never loses her outward composure, her letters keep up a relaxed, even cheerful tone, and for the most part she is reticent even in her journal. Anne too is outwardly unruffled. Again and again she reasons herself into the right frame of mind and controls heart-stirrings that are the most intense of any Jane Austen heroine. If an impulse does get the upper hand, a reluctance to admit weakness makes the women try to rationalise it. In a Bath pastry shop Anne wants to see if Wentworth is in the street outside: 'She now felt a great inclination to go to the outer door; she wanted to see if it rained. Why was she to suspect herself of another motive? Captain Wentworth must be out of sight.'[96] Katherine wishes to be alone with Pechell on a summer evening in London, but, in a passage already quoted, invents other reasons for going outside: 'It was a very fine night, I went out for a few minutes before we all went to bed, as the window was wide open. I never shall forget those moments.'

With their fate uncertain, the lovers try to snatch such moments together while in larger groups. Katherine's notation of these occurrences is too cursory for us to see how brief exchanges of words or shared walks are contrived, but in *Persuasion* the concert room scene unfolds what many undeclared couples must have experienced. Seated on a bench with her family party and the Dalrymples, Anne seeks unobtrusively to make eye contact with Wentworth, who is standing a little way off, but she glances across just as he looks away, and then the orchestra strikes up. They stay behind during the interval as the others go in search of refreshments, and when the others return she is able to place herself near the end of her bench. He, irresolute at first, slowly makes his way over, and they exchange some private words. Soon Mr Elliot touches Anne's shoulder and asks her to translate the lyrics of an Italian song, and the moment is over.

The force of Anne's emotional struggle is such that when it seems that her hopes might be fulfilled she is almost overwhelmed. She feels 'joy, senseless joy' when she realises Wentworth is unattached and may yet be hers.[97] Then she catches sight of him at the Bath concert: 'Anne saw nothing, thought nothing of the brilliancy of the room. Her happiness was from within. Her eyes were bright, and her cheeks glowed, – but she knew nothing about it.'[98] Anne has regained her lost bloom, and when everything is at last resolved on the retired gravel walk by Union Street she and Wentworth are 'more exquisitely happy' than when first engaged.[99] Katherine has no narrator to describe her state of mind, and she does not entrust all her feelings to her journal, but we know enough of her to be sure they are the same, and at her wedding she too is blooming despite the flight of youth, '*very very* handsome' in Lady Zouche's words.

When she marries Pechell, Katherine does not spurn her mother for having opposed the match, or rue her own acquiescence. She understands her mother's reasoning and respects her principles and experience, though she thinks she was mistaken. Likewise Anne has no wish to blame Lady Russell for persuading her to give up Wentworth, or herself for being persuaded, even as she wishes she had felt able to follow her own heart. Later she tells him she cannot reproach herself for accepting the guidance of someone who was 'in the place of a parent', for to do otherwise would have lain heavy on her conscience. She also says that although she would not give the same advice as Lady Russell in a similar case it was not necessarily wrong: 'It was, perhaps, one of those cases in which advice is good or bad only as the event decides.'[100]

This sentence is crucial. Foresight is difficult, hindsight all too easy. Financially, the choice of marriage partner was momentous for a well-born woman, who had no opportunity to earn her own living or escape from an impoverishing alliance. It was far from certain that Wentworth or Pechell, on their first application, would have been able to support their wives adequately, or even lived long enough to attempt it. The navy was indeed 'a most uncertain profession', as the early death of Charles Bisshopp demonstrates. However, to an enterprising man with luck on his side it offered considerable monetary rewards, the aureole of heroism, and an increase in social status, so the risk of conferring a daughter on such a man might be worth taking, especially if they seem deeply in love. As years of solitude go by Anne and Katherine grow increasingly sure they would have been better off married than single, and their frustration is understandable.

When the men return to England a second time, advanced in rank and enriched by prizes, the conflict between romantic inclination and prudential motives is removed. Anne's and Katherine's choices, whatever they might once have been, are no longer unwise on any reasonable scale of values. Their families change tack accordingly and the long-awaited weddings take place. But the sober truth is that if the men had failed in their careers, marrying them would still have been impossible. Jane Austen never advocates marrying for love without money; indeed the closing chapter of *Persuasion* deprecates the incidence of this:

> When any two young people take it into their heads to marry, they are pretty sure by perseverance to carry their point, be they ever so poor, or ever so imprudent, or ever so little likely to be necessary to each other's ultimate comfort. This may be bad morality to conclude with, but I believe it to be truth.[101]

The case of Wentworth and Anne is different, the narrator continues, because of their maturity of mind, their settled, justified preference, and Wentworth's independent fortune. The same can be said of Pechell and Katherine. Indeed, Katherine is no less opposed to rash marriages than Jane Austen, as a scandal in her family will make plain.

The final conjunction of personal and financial eligibility in Wentworth is one of the features of *Persuasion* that make it a classic love story. Another is the suggestion that he and Anne are better qualified for and more deserving of happiness when they finally achieve it than when he first proposed. We know too little of Pechell during his bachelor years to make a similar claim for him, but certainly Katherine seems to grow in moral stature during her long travails. After the death of her brother Cecil in 1813 her grief, though natural, became a fixed attitude of despair and indifference to the world, with more than a trace of self-indulgence, not unlike Captain Benwick's exhibition of sincere but shallow grief for his deceased fiancée. The stern test of disappointment, uncertainty and loneliness in Katherine's love for George adds steel to her character, as does the need to suppress rather than display her emotions. Another source of strength, for her and Anne, are the patience and resilience gained from nursing an invalid sister.

As wives they will bring all their qualities, inborn and acquired, to bear. They will be strong, capable partners to strong, capable men. During their spinster years they were casting around for a meaningful role, for a fit object to love; they were adjuncts, however important, to other people's lives. Now they will be at the centre of their own 'little social commonwealth', channelling their intelligence and energy into the only realm that provides a gentlewoman of their generation with a range of fulfilling duties and the reward of social esteem. Because *Persuasion* ends where a romantic novel must we cannot observe Anne as a married woman. It has been suggested that the Crofts offer a picture of her future with Wentworth; however, the young protagonists are far finer-grained than this jolly, kind-hearted couple, who are affectionately presented but never evolve beyond fairly simple, sometimes comic 'character parts'.

A more illuminating model for Anne's future is Katherine, with whom she has so much in common. In the same way, Harriet and Robert Curzon show how the lives of the younger Musgroves and their children might develop. Imagining the later years of Jane Austen's characters is tempting because they are so lifelike, or, as Virginia Woolf puts it, 'so rounded and substantial that they have the power to move out of the scenes in which she placed them into other moods and circumstances'.[102] The continuing tale of the Bisshopp sisters and those around them can aid this imaginative process by showing directions in which their fictional counterparts might travel.

4

Marriage and Children

1827

The Pechells' life together continued as gregarious as it had begun, and Katherine's journal is brimful of parties attended, visits made and dinner guests invited. This gazette reveals the important part the couple's neighbours played in their lives, many of them people Katherine had hardly known previously: the Burrells of Knepp Castle and West Grinstead Park, Mr Gratwicke of Ham Manor, the Howards of Aldingbourne, the Kings of Fryern, Lady Newburgh of Slindon, the Primes of Walberton, the Walkers of Michelgrove, and so on. The journal shows too that after her marriage Katherine became a more regular churchgoer, mainly attending services at St Mary's in the tiny village of Clapham, close by Castle Goring. This change was not due to George's influence, for he appears to have been rather light in religion.

There was regular traffic between Castle Goring and Parham, just seven miles north and a little west, and Katherine also saw a good deal of George's family, who took her to their hearts now that she was his wife. George's elder brother Samuel had returned from the Mediterranean in the autumn of 1826 and saw no further service afloat. On succeeding to his father's baronetcy he elected to use his middle name, becoming Sir John Brooke-Pechell, though in the family he was still called Sam. His inheritance, together with large sums in prize money, made him comparatively wealthy, but although he could afford to marry, he showed no sign of wishing to do so. He had a warm, easy relationship with George and Katherine and was often under their roof. They also got on well with George's sister Fanny, who in 1824 had married Robert Tredcroft, rector of Tangmere near Goodwood; and with the widowed Lady Pechell, who still spent most of her time at Hampton Court Palace.

During the winter Katherine experienced the first shock of her married life: 'My dear George had a dreadful fall out hunting. I never shall forget the distress of that day and therefore need not record it.' He needed over a week to recover, but she was determined not to cling to him or trouble him with fears on his account, and his frequent, often lengthy bouts of hunting and shooting and the 'man dinners' that went with them received no check from her.

KATHERINE TO HARRIET
CASTLE GORING, 7 MARCH 1827
My dearest Harriet – I am truly sorry to hear of your stiff neck and rheumatics. I hope you will take care of yourself for there is nothing so trying as the month of March. It blows and rains beyond every thing, however George is gone off to hunt which he has not done for several days, and I think it will do him good for he has been worrying himself with mending the gutters at the top of the house ...

George dined and slept a week ago at Mr Primes, and the two Miss Streatfields went in the evening to a ball at Lady Henrys in black gowns with red sashes and necklaces and he said it looked very pretty. I believe I did not tell you how well I behaved about George going off *en garçon*, but Col. Wyndham in the field suddenly offered himself to Mr P[rime] for the next day. He poor man was desolé as there was nobody to meet him, and he turned to George and said if he would but come he would send his carriage for him. However I recommended George to go with a good grace [in] his own gig, which he did and helped to play at whist ...

For several weeks in February and March Harriet had her mother for company at Hagley while Robert and Little Bob visited family friends in the Midlands and then went to London. On 17 February Robert wrote to tell Harriet that Lord Liverpool had suffered a stroke, and he followed this with regular bulletins. The prime minister regained the power of speech and the use of his limbs, but a clouding of his mind obliged him, at the age of fifty-six and after fifteen years in office, to resign. His half-sister Lady Verulam expressed herself with her wonted dignity: 'I trust in God's mercy that his precious life will be spared to his friends. As a public man he must cease to live, which to the nation is I may say an irreparable loss.' Lord Liverpool had a second stroke in the summer; the third, in December 1828, carried him off.

In April Harriet stirred at last, travelling to London for her first stay in the newly decorated and furnished house in Upper Brook Street. Then she went on to Parham with Little Bob, and from there visited Castle Goring.

KATHERINE'S JOURNAL

26 May. – On this day my dear sister performed her journey from London to Parham after an absence of 10 years and a half, having been kept away from 8 years of illness and other previous impediments.

27 May. – We went to Parham to meet her. It was truly affecting to see her there upon crutches, so different from the youthful and active creature she was when she left it, but the happiness was great to see her there at all after her severe sufferings and the very uncertain hope of her ever coming again. To our great delight and no little surprise she expressed a wish to come to Castle Goring the very next day, so on Monday the 28th of May George and I returned home and brought Little Bob with us in the expectation of her immediately following us. However the rain in the evening prevented her coming to us, but on Tuesday the 29th of May we had the happiness of seeing her at Castle Goring, and it was indeed a great pleasure to me to have the comfort of her presence under my own roof. My mother accompanied her and left us on Wednesday the 30th of May. Dear Harriet enjoyed herself and was amused with seeing our residence. George prevailed upon her to set out of doors at the south front of the house. She admired the sea view and we were very happy.

31 May. – Harriet was very ill in the morning but she recovered as the day advanced, and at four o'clock she was sufficiently recovered to return to Parham. I accompanied her as George was so kind to let me go, and I came back to him Saturday the 2d of June.

Harriet continued to improve, and Lord Verulam rejoiced in his journal to see her looking stronger and walking without crutches.

For the rest of her life these good spells alternated with periods of debility.

In June George and Katherine visited Lady Pechell at Hampton Court Palace and then stayed with the Curzons in London for a taste of the Season: 'We returned home having been absent three weeks and two days, and having enjoyed our tour extremely, and still more our return to our beautiful and comfortable home.' Katherine's journal contains many such expressions of affection for Castle Goring, and she hardly minded the disturbance caused by renovation work during their first years there. George's agent Jeremiah Hemmingway had died soon after being engaged, so George managed the workmen himself as they sank a new well to increase the water supply, fixed gutters damaged by pigeons, and replaced stolen lead pipes. Fortunately fears of dry rot proved groundless, and all in all the expense of repairs fell below what he had expected.

More irksome was the friction with John Bright, a tenant farmer on the Castle Goring estate who acted as the owner Sir Timothy Shelley's factotum there. When George signed the lease only the garden and a small park were attached to the house. Afterwards he arranged to add seventeen acres of woodland previously allocated to Bright, from whom he rented further parcels of land directly. However, complicated disputes about boundaries and access soured relations between the two men, and they were at odds about the best means of protecting game and keeping off trespassers. Bright further resented George's right to sport on the whole estate, which had been his sole preserve before the house was occupied, and he tried to make things awkward for him. A low point came when Bright, in what could be passed off as a mistake, shot some of George's tame pheasants.

George complained about these matters to Sir Timothy, and he did so quite often. Never, though, did this insistence on defending his rights make his landlord impatient. Sir Timothy has been portrayed as an ogre in biographies of his supremely gifted son, who died in 1822, but most of his acquaintance knew him as a fair-minded man who was punctilious in attending to business, kind to his tenant farmers, and charitable to the poor. His letters to George are sometimes a little pompous, but always courteous and considerate, showing a real interest in his lessee's comfort along with a desire, which the latter no doubt shared, to 'keep far from lawyers and surveyors'.

In July George was appointed a justice of the peace for Sussex and went to West Grinstead for the quarter sessions. Then George Bisshopp brought his wife and children from Ireland for a two-week stay, divided between Parham and Castle Goring; they were taken to see beauty spots like the Roman pavement at Bignor and introduced to the local gentry at dinner parties. September brought an invitation from the Duke of Norfolk and a Channel crossing.

KATHERINE'S JOURNAL

2 September. – We went to Arundel Castle to stay. The Duke walked all about with us in the gardens and shewed them off, I was much amused. I never admired the library so much as I did that day and it was a pleasure to me to shew it to my dear George who had never seen it before.

3 September. – I went to Parham and the men went out shooting … I returned to dinner at the castle. Our party was very small this day, our two selves and the Duke, Capt. Wollaston and Mr Edward Howard. I was much amused, and did not mind being the only woman. The Duke was extremely cordial and pleasant and seemed anxious to make me comfortable. I brought away a most agreeable impression of this place, having entered with a feeling that I should be tres ennuyee.

15 September. – We embarked on board the Talbot steam packet for Dieppe and landed about 8 in the evening. I was extremely amused with being actually in La Belle France and beautiful the country is. The noise of the people astonished me very much. Their extreme gaiety and screams and cries of joy upon the appearance of the steam boat which they certainly must see three times a week was extremely ridiculous. We took up our abode at Taylors English Hotel.

16 September. – We went to the Church of England service and heared it performed in English. Lady Granville was there. We afterwards drove about the town in a coach.

KATHERINE TO HARRIET
DIEPPE, 16 SEPTEMBER 1827
My dearest Harriet – I wrote to you from Castle Goring in such a hurry and such a state of astonishment at what I was going to undertake that I fear you thought it was very shabby of me, but I begged dear Snugest to explain my case to you. Lady Warren

is in fear of a chancery suit if a Mrs Perkins finds out she is out of England. Lady Warren wrote to me a fortnight ago to ask if I would spare George to go to Dieppe with her for a few days, and that she was coming to Parham and to Castle Goring. I thought I must comply, an odd proposition, and the more so as she said so much about secrecy. I therefore wrote her word George was much at her service but *not* with my consent unless *I* was also of the party. Knowing them both as I did I knew she would persuade him to go how ever much he fancied he should persist in declining, and so it turned out. She gave me I must say the kindest invitation to accompany her and George, and she pays our passage there and back.

My poor George hates it beyond expression, is excessively sick and more bored. We got into the steam vessel at six in the morning, I was most dreadfully sick till ½ past ten, when I was obliged to go into the cabin, and I made them put a blanket on the floor, where I laid very comfortably till 7 in the evening. We then landed on the peer, and though I was scarcely able to stand I was extremely amused at the appearance of the people. The cheerfulness and screaming and gaiety beyond any thing I could have conceived. The coast is more like Hastings than any other place, and much prettier than I was prepared to expect. All the women in snowy white cap's, very coarse and unbecoming, and not a bonnet to be seen. Consequently they are all sunburnt and ugly, but then George says only look at their shoes and stockings.

When we got to the Hotel d'Angleterre we found all the best rooms occupied and nothing but little French beds for single people. I was so ill I was delighted to be just any where, and I locked my door and said I should not mind, but when I awoke in the middle of the night and found myself quite alone in a foreign country you cannot think what an odd feel it was.

I was awakened about five in the morning again by a great dispute in French about a washing bill, which was as good as the French play. We have found out a double bedded room for tonight, so I shall be more sociable. This morning we went to the English Church, where we saw Lady Granville and Lady Hardy and Lady Nelson the widow. Then we drove about in a coach and ended with the cathedral, which is very beautiful, and it is curious to see a *great* Roman Catholic church all dressed up with flowers etc. etc. I am in fits of laughing at the grotesque appearance of the people.

This evening we are sitting very dull at the inn, Lady Warren talking scandal, George reading and I writing to you. Lady Warren proposed taking us gratis to Paris, but George has declined for many reasons, the principal one the lateness of the season and the danger of the steam vessels in a high wind, which is inevitable at this season ... This hotel is kept by English people, which is a great take off to the novelty one anticipate's in going abroad. I have however made acquaintance with one French housemaid and I find I get on quite well with my French ...

For four days they looked at the shops, went to the theatre, and mixed with other British visitors, including Countess Granville, lately Britain's ambassadress in Paris. Then it was time for the homeward passage.

KATHERINE'S JOURNAL

21 September. – We embarked on our return on board the Talbot. We had a very bad passage of 22 hours, as we were obliged to lay to all night, the weather being so bad the captain could not attempt to land either at Brighton or Newhaven. I was dreadfully ill during the voyage and was most happy to land safely the next morning at the pier in Brighton, and returned to our clean, beautiful and comfortable home. I was much struck with the richness and beauty of the country and the cordiality of the people. I felt as much at home at Dieppe as if I had always lived there, indeed more so than I ever felt before anywhere in England ... The baths are very delightful, and altogether I am glad I have seen a little bit of the opposite coast although it was a great disappointment not going on to Paris and the more so as Lady Warren offered to take us gratis, and I should have liked of all things to have gone. Lady Granville's good nature to me would have insured my amusement in the society of Paris.

It sounds as if George, who by this time had had his fill of foreign travel, seized on any available pretext not to continue to Paris. A trip to Cherbourg four years later would be Katherine's last sight of the Continent. Eager to venture further, she knew that her husband was not.

At Hagley Harriet was a magnet for family correspondence, with her husband, elder son, sister, and mother writing from a variety of locations. In August her parents, now seven years without a London home, took up her invitation to use Upper Brook Street. They were 'all admiration' for the way it had been decorated, Lady Zouche wrote, and very thankful to be allowed to stay. Her letters to her favourite child were more adoring than ever and filled with the humble gratitude of old age for the kindness of the younger generation. This change is somehow poignant, as are the incoherent lines penned by Lord Zouche during a pause in one of his wife's compositions. He no longer went away on his own, but stayed close to her; and she, after all the mortification he had caused her, now felt sorry for the muddled old man.

In September Robert and Little Bob made an educational tour of Wales. This was more duty than pleasure for Robert, who no doubt recalled his earlier travels with Penn Curzon. Little Bob, on the other hand, enjoyed it greatly, foreshadowing the extensive roving of his adult life. At seventeen he was at last rebelling against his diminutive nickname: '*He* does not like to be called *little* as he intends to grow into a tall man,' Robert told Harriet. His own letters show him quite capable of poking fun at himself for his lack of inches and other defects, but very sensitive to criticism and mockery from others.

The Pechells passed the rest of the year in visits made and received, hunting and shooting expeditions for George, and ladies' outings for Katherine. She often saw her parents, now back at Parham, but George rarely accompanied her there and usually absented himself when they came to Castle Goring. Lady Zouche noticed this and vented her feelings to Harriet: 'I think it does not answer to obtain company against their will, and it is so tiresome and bad hearted not to amuse and oblige people with one's society when they request it.' Perhaps she was secretly glad not to see much of George, for closer acquaintance had confirmed a lack of sympathy between them. She found his rather brisk personality devoid of charm, and although he was civil his attentions fell short of what she expected in a son-in-law. There is no evidence for his feelings, but he cannot have forgotten the setbacks he had suffered at her hands.

1828

In February Robert took his sons on a sightseeing tour of Warwickshire and Oxfordshire. Then they visited Lord Howe at Gopsall, where Robert II, as we shall henceforward call him, had a taste of fox-hunting.

ROBERT CURZON II TO HARRIET
GOPSALL, FEBRUARY 1828
My dear Mama – We arrived here prosperously at Gopsall on Friday and Knighton was not at all tired, and yesterday I went out a hunting for the first time in my life, and was in at the death, and had my face blooded. I think hunting is very good fun, only the leaps tire one very much. It is a great exertion to stick on so tight so very often. My horse was 17 hands high and leapt like a greyhound. I went over one hedge as high as my horse with a large ditch on the other side. I had no idea that a horse could possibly leap so high. I hope you are pretty well and find some thing to amuse you at while you are all alone at Hagley. I am pretty well, only very stiff.

I remain

My dear Mama

Your affectionate son

R. Curzon

In the summer Harriet repeated her journey of the previous year to London and Parham. The days with her mother at Parham became a precious memory as soon as they were over.

HARRIET TO LADY ZOUCHE
UPPER BROOK STREET, 4 JULY 1828
… How very kind my dearest Snugest you are to write me the dear letter I received yesterday and which I should have answered, but somehow I was ten times more tired than the day before, and yet longed to thank you so much. Bob went to Penn yesterday and Little Bob to the British Museum, so I put myself into my bath and dined with Bob at five o'clock for him to return afterwards to Croydon in the barouche, which he did, and I was all by myself wishing I was with you at dear quiet Parham in the *green ameni prati*.[103] However the time *passed itself* somehow and I thought Bob never would come home, but he arrived after ten and I was in bed.

How good you are dear Snugest about every thing, but just now it is about the venison I mean. I dare say I shall, like you, be often thinking of the many things we might have talked over. The very little time we were together was however very comfortable, and as poor Mrs Lister writes me word it is best not to dwell upon the blessings that one has lost but be thankful for the many that remain, so I try to comfort myself for my continual separation from you by the thoughts of how much worse it would be if I was still farther, and the consolation of your being so well, and dear Grumpus so much better than when he was here ...

In the early months of the year Lord Zouche's health had appeared to be breaking up, but by the summer he was better. During his illness Katherine spent time at Parham while George put in more hours as a magistrate, and in May they went to London together for a snatch of the Season. The house in Hertford Street that Katherine had inherited from Mrs Hugh Bisshopp was being let, so they stayed with friends. 'I passed several pleasant evenings,' Katherine recalled, 'my dear George always going out with me and making every thing pleasant to me by his kind care and attention.' In August they rattled merrily around Sussex, but early in September Katherine returned from a party at Arundel Castle feeling unwell, and the next day she was bled and ordered to lie on the sofa, where she remained for seven weeks.

LADY BROOKE-PECHELL TO KATHERINE
HAMPTON COURT, 8 NOVEMBER 1828
My dear Kate – I feel such real pleasure in the prosperous state you are in that I cannot deny you any request, and certainly not that which will (you say) relieve your mind from anxiety on your mother's account. She herself proposed me to attend you, so that I have strong motives for hoping that I may prove a comfort to you all, but the best recommendation I have is good luck and experience. The latter end of your letter quite frightened me, had I not seen the line added at the outside saying you were better. Now from this time I insist on your not setting up to write to me any more for some months. No news will be good news, and besides I shall no doubt hear sometimes from George. I think if you please that it is better not to communicate the state you are in till after the 4th month, viz. after you are sure of *feeling*

tokens of life. Then there cannot be any mistake and no doubts. To ensure that desirable moment you will be kept on the same system as at present, which agrees with you. I think after the 5th month it will be time to engage your nurse, and if Morah has not one that he is particularly anxious to place about you I can vouch for the merits of Mrs Newman of Chichester. She is a very excellent nurse in every way that her talents can be required ...

It is this letter, and another from Lady Pechell to Lady Zouche, which reveal that Katherine was pregnant; in her journal coyness or superstition prevented her going beyond mentions of feeling unwell and needing to lie down. She had miscarried twice already, and at almost thirty-seven she was anxious to bring her pregnancy to term this time. The reason she asked her mother-in-law to take her mother's natural place with her when her child was due the following April was that her father's health had deteriorated again and her mother might be unable to leave Parham.

Lord Zouche faded faster than expected. In early October he was well enough to visit Castle Goring, where he was astonished to find Katherine confined to the sofa but delighted with the cause, and then travel to London with his wife to see a clerk in the court of chancery. On his return he fell, possibly as the result of a stroke, and his health took a sharp turn for the worse. By the end of the month his digits were affected by dry gangrene, a sign, the doctor said, that the end was near. In his final days he was as temperamental as ever, as Lady Zouche told Harriet: 'I was much affected last night when poor Grumpus called me to his bedside and said I only want to look at you, but to day in the end parlour he said I only made faces etc. etc.' Harriet was too infirm to make the journey from Hagley, and there was no question of Katherine covering even the short distance from Castle Goring. Only his long-suffering wife was with him when he died, without pain, on 11 November.

George visited Parham daily to assist Lady Zouche until the Curzons arrived. There was a small funeral, with Lord Zouche's sons-in-law as chief mourners, and his remains were deposited in the family vault. Later Katherine added a sentence to the short biography she had written in the printed list of Parham's pictures: 'This was my dear father who never spared any expence or exertion to promote what he considered to be the aggrandisement of his children and family.' Not much of an epitaph, but more than he deserved, and the best she could think to say of him. Lady Zouche afterwards discovered some old family letters that showed how miserable his childhood had been. How much of his strangeness, she wondered sadly, was due to neglect by a rancorous and divided family.

The breath was not long out of Lord Zouche's body before his tangled affairs threatened to overwhelm those he left behind. Latterly there had been delays in the payment of his daughters' allowances, and a bill of sale around the time of Katherine's marriage indicates a further shedding of possessions. His will, leaving his personal property to his wife, was an irrelevance as he had no money and almost all his moveable effects had been signed over to his daughters so as to shield them from creditors. However he left a large estate, to which Harriet and Katherine were by right co-heiresses, while his widow was to receive a jointure paid from its income. But how could such a complex property, spread across Sussex and Oxfordshire, be divided equally? Who would own Parham itself? And to what extent were Lady Zouche, her daughters and their husbands liable for Lord Zouche's debts? 'I was now involved in a multiplicity of business,' Katherine recalled, 'and my time chiefly passed alone in looking over old papers.' Years would pass before it was all sorted out.

There was also the question of the deceased's hereditary honours. In the absence of a surviving son his baronetcy went to George Bisshopp, but the Zouche barony was held 'in fee' and could pass through the female line, though the abeyance would have to be terminated again. Robert and Harriet were willing to undergo the trouble and expense of this, and were shocked to learn that the Pechells intended to make a rival claim. With no explanation in their own words or in the Curzons' we can only guess at their reasons. Perhaps George felt a decision in Katherine's favour would reward his naval service. It was a foolish venture, for although there was no firm rule in such cases that the peerage be awarded to the elder daughter, it was natural to assume it would be. After the difficulties about the marriage settlement the sisters had grown close again, but the succession dispute cleaved them apart a second time. All the while Katherine's difficult pregnancy was darkening her mood.

KATHERINE'S JOURNAL

19 November. – My own family all arrived in a body to see me. I thought I would have died at the entrance of five persons in deep mourning, and I who have been so long in seclusion felt perfectly unequal to the exertion. My mother seemed quite well, my sister much over harassed in a state of nervous excitement which did me no good. This unsatisfactory meeting terminated to my great relief in a couple of hours. I did all I could to prevail upon my sister to pass a week with me or even a day, but she would not consent. She however came to see me again on the Saturday the 22d for an hour and returned to London Monday the 27th. My mother remained alone at Parham for a fortnight and then came to me for a week on the 8th of December.

15 December. – My mother went to join my sister in London. Since then my time has been passed in great anxiety and vexation, but the great duty of taking care of my health under present circumstances has prevented my giving way to many painful and wretched feelings, and with so affectionate a husband as it is my lot to possess I ought not to repine at the unkindness of others.

The Curzons hastened to submit their claim for the peerage. Before his father-in-law was buried Robert wrote to Sir William Knighton, who immediately approached the king and received an undertaking that he would confer it on Harriet. Of course the matter had to pass through the right ministerial channels, and Sir William told Robert what to do at each stage, while the prime minister the Duke of Wellington and the home secretary Robert Peel assured him of their backing. The Pechells did not, in fact, put in a full claim, but applied for a stay in the proceedings so that their case might be heard. This was dismissed, and on 13 January 1829 Harriet's succession was announced in the *London Gazette*. The cost of stamps and fees was £560, excluding charges for work done by the College of Arms and the attorney general's report. But the Curzons felt that such a fine adornment, which their elder son would one day inherit, was worth the expense. Sir William wrote to Robert to congratulate his 'dear little wife' on becoming the 13th Baroness De La Zouche.

1829

The two Lady Zouches (we shall continue to refer to the dowager by that name) passed the winter and part of the spring at Hagley.

In March Robert left them for parliament, where the question of Catholic emancipation filled every mind. His principles were no more favourable to a Catholic Relief Act than were those of Wellington and Peel. However, faced with the prospect of civil strife in Ireland, the two Tory leaders resolved with heavy hearts to push the measure forward; and Robert, unwilling to oppose men to whom he was under an obligation or a policy he knew must one day prevail, abstained after the second reading. This perturbed Harriet, who hated anything that might imperil Anglican supremacy. He reassured her: 'Do not be uneasy at the idea of the papists lording it over us, they will not be able to do any such thing. In questions of worldly or spiritual interest 5000000 of raggamuffins will not be able to dictate to 16000000 of comparative wealthy and well educated persons.' On 24 March the Act was passed.

He put a brave face on it, but the controversy was a disheartening experience for Robert. Fear of Catholicism was deeply ingrained in the English mind, and his acquiescence to emancipation set him at odds with friends whose general outlook he shared. This increased a weariness with his parliamentary duties that he had felt for some while, and he told Harriet that with the peerage obtained it would be no sacrifice to give up his seat. He was a plain Staffordshire squire, happiest at his own hearth or mixing with friends and neighbours, and national politics held little appeal. He did not enjoy living in London, especially as Harriet was never well enough at the close of winter to accompany him there. 'I beg to be vastly tired of it,' he told her.

Meanwhile Katherine remained fixed to the spot at Castle Goring, being looked after by the Parham housekeeper and visited by friends: 'I have now passed five months upon one floor and hope to have patience to pass the next three in the same quiet manner,' she wrote in her journal in late January. George still went hunting or shooting for days on end, though he sometimes felt abashed at leaving his prostrate wife. 'I have just had a letter from him,' Katherine told Harriet in early March, 'in which he says as I have got *Mrs Janet* to take care of me and there is no frost he shall not return till Friday, and then *he will never leave me again*, which amuses me so very much for I am sure dear love I am so glad he has a little change so long as he makes me feel I am always in his thoughts and am not neglected by him.'

Harriet and Katherine avoided falling out over the peerage by keeping silent on the subject. The partition of the estate promised to be far more problematic, and until it was complete Parham was an awkward joint responsibility. They agreed that their mother, now without a home of her own, should live there as much as she liked, but how to run the household proved a vexed question, and half-explained squabbles about servants, horses and keys echo through family letters. George knew the place had been sloppily managed, even since Robert had taken a hand in it, but he had a tactless way of making suggestions, and Katherine a tactless way of endorsing them, that irked Harriet and Lady Zouche. They took offence where none was intended, as when George referred to the dowager's jointure as an encumbrance and Lady Zouche understood him to mean that she was one herself.

As Katherine's pregnancy advanced they all tried to avoid contention, and Harriet sent gifts for the unborn child.

KATHERINE TO HARRIET
CASTLE GORING, 2 APRIL 1829
My dearest Harriet – I was delighted to hear from dear Snugest that you had been down stairs, though I thought it was rather soon after so severe an illness as you have had. I hope you really will take care of yourself now, you have nothing required of you but to take care of your health, and I hope you will stay quiet and not catch cold. I was longing to write to you yesterday to thank you most gratefully for your beautiful present of the dear child's things, which I unpacked and looked over the day before. The two little dear caps I could not part with all day, they really do look as if something was coming to wear them. I see you have been so good as to include things for me and two thick petticoat sort of things which I did not know by sight ...

George was absent at Brighton when I looked over the things and yesterday we were very busy and today he is gone [to] a shooting party, but I must make him look at them and make him understand that you have saved him £50 or £60, which I am sure he will be very grateful for when he comes to comprehend it ...

Two days later she gave birth.

KATHERINE'S JOURNAL

2 April. – George went to dine at Mr Primes. I felt ill all night and on the morning of the 3d I sent for Mr Morrah my accoucheur. He gave me laudennum and brandy and water, mutton chops and everything to support me, and I got through the day with some few intervals of ease. Jannett Freeman the housekeeper from Parham came to me by a previous arrangement. At 12 at night I became so ill that I have lost all consciousness or recollection of how that dreadful night was passed. Jannett sent for Morrah, for Captain Pechell and for my monthly nurse, and I was seized with the pains of premature labour and my dearest baby Henrietta was born at 7 o'clock in the morning of the 4th of April. I had the happiness of suckling her till the 28th, when she was seized with convulsive fits, and Lady Pechell and George and Morrah sent for a wetnurse. My baby was also baptised by Mr Calhouse and registered at Goring. She recovered but I became very ill and suffered severely from weaning her as I had so much milk.

While his wife tasted the joys and discomforts of motherhood, George broadcast the news and reaped a harvest of congratulations. Some friends offered advice, especially on the need for the mother to stay still. 'Do not let Kate fancy herself well too soon or exert herself in any way,' Frances Vernon told George. 'Tis better to take two months rest after being in so delicate a state with a first child, and may *establish strength* for *future performances*.' The desirability of further childbearing was stated even more baldly by Sir Timothy Shelley: 'This is the first opportunity I have of giving you joy of a first born at the Castle, and that you may lay another upon the stocks, a fine boy, within the year.' But Katherine did not regret her baby's sex, and one imagines her smiling at Mr Gratwicke's praise for her 'very fine and *beautiful* daughter' and Mr Prime's facetious comment to George that her good looks gave him the prospect of 'establishing her well' at a young age.

Katherine recuperated slowly, and for weeks her limbs were swollen. Lady Pechell assisted her ably, creating new warmth in a relationship that had not been without awkwardness. The death of Lord Zouche in November had released Katherine's mother to attend her, but the existing arrangements were not changed. Lady Zouche was at Hagley at the time of the birth; presently she returned to Parham and then went to Castle Goring. 'The little girl seems to be a miniature of Kate, has fine large eyes, a very small head, and a sweet quiet smiling look,' she wrote to Harriet. 'I think her remarkably pretty, but Jannett and the nurse both said she had amazing long legs and arms and was 21 inches in length.' A few days later she made another positive report: 'Now as to dear Kate, she is certainly as well as possible and the child sucks most prosperously, Lady Pechell says without giving the dear mother any pàin, but Katherine does not quite agree in that account. However, she certainly has had no swelling, no stiffness or soreness in her bosom.'

Harriet was asked to be a godmother alongside Katherine's friend Henrietta Howard, after whom the child was named. Katherine hoped George's brother Sir John would consent to be her godfather.

KATHERINE TO SIR JOHN BROOKE-PECHELL
CASTLE GORING, APRIL 1829
... G. has probably told you that I have several weeks intended to write to you, first to thank you for all your kind enquiries about me during the illness which I most miraculously struggled through, and also to bespeak your affection and protection towards my little Henrietta, who is I assure you a very pretty and promising little personage. I will not affect to have forgotten all the dislike I have heard you express upon the subject of standing godfather to the children of your relations and friends, but as you are the person of all others I wish to select to be the godfather of my little girl I cannot help expressing my wishes to you in the hope that you will do George and myself that favour. If you are so kind as to acceed to my request my sister and Henrietta Howard will undertake to relieve *you* from all the *responsibility* I have heared you say you disliked. Should you refuse or accept the office I am so desirous of conferring upon you I hope your niece will in either case have the happiness of your advice and affection upon all occasions and I shall have the greatest pleasure in showing her to you whenever you come to us, which will I hope be very soon ...

In his reply Sir John, like George something of a free thinker, said it would trouble his conscience to assume a responsibility '*nowhere enjoined* except by the pomp of our churchmen', but regard for his sister-in-law outweighed his scruples and he accepted the position so flatteringly offered.

Henrietta's birth temporarily softened Harriet towards Katherine, and she sent loving congratulations. However she and their mother disliked George – the 'Wasp', as they called him – more than ever. After her return to Parham Lady Zouche clashed with him on various matters, and the need for a survey and audit of the estate prior to its division promised further friction between him and the Curzons, who had already rejected suggestions he had made about Lord Zouche's debts and the tenanting of the farms. George was a busybody who acted as though he and his wife owned Parham outright, his antagonists agreed, and Robert counselled keeping aloof: 'If G. P. continues to go on in this way he will get everything into such a state as to make him *feel* the inconvenience of an undivided property. We have only to remain quiet.'

The Curzons steered clear of the Pechells during the increasingly strained discussions about the estate: Harriet avoided her sister as much as she decently could and Robert found pretexts for declining invitations to Castle Goring. Their dislike of direct confrontation was combined with a resolve not to give way on the points at issue, for they saw no justice in the Pechells' conduct and hoped it would become more reasonable. Harriet in particular had a stubborn sense of rectitude behind her mildness of manner, and she readily attributed Katherine's stance to the stresses of pregnancy and motherhood or to George's nefarious influence. Lady Zouche agreed: 'The dear Kate is a most agreeable companion and means to be a friend, but her views and principles are somehow or other *strangely perverted*.'

Katherine certainly accepted George's authority, but Harriet was even further from asserting herself despite having a less forceful husband. During her father's last illness she had thought of going to Parham, but Robert decided the journey would be too taxing: 'So I am easily checked you know,' she confessed to her mother, 'and set down like a dog in the kennel till my dear master lets me out.' During the quarrel with the Pechells this trait became more pronounced. When Harriet and Robert were apart she sent him copies of letters she had written to Katherine so that he could see if she had done right. His replies elated her: 'How shall I thank you as I wish and feel for the approbation you are so good as to express to your poor Fright, and which fills me with delight.'

The extant documents tell only one side of this sorry story. George left no recorded opinion of his in-laws' behaviour, and Katherine's journal contains only vague or inscrutable remarks. Lady Zouche hinted that a sense of injustice had been festering in her younger daughter: 'Dear Kate always thinks she does everything for others, and that nobody is kind enough to her.' Certainly Katherine made no secret of her surprise that her mother had chosen not to be close by at Henrietta's birth. Harriet suspected she was also bitter about the long deliberations over her marriage settlement and, retrospectively, about the gift of the Welbeck Street house to the Curzons. Given all that had passed in the years before she became George's wife, further resentments may be imagined.

At the end of April Harriet joined her mother at Parham, and from there she drove to Castle Goring several times to see Katherine and her girl. In mid-May Lady Pechell left after an attendance of five weeks, but Henrietta Howard came and helped her little godchild through an illness. Katherine tried to get stronger herself with rides on the gravel paths round the house and dips in the sea at Worthing. In early June she and George went to Parham, her first visit since her father's death. The atmosphere was hostile, as it was when she called alone a week later: 'I went to see my mother and sister at Parham and received great unkindness from them, which I thought unfair considering my very bad state of health and my temporary state of anxiety for my baby then under vaccination'.

We know not what this 'unkindness' was, but Harriet, having accused Katherine of being unreasonable, was laying herself open to the same charge. She panicked on learning that George was to inspect the Oxfordshire estates and might go to Oxford, where her son was studying: 'I wish you would write to dear Little Bob,' she urged Robert, 'and caution him that G. P. is likely to come and not to be taken in to make promises or *sign any thing*.' She even cast a slur on her sister's character: 'Katherine thinks if she can get hold of you she can do wonders with you – or any man, she once told me.' This conflation of a youthful boast with ostensible present motives reveals an unexpected streak of malice in Harriet, who had never before been jealous when Robert and Katherine were alone together. She also showed a subtlety at odds with her bland manner: in the perplexed, doleful tone in which she told Lady Zouche of Katherine's misdeeds – a tone calculated to arouse indignation; and in asking her repeatedly not to tell Katherine what she had said, thereby forging a bond of confidentiality from which her sister was excluded.

She had no need to worry that Lady Zouche's loyalty would waver. Harriet was, she said and repeated, her first of loves, the pride of her life, her admired and accomplished daughter, the comfort of her wounded spirit, her best and most indulgent friend. She was also grateful to Robert for always considering her and echoed Harriet's craving for his good opinion: 'You may be assured, dearest of loves, that while you and dear Mr Curzon love [me], and continue your kind approbation of my conduct, I care very little about anything or any body else.' For his part Robert was genuinely fond of Lady Zouche, whom he still called 'Snugest'. The old lady was in poor health this year, suffering from dizziness and spasms, and Harriet, more able-bodied than for a long time, was glad of the opportunity to care for her rather than requiring constant attention herself.

Towards the end of July, Harriet decided her mother was well enough to be left alone at Parham and joined Robert in London before returning with him to Hagley. Once there was distance between her and Katherine she looked forward with greater equanimity to their differences being one day resolved.

HARRIET TO THE DOWAGER LADY ZOUCHE
HAGLEY, LATE SUMMER 1829
... Poor dear Kate! She feels she has got all wrong with you and I, and tries to make out that we are the occasion of it. She so really admires and likes Wasp's gay ways that I trust he will never make her unhappy, and personally attentive as he is in the greatest degree to her I hope proves that she is as much his taste as he is hers, for all one's consolation in the match is that she should continue to be satisfied with it. In the mean time nothing can be more tiresome and distressing than her writing in that complaining manner of old grievances. If they were grievances they are over now or at least should be, and now to revive the history of the peerage is quite nonsensical. I am very sorry indeed that subject should be such a bitter one to her, but I think with you it is better not to enter into any discussion in writing to Kate, and to let matters get smooth by time, if they can, which with the blessing of God they will ...

Luckily for Katherine, she had plenty to distract her from the family rift.

KATHERINE'S JOURNAL

23 July. – We removed to Cowes, where I recovered my lying in by constant sailing. I passed many pleasant days during August, several on board the Falcon, Lord Yarborough's yacht. Everybody admired my baby, and my returning strength made our stay at Cowes very satisfactory to me. We returned to Castle Goring the 23d of August. I drove to see my mother at Parham several times before she removed to London the 12th of September.

2 September. – George and I went to Aldingbourne to attend the ceremony of Isabella Howard's marriage with Lord Andover. The bride looked very pretty and it was altogether a most gay wedding. On the 20th of September we went to stay a few day's at Parham. I was very glad to walk about that dear old place and really to see it after a twelvemonth's absence, for those melancholy morning visits to my mother and sister were distressing to me in the extreme. I was also glad to take my dear baby to the home of her ancestors. On the 30th we returned to Castle Goring.

October. – During this month we dined and slept at Mr and Mrs Prime's, Walberton House, and stayed two days at Binsted Lodge, Mrs Smith's. Lord and Lady Mayo are living with her, all very pleasant people.

17 November. – The Burrells came to us. On the 18th I was honoured with an unexpected morning visit from Princess Augusta, who is staying at Worthing. I felt very glad that Mrs Burrell was with me as Captain Pechell was out hunting. Her Royal Highness appointed us to go to her on Saturday the 21st, which we did though reluctantly on George's part as it was hunting day. After an hours conversation we sat down to luncheon and were then dismissed. Princess Augusta came to Castle Goring on the 1st December to pass the morning. We had Sir William and Lady Jane Houstoun to meet her. Her Royal Highness was particularly agreeable and played upon the piano forte. I received several visits from her in the course of the winter without notice, and nothing could be more friendly and considerate than she was to my bad state of health. My confinement has not however been so severe this winter as it was the last, for I have generally been able to go out in the carriage once a week.

Katherine was indeed pregnant again, and Lady Zouche took account of this in her plans for the next few months.

THE DOWAGER LADY ZOUCHE TO HARRIET
UPPER BROOK STREET, 18 DECEMBER 1829

... I now incline to think I shall take a house for February and March and go to Parham in April, as I see plainly that K. will resume her complaints of last year if I am not within distance of her towards the latter end of her grossesse, till Lady Pechell comes. I take the liberty of mentioning *this* to you presuming on yours and dear Bob's leave to rest my bones at dear Parham in spring, and I trust soon after if not then it will be yours entirely ...

G. P. in passing thro' London Sunday sent me two pheasants with his compliments, so I *politely* wrote by Mondays post that I was much obliged, as indeed I felt. K. wrote by return the most absurd palaver that G. was always most happy to show me attention *whenever I gave him an opportunity*. Now really, to think of refusing me the [*illeg.*], his impertinent absurd attacks about key's, cart etc. and the plate the other day, it is so terribly insincere that my only refuge is perfect silence on the matter. If it was not for Kate's present situation I should not wish to go into the same county, but if she should be very ill at that anxious moment, or any thing fatal should happen, I should be miserable not to have it in my power to embrace her poor dear soft face ...

1830

Lawyers and land agents were now conducting the negotiations about the division of the estate; direct discussion between the parties had ceased. The Curzons wanted the house to go with Harriet's peerage, and the Pechells agreed to this but demanded something of similar value in return. The Curzons pronounced this an extraordinary idea, though as the estate was to be split equally neither side was likely to surrender its centrepiece without compensation. Another question was who should have the Oxfordshire farms, the poor state of which George's recent inspection had confirmed. A settlement of some sort was becoming a financial imperative, at least for the Pechells. 'I hope after buzzing so far, G. P. will come to his senses at last,' wrote Harriet, 'for it is so evidently to his advantage to come to a partition of the estates that he must see it.'

At Castle Goring Katherine continued to find her second pregnancy easier than her first. Her journal reports no ill health, and she stayed with friends for days at a time. In April she and

George passed a few weeks at Parham with Lady Zouche before taking her back with them to Castle Goring. In May George was in London or sailing with the Vernons while his wife waited at home for the arrival of their child.

KATHERINE'S JOURNAL

22 May. – My mother left me, having stayed with me seven weeks. On this same day Saturday the 22d 1830 Lady Pechell was so good to come to attend me during my confinement. I trust God will give me strength to go through this dangerous illness, or that if he should be pleased to deprive me of my life my dearest little Henrietta will be taught to love the memory of the mother who adores her and whose greatest regret is to leave her, and that she may grow up to be a blessing and comfort to her dear father, and never to depart from the strictest principles of virtue and religion, which it will be the chief occupation of my life to teach her if I recover from the illness that awaits me.

26 May. – My boy was born at twelve o'clock in the day.

31 May. – My mother came from Aldingbourne to see me.

2 June. – I was very ill for several days with the milk fever and am grateful for my recovery, which was doubtful for a night.

12 June. – Lady Pechell left me after three weeks kind attendance and returned again in a week to enable George to go to London.

26 June. – George returned.

29 June. – My baby was christened by Dr Penfold in the presence of Lady Pechell and several of our immediate neighbours. His name is William Henry Cecil George, his godfathers the King and Lord Napier and his godmother my dear friend Lady Charles Somerset.

Lord Napier was the son of Lady Pechell's sister Maria; the king was William IV, formerly Duke of Clarence, who had acceded to the throne just three days before his namesake's christening. The reign of the Sailor King was a good time to have naval connections, and a royal godfather was the first of its blessings for the Pechell family. The second came a day after the christening in the form of a letter from Sir John Pechell, an old intimate of the new monarch and now a lord of the admiralty, informing George of his appointment as a gentleman usher of the privy chamber.

Amidst this happiness was the continuing sorrow of the breach with Harriet, soon widened by a fresh misunderstanding about Parham.

KATHERINE TO HARRIET
CASTLE GORING, 6 AUGUST 1830
... I have been so extremely unwell all the morning that I did not intend to write any letters today, but yours just arrived at two o'clock (as it was directed near Arundel) in which you say Capt. Pechell and I have put an end to your being at Parham with any comfort this summer though it was an object to you to be there cannot remain unanswered a single moment. I can only beg you not to give way to such an extraordinary and unfounded fancy. If you wish to go there why not set out and go, surely there is nothing to prevent you. You cannot suffer what you did last year, for if Snugest is to join you there she is now in perfect health and spirits, and George has assured you that as far as he is concerned he will do everything to make it agreeable to you, and you cannot doubt that I would too, though I do not see why either of us should ever venture to say this to you about your own home, excepting that you say we prevent your going there. I hope you will forgive me if I say any thing to vex you. While we have any share in Parham it must always be the greatest pleasure and delight to us that you should occupy it, and if it was absolutely necessary to your comfort that we should cease to have any interest in it before you could go there for the summer, why not make an arrangement, what George calls 'terms', which you said you did not understand. I mean any plan upon a sheet of paper like people being married upon articles while the concern of the partition of the estate is going on ... I only hope you will do me the justice to believe that if you do go away from Parham this summer it will be a very severe disappointment and affliction to me ...

Harriet did not go to Parham; instead she went alone from London to Hagley while Robert took their sons on a tour of Germany. Robert II had completed a few terms at Christ Church, but without much profit, and his tutor told him he should probably not try for a degree. He had failed to master Greek, and despite having a cultivated mind he was too indolent to apply himself to a serious course of study. Edward had just left Harrow and, like his brother, would be tutored at home before going to Oxford.

The previous year Harriet had resumed her journal. At first her entries were patchy, but she covered the second half of 1830 as fully as the decade after her marriage. Her chief amusement was a recently acquired lapdog named Ri.

HARRIET'S JOURNAL

10 August. – At a little before eight got up to be with my dear Bob and see my two dear boys before their journey. The parting very sad to me, dear Bob most kind and my beloved boys, and they left me about ½ past nine to embark at the Custom House or near on the river for Ostend. May God keep and bless them. Mr Parker came. I was very unhappy but tried to be rational and put my trust in God. My dear Mother came to dine with me, all the servants busy packing.

11 August. – So very much depressed I feared I should not be able to set out, but at last every thing being ready and the coach and servants gone I departed in the open carriage, taking both my maids, Ri and Richard with me. Left London about ½ past twelve, intending to sleep at Wycombe. Went by Southam and Gerards Cross, but finding it was not five when I reached Wycombe Richard encouraged me to proceed. Before we got to Tedsworth there was a little rain, which increased and continued. Arrived at Oxford, the Kings Arms, a dirty inn, unluckily crouded and the people careless. A little *poky* room by the door the only setting room I could have, but as it rained I thought it best to be contented and took refuge with my maids in a tolerably spacious double bedded room, when I lighted a fire and had some tea and cold chicken. Ri approved very much of the fire.

Her onward journey took Harriet to Walton Hall in Warwickshire, where she spent four days with Sir John and Lady Mordaunt. The weather remained wet, so she and the other guests occupied themselves indoors. She admired the Mordaunts' collections of shells and old coins and smiled at their daughters' delight in Ri, 'who was very good and in beauty, being just washed previous to his journey'. She then proceeded to Hagley, where she found a letter Robert had sent from Ostend, 'quite a cordial to me'. Over the next weeks he wrote from various stops to assure her that he and their sons were well. Continental travel still held few charms for him: 'Not so much enchanted with the scenery of the Rhine as people sometimes are' is Harriet's summary of his letter from Coblenz.

She was joined at Hagley by Lady Zouche, as in the last few years, and together they drove about the neighbourhood, entertained visitors, went to church, and sat in companionable silence in the library. One day they dined with royalty at Kedleston Hall, the Derbyshire seat of Lord Scarsdale. In July Charles X of France had been overthrown and fled with his family to Britain, and the guest at Kedleston was his daughter-in-law the Duchesse de Berry. She was the doughtiest of the clan, and two years later she attempted to restore the king to his throne by means of an insurrection in the Vendée.

HARRIET'S JOURNAL

22 September. – In the afternoon the Duchesse de Berri arrived. She is attended by the Countess de Bouilli and the Comte de Ménars. I was presented to Her Royal Highness before dinner and renewed my acquaintance with Monsieur de Ménars, whom I had known previously at Kedleston when he was an emigrant from France before the last King was restored, and has married an Englishwoman and lived near this place in the house Alfred Curzon now inhabits. The Duchesse de Berri is a plain shortish woman, very fair and rather fat. Her manner very good natured and seeming desirous to please. At dinner Lord Scarsdale sat next to her on one hand and Lord Shrewsbury the other side. I was placed next to him and Comte M. by me, and we had a cheerful pleasant party, for the Princess was anxious to wave all ceremony.

In the evening we sat in the great drawing room, which was lighted up and very handsome, and as I had never seen it so before I was much pleased. The Duchess spoke to every one in turn, in the latter part of the evening we had a song or two from Alfred and then cards. She seemed a little tired, but to enjoy both and spoke with delight of all she saw in England, enlarged upon the beauty of the country, the verdure, and particularly the cleanliness of *everything everywhere*. The party had been to Liverpool, where the dock's made great impression upon her.

23 September. – This evening she was rather better dressed and we were all pleased by her wish to please, but the spirits she tries to assume fade away before the least circumstance that can revive her sad reflexions, poor thing. She seems to look up to Monsieur de Menars, to whom her dying husband recommended her, with great regard. He is become very old, and seems worn. Madame de Bouilli, a lively, clever Creole with dark handsome features and the manners of a genteel Frenchwoman, was very agreeable ... The evening passed nearly as the last, except that we had no music and it was later when the Princess took leave of us all, which she did very gracefully, the only time indeed in which she did assume *the Princess*, and I went to bed heartily tired tho' I had been very much interested and entertained.

In early October Robert returned to Hagley from Germany, having left his sons to winter at Dresden. At the end of the month he departed again for London and parliament. The election prompted by William IV's accession in the summer had yielded a Tory majority, but party divisions allowed the Whig leader Lord Grey to form a government and push ahead with his cherished project of parliamentary reform. During the long negotiations that yielded the new administration the popular clamour for a widening of the electoral franchise, combined with economic distress and the recent events in France, led to outbreaks of violence and the fear of a general uprising. Sussex was one of the worst-affected counties.

KATHERINE'S JOURNAL
18 November. – I was much alarmed by the mob besetting our door at 8 in the morning. George went into the midst of them and made them a speech which appeared to pacify them for the moment. During the whole of this month I was distressed with various apprehensions, as ricks were set on fire by unknown incendiaries in all directions, and the flames I repeatedly saw blazing in the evenings while George was out patrolling caused me great alarm as I continually fancied Parham was burning.

The situation became calmer in December and the Pechells resumed their usual activities. At Hagley Harriet fretted for her sons, alone abroad for the first time, and for her mother, who fell again in early November and took a while to recover. The giddy spells to which she had long been subject were becoming more frequent, and colds and other indispositions more troublesome.

1831

This year Harriet abandoned her journal again, but we know from other sources that Robert II and Edward returned safely from Germany in January, and that in February she travelled to London via Gorhambury, the first time for many years that she had ventured from Hagley so early. The partition of the Zouche estate was at last close to being agreed, but there were still a few unresolved points: deficiencies in buildings, the sum owed to the Pechells for relinquishing their half-share of the Bisshopp heirlooms, and the value of timber in various locations. The recent disturbances had exacerbated a long-term depreciation of land in Sussex, so Robert requested that certain calculations be made afresh.

An equitable solution could have been found far earlier had it not been for temperamental differences between the couples, in particular between the husbands. George was a stickler for detail and determined to defend his interests, making him an 'illiberal and griping person' in the opinion of Robert, who preferred to glide over complex matters in the hope they might sort themselves out, but, like many such people, would suddenly grow anxious that he had sold himself short and then revisit bases of agreement already in place. The wives took their husbands' parts and remained at variance, though relations never broke down entirely. Katherine gave Harriet the portrait catalogue she had lovingly compiled over several winters so that it could be kept at Parham. On the flyleaf she wrote an inscription asking her 'Dear Sister' to find a place for it in the library 'notwithstanding its imperfections'. There is no record of Harriet's response to this gesture, but the book did stay at Parham.

In mid-January the Pechells were among a party of forty invited to the Pavilion by King William and Queen Adelaide. Present too was the king's sister Elizabeth, the widowed Landgravine of Hesse-Homburg: 'They were very civil, and the Landgravine said to the Queen I was like an antelope. Seeing me fluried, she added, a beautiful antelope.' In early February a hailstorm shattered the new windows on the sea-facing front of Castle Goring, but only two days later guests came to dine and sleep. When the Pechells went on overnight visits they took their children with them, but on their removal to London at the end of April they left them with Lady Pechell at Hampton Court Palace and went to stay at Sir John Pechell's apartment in the admiralty. George, after less than a year as a gentleman usher, had just been made an equerry to the queen, and between balls, dinners and visits to the theatre he began his new duties.

The Curzons also spent the spring in London, and it was Robert's last as member for Clitheroe. He had long wished to stand down and the election that took place shortly after Robert II attained his majority in March provided a chance to do so without sacrificing the family interest. To rehearse for his candidacy Robert II assisted a friend on the hustings at Bath: 'I had intended to make a long speech which would have had an electric effect. It was truly sublime, but when I got up I was in such tribulation that I only treated them to what I intended for the preface, but luckily it was much better as it was. I only pity the audience that they should have lost so fine a specimen of eloquence.' Fine oratory was not required to return a Curzon for Clitheroe; nor was any real interest in politics. Offering neither, Robert II won the seat.

In June the division of Lord Zouche's patrimony was finally agreed, though the paperwork would not be complete until the following spring. 'Of this I am quite confident, that more attention and anxiety could not have been devoted to any business than has been to this partition,' wrote Robert's solicitor. The Curzons got Parham and most of the Sussex property; the Pechells got Angmering in Sussex and the Oxfordshire farms, which they had been persuaded to take after all. Because of a small disparity in purchase value between the two schedules the Curzons paid the Pechells £963, leaving each party with land and assets worth £141,579. The mortgage of £42,000 at 4% annual interest was divided equally, and there was a joint arrangement for arrears in rent and necessary repairs. The weeks leading up to the agreement Katherine spent answering 'vexatious letters' from the Curzons, who in her view caused 'much needless trouble and annoyance' to the last. 'I awakened from a dream of affliction,' she wrote when it was all over.

The partition marks the high point in Harriet's fortunes. At forty-three she was a baroness and the mistress of two country seats, one of them her own possession. She and her husband also had a large house in London and a son in parliament. The contrast with her sister, who lived in a rented country house and had no London abode, was great. At around this time Harriet had her portrait painted by the Cornish artist Richard Pentreath. It shows her as an attractive but already matronly woman, with the wide-set eyes and long, oval face of the Bisshopps; her pose is dignified and confident, her dress rich but restrained, and the draperies and romantic landscape behind her are in the best traditions of elegant society portraiture. On her lap is her beloved Ri.

This summer there was pleasing news from Ireland, where George Bisshopp, now the ninth baronet of that name, had won the good graces of the current Lord Lieutenant the Marquess of Anglesey.

THE REV. SIR GEORGE BISSHOPP TO THE DOWAGER LADY ZOUCHE
DUBLIN, 28 JUNE 1831
My dear Lady De La Zouche – Not knowing exactly where you may be at present, I think it best to send this to Brook Street, whence I make no doubt it will be forwarded to you, as I wish to give you as speedy information as possible of a most agreeable occurrence, and think you are one of those friends who will fully participate in the pleasure which it has caused in my domestic circle. The deanery of Lismore in the County of Waterford became vacant on Saturday last, and on Sunday Lord Anglesey did me the honor to confer it upon me.

The manner in which it was done was most gratifying. On Sunday I preached before him as usual at the Castle Chapel, and when the service was over he sent his Aide de Camp to me with an invitation to dinner. Accordingly I went, and I could perceive nothing in his manner towards me that was at all different from what it usually is, except that he seemed rather more thoughtful and talked less at dinner, which probably was owing to the great press of public business at present. There were about 14 or 16 people at dinner, and when the servants had withdrawn, he said as if quite casually, 'So at last we have lost the poor old Dean of Lismore', who was his cousin and had been promoted by him when he was last in Ireland. 'Well', he continued, 'we are all mortal, but suppose we drink the health of the future Dean.' Every one of course assented, and as there were three clergymen present besides myself, and all aspirants, you may conceive it was a nervous moment. When all was ready Lord A. said, 'I will give you Gentlemen the health of Sir George Bisshopp, Dean of Lismore.'

I must now close the scene, for it would be difficult for me to describe my feelings or to recollect what I said. All that I will say is that I am most truly grateful. The value of the deanery is rated at from £12 to 1500 per annum, situated in one of the most beautifully picturesque parts of this country, on the banks of the Blackwater close to the Duke of Devonshire's estate and midway between Cork and Waterford, from each of which it is distant about 25 miles. There is likewise some patronage attached to the deanery, which is not an unpleasant thing to have. In fact it is one of the most delightfully circumstanced preferments in this country, and you may naturally suppose that it has put us into very good spirits ...

Katherine and George spent the summer at Cowes and sailed in yachts belonging to friends – the Duke of Norfolk's *Arundel*, Lord Vernon's *Harlequin*, Lord Belfast's *Louisa* and Lord Yarborough's *Falcon*. Katherine loved nautical life, with its jolly regattas, lunches afloat, summer fireworks and balls at the Royal Yacht Club. She was a more intrepid sailor than most wives, and one day on the *Falcon* she noted with satisfaction that she was the only woman present. She had always liked male company, and her marriage enabled her to enjoy it in a relaxed, convivial way that had previously not been possible.

August brought the excitement of the Cherbourg Regatta organised by Lord Yarborough, the first commodore of the Royal Yacht Club.

KATHERINE'S JOURNAL
25 August. – We sailed for Cherbourg, an expedition long projected and of which I never really thought I should form a part, as I could not bear the thoughts of being separated from my children in a foreign country, although I was promised I should return in four days at furthest. When the morning arrived however the weather was so bright, and George encouraged me so much to go, that in half an hour I found myself under weigh on board the Harlequin with him, Lord Belfast and Augustus Smith. We sailed in two lines from Cowes by Spithead to St. Helens,

one line headed by the Falcon and the other by the Harlequin. I looked back upon both lines from the Harlequin's deck, and our little squadron consisting of about 35 or 40 yachts formed a most beautiful sight. A number of large ships were at this time anchored off Portsmouth, which added to the magnificence of the scene ...

An unlucky puff of wind dispersed our little squadron and frightened all the ladies, who were most of them set down on shore and reached Cowes in poney carriages. I was neither sick nor frightened being in such a large vessel. The Falcon went on, we anchored off St Helens. Lord and Lady Anson joined us on board the Harlequin, some accident having occurred to the Louisa, in which they were performing their voyage. At eleven at night we went to bed and to sleep, and in the morning we were becalmed 13 miles from Cherbourgh. In this state we remained the whole day, making no sail, and we did not anchor off Cherbourg till 10 that night. This was a tiresome day, the heat upon deck was insupportable, the stink and stuffiness below still worse. The pilot came on board, he spoke Danish to the English sailors. I could not stand from faintness. At last we went to bed.

27 August. – I went on shore with George to take a walk about the dock yard and saw the bason etc. etc. and returned to the Harlequin in a boat. Lord Anson and George went on board the Louisa to run for the Gold Cup, which was won by the Eliza, Captain Garth, and I went on shore again to several shops with Lady Anson. Lord Belfast and Mr Smith accompanied us. We dined on board the Falcon and in the evening we went to the ball given by the inhabitants of Cherbourg to the English. Returned on board to sleep.

28 August. – George went on shore with Lord Yarborough to see the shipping. Lord and Lady Anson ordered the boat to go to some shops, and I took the opportunity of going to see the cathedral[104] accompanied by Augustus Smith. I was much gratified by the splendour of the Catholic service, though I could not perceive much devotion as the military band played opera music between the prayers. We joined the rest of our English party upon the Champs de Mars, where a review took place. We returned on board the Harlequin and had a delightful sail round the breakwater. In the evening we went to a concert in the same room where we had attended the ball on the preceding night. The room was decorated with the tricolor flags and beautifully fitted up with the combined emblems of England and France. We slept that night at the prefeture.

29 August. – New wonders to me in the shape of a French breakfast!!! ... That night the English gave the French a ball, after which we returned to the Harlequin, went to bed and got under weigh about four in the morning, and after a most rapid and rough passage were off the Needles at eleven o'clock and landed at Cowes again two hours after. I had the inexpressible happiness of finding my dearest children quite well after this memorable separation of five days, so successfully accomplished. We went that evening to a party at Lady Belfasts. It was odd enough to reflect that we had been at a ball in France all the preceding night.

With the question of the family estate resolved, the sisters sought to mend their frayed relationship. In the autumn George was often away from home, mainly performing his duties as equerry, and during his absences Katherine took her children to Parham to see her mother and the Curzons. One of these visits lasted five days, which suggests a renewed cordiality. Harriet and Lady Zouche made return visits to Castle Goring, and in October Lady Zouche went there for a longer period.

Towards the end of 1831 Robert and Harriet, back at Hagley, faced the spectre of incendiarism that had unsettled Sussex the previous year. The targets of the malcontents were properties of Staffordshire landowners known to oppose Lord Grey's Reform Bill. Haystacks and outbuildings on the Hagley estate were set on fire, though the house itself was not damaged. Robert's reputation as a kind landlord and benefactor of local charities aroused strong indignation towards the perpetrators, and a town hall meeting in Rugeley agreed a reward of £175 for information leading to their capture. 'I am very sorry you think it necessary still to take precautions against the incendiarys,' Katherine wrote to Harriet on Christmas Day. 'I trust we shall hear no more of such horrors as the winter gets on, for it is generally in November and December that all the shocking things happen.' The attacks were not repeated.

1832

A large part of Katherine's journal at this time is devoted to her daughter and son, especially their health and milestones in their development. She also learnt to play the organ, Sir John Pechell having given her the instrument at Aldwick when he sold the property after his father's death. George's position in the queen's household often took him from home. If it was to Brighton his wife and children accompanied him, but if to London he usually went alone.

A selection from Katherine's journal takes us to the end of May.

KATHERINE'S JOURNAL

7 February. – We went to stay till the 10th with Mr and Mrs Prime at Walberton. Met Mr and Mrs Clerk Jervis and Lieutenant Hardy who wrote Travels in Mexico, all very agreeable people. We found our dear children in great health and beauty when we came home.

15 February. – We dined at the Pavilion, about 25 at table. The King and Queen and Princess Augusta, Lady St Germans, Baron and Baroness d'Ompteda, Lady Sophia Sidney and Miss d'Este, the rest household … The Queen worked in the evening, and after a short time sitting in a circle we were called to play commerce with the King and Princess Augusta. The Kings good humoured and kind manner is particularly delightful.

21 February. – George went to London for the levee and birthday … I remained quite alone till Georges return on the 25th. I find so much to do that although I regret his absence I do not wish for society while he is gone. The children are a constant occupation and I have taken to play a great deal upon the organ.

14 March. – George went to London to attend the Queen's drawing room, which was suddenly postponed on account of Princess Louise of Saxe Weimar's severe illness at Windsor. He returned Friday 16th. During his absence I received a subpoena to appear at the assizes at Lewes on the following Tuesday to give evidence upon some of my father's concerns in the year 1825. This gave me great anxiety and uneasiness as I was obliged to recapitulate all the circumstances of a most painful retrospect, though I did not go to Lewes, having a certificate from Morrah that I was not well enough to attend in person. George went.

22 March. – Lady Warren came from Brighton. I had the pleasure of showing her my two children, a most delightful addition to our family since she visited us before four or five years ago.

25 March. – Young Mr Kinderley came with the partition deeds of the estate, which we signed before his departure a few days after, and I now hope to hear no more of law matters for many years.

1 April. – I went out with George in the gig. We went to Little Hampton and got out at the wharf to look at the Duke of Norfolk's yacht the Arundel, which is undergoing alterations, having been lengthened 7 feet in her bow. She is a beautiful vessel, her mast a beautiful piece of Virginia Pine two feet and a half in diameter.

13 April. – My little Henrietta was taken ill. I carried her in the chariot to Worthing to see Old Morrah. He thought nothing of her indisposition, but on Saturday morning it proved to be the chicken pox, which she has taken very favourable. Henrietta is three years old. She has 20 teeth, she is three feet in height, she says her prayers perfectly well, can read her letters large and small in any book, and she can repeat several little sonnets or poems for children.

25 April. – Mr Bennett the organist came to show me how to play upon the organ.

4 May. – From the unusual circumstance of no other person in the house having caught the chicken pox, not even the baby, I cannot help fancying that they have been saved by vaccination, and that my little Henrietta has had a mitigated small pox, that disorder being now in all the neighbouring cottages.

16 May. – George went to London for the Queens drawingroom on the 17th and a ball on the 18th and returned on Sunday 20th.

26 May. – My dear boy was two years old.

30 May. – My dearest Henrietta fell down, and though only on the carpet knocked out her front and side teeth. They are much missed, and I must have the mortification of seeing her in her present disfigured state till she is 7 years old and has cut her new teeth.

Latterly George had joined Katherine in her efforts to repair ties with the Curzons. Because of his proximity to Parham he could keep an eye on it when they were elsewhere. He offered to have notices served on trespassers and to make sure the gamekeeper did his job. 'I beg you will not suspect me of any evil of interfering in any way,' he wrote to Robert, who responded cordially. Soon the two men were corresponding about various matters, including an outbreak of foot rot in sheep that threatened the livelihood of tenants, some of them already in arrears with their rent. The Curzons also feared that some of Parham's poultry had fallen prey to foxes, and George said that if this was so he had cocks and hens to fill their place: 'Harriet shall not lose her eggs.'

One member of the Curzon family who had always found it difficult to dislike the Pechells was Robert II, and when the fog of discord began to lift he visited Castle Goring to see his 'Aunt Kat'. He now lived in London but felt no enthusiasm for his parliamentary duties. Since his election the previous spring he had made no speeches in the Commons, though he voted reliably against reform and in March of this year became a founder member of the Carlton Club. When the Reform Act received royal assent in June his seat was swept away, and he never held another. A few weeks later he crossed the Channel with Walter Sneyd, the scion of another old Staffordshire family. So far the young traveller had seen parts of Germany and Ireland and made a trip to Paris. This time he would range much farther.

While the Reform Act ended Robert II's political career, it allowed George to hope that his was about to commence. Brighton, hitherto unrepresented, was now a borough returning two members, and when local dignitaries sought his candidacy at the forthcoming elections his hesitation was as short as good grace permitted. He knew something of the rough and tumble of canvassing, having assisted his friend Henry Howard at New Shoreham in 1830 and 1831, and he enjoyed the support of the king, who as a Brighton resident for part of each year had some influence. In an open letter to the electors George declared himself 'favourable to a repeal of taxes which press on the industrious part of the community', a sentiment likely to appeal to a constituency dominated by tradespeople. As well as George, standing as a Whig, there were two Radicals and two Tories.

The decision to enter the political fray was made amidst the balls and dinners of the Season, which the Pechells frequented for a few weeks in June. Katherine had been enjoying these annual bursts of metropolitan activity more since her marriage than before it, and although George liked them less, he was content to accompany her in between his stints as a courtier. She also had the satisfaction of watching him perform these duties, sometimes at royal drawing rooms and once at a military review in Hyde Park, which she saw from a friend's house in Park Lane. This year they had the added pleasure of staying in their own house in Hertford Street, briefly available between tenancies.

In the summer George used his nautical expertise to trial the *Waterwitch*, a racing brig constructed on new principles for Lord Belfast, vice-commodore of the Royal Yacht Club. The trials took place off the coasts of Cornwall and County Cork, and the *Waterwitch* outpaced all the crack naval vessels ranged against her. Chastened, the admiralty ordered that men-of-war of the same size must have their sails cut in a similar manner, and two years later it quietly purchased the brig from Lord Belfast. This is an instance of how yachts built for members of the club – renamed the Royal Yacht Squadron in 1833 – contributed to advances in small ship design for the navy. In this sense their privilege of flying the white ensign was well merited.

In the final months of the year, George and Katherine saw family and friends in Sussex. There was also a dinner at the Pavilion at which Katherine, who was pregnant again, received another mark of royal condescension: 'The Queen's kindness to me was more than I can express. She seemed to feel for me the distress of my unwieldy state and my inability to stand, and commanded me to sit while others were standing.' The main activity was electioneering, in which Katherine joined despite her condition. Prior to her marriage she had shared her family's Tory outlook, but now she made her husband's Whig politics her own. As polling day approached her nerves jangled.

KATHERINE'S JOURNAL

3 December. – [George] went to Brighton to remain till after the election was over. My heart sank to see him go!

5 December. – I joined him at the York Hotel and devoted the four next days entirely to going about in the carriage and canvassing. In the evening the lawyers came and helped to cast up the numbers. I was very anxious indeed and felt or fancied our cause was not in a prosperous way. I hoped however it was only my bodily infirmities which made me see every thing in an unfavourable light. Sunday morning George got up with such a hoarseness as to be almost speechless. He stayed in the hotel the whole of that foggy day, and was well Monday morning the

10th and went to the hustings accompanied by Sir James Lloyd and other friends to the nomination.

I settled to return home this day, fearing the inevitable anxiety of staying to witness the election might be attended with bad consequences to my health at this critical period. I saw him on the hustings, and can only wonder at the bad taste of those who preferred the other candidates.

We lost the election, to my great mortification. I preferred remaining at home alone during the two days poll at Brighton to accepting the kind invitations of those who wished me to remain nearer the active scene. I rather anticipated an unfavourable result, being convinced that Georges straightforward, honourable character was not fit to cope with the ungentlemanlike tricks of those unprincipled Radicals his opponents. Yet when I found it really was all over and that he was defeated I was as much surprised and afflicted as if such a termination to all our trouble and anxieties had been impossible.

By returning two Radicals Brighton put itself firmly on the political map. But George had not wasted his time. He finished third with almost a quarter of the votes and established a bridgehead for future advances.

We know little of Harriet's life this year beyond what is set down in Katherine's journal, which shows she was well enough to move between Hagley, London and Parham and go into society. Of the other Curzons, Robert was grappling with the many problems of his wife's Sussex estate; Edward had just passed his 'Little Go', allowing him to begin at Oxford; and Robert II was gathering impressions of Belgium, Germany, Austria, Switzerland and Italy in the genial company of Walter Sneyd.

1833

For her third and final lying-in Katherine, now forty-one, had no female attendant from her own or her husband's family, and the day when a man permitted the birth of his child to disrupt his routine had not yet dawned.

KATHERINE'S JOURNAL
On the 2d 3d and 4th of January we had shooting parties and dinner parties of men. On Saturday morning January 5th 1833

my dear little Adelaide was born about ten o'clock. The pains and miseries of labour had commenced about three o'clock, Mr Morrah was sent for and remained in the house till this very fine girl was dressed. On this day George went and dined at the Pavilion. He dined there again Sunday 6th and returned home Monday. He went this week to dine and pass a day at Warnham Court, also Aldingbourne. I felt very well but solitary, several parties at the Pavilion to which George went. We received an intimation from the Queen that she intended us the honour of being Sponsor to my infant. Col. and Mrs Fremantle and several men dined with George this week, the noise in the house was quite distracting. I was however able to come into the drawing room on the Monday fortnight after the birth of my child.

8 February. – My mother came from London to pass a week with me.

9 February. – Our little girl was christened by Mr Calhouse just before dinner. My mother stood for the Queen, Lady St Germans was the other godmother and Col. Fremantle stood for Sir George Bisshopp. Our dinner party consisted in addition to ourselves [of] the clergymen and sponsors, Mrs Fremantle and the Gorings of Highden. In the evening my mother went to bed early and I was too much exhausted to make any attempt to entertain my company. I therefore played on the piano forte and they all danced. My eldest girl and my boy were present at Adelaide's christening.

16 February. – My mother returned to London.

22 February. – George having been at Brighton brought home a very handsome silver tea pot which the Queen had commissioned Lady Mayo to give to us for Adelaide, Her Majesty's god-daughter.

24 February. – We received a letter from Sir John Pechell announcing his intended marriage with Julia Petre, which we had long anticipated.

Since becoming a lord of the admiralty Sir John had done even more for the navy than during his years at sea. In particular he improved the maintenance and operation of ships' guns by instituting a course of training on a vessel docked at Portsmouth. According to the *Dictionary of National Biography* he was 'one of the architects of the professional navy of the later nineteenth century'. He also went into politics, representing Helston in

Cornwall and then Windsor as a Whig. Outwardly successful, Sir John endured the private misery of gout, from which he suffered so acutely that he was often unable to tackle stairs. The life of an invalid bachelor was dreary, and he decided, in his late forties, to try matrimony. His bride was Julia Petre, a niece of the Duke of Norfolk. They married in London in April and honeymooned at Castle Goring.

George and Katherine spent the summer in Sussex and on the Solent.

KATHERINE'S JOURNAL

2 July. – The Waterwitch passed by Castle Goring about half past eleven in the day. It was a beautiful and interesting sight to me to see this brig, and I fancied I saw Captain Pechell looking over the bulwarks. He lay to off Brighton, where he landed and stayed two or three hours, and sailed for Cowes in the afternoon. The evening was very showery and I saw the Waterwitch beating about to the east of Worthing at 8 o'clock. She did not reach Cowes till 12 the next day.

5 July. – I returned [from Parham] to Castle Goring and found my dearest Henrietta ill of a fever. May God spare her to me. I fear I have not been sufficiently grateful for the great blessing of possessing so great a treasure.

6 July. – George returned. Henrietta safe through Morrah's skill, he has attended her twice each day.

16 July. – This was the day George accompanied the Duke of Norfolk to dine at Norris Castle with the Duchess of Kent. The account of this party I received in a letter from him a day or two after. The Duchess had desired Sir John Conroy to find out whether I was at Cowes that I might be invited also. Her R. H. was very civil in her enquiries after me and told Captain Pechell she should have been very glad to have seen me with him. He played at whist at her table.

18 July. – I was still very anxious about my little Henrietta's health. She however thank God gains strength daily. I have been obliged to cut off her curls to keep her head cool.

20 July. – My dear George came home. He is now a member of the Royal Yacht Squadron and is very busy new rigging his little yacht the Emily of 33 tons, altering her from a frigate into a brig.[105]

21 July. – We rode out upon the two ponies, which we have frequently done this summer.

23 July. – One day last week I carried my beautiful baby Adelaide to Offington House in the chariot to shew her to the monthly nurse who had attended me at her birth and now staying there. This was the first time of this dear little child going out in the carriage, and Offington is the first house she has gone into. She is the finest, fattest baby possible and has already one tooth.

29 July. – My mother and Harriet came to me at Castle Goring, also Mr Curzon and Edward. Robert is travelling and gone to Egypt. Harriet admired my little Adelaide extremely.

7 August. – George sailing with the Duke of Norfolk.

10 August. – George came home with a dreadful inflammation on his face and the side of his nose, having had a coup de soleil. He had violent headache and was very unwell for several days.

17 August. – Sent off all the servants and cart to Portsmouth to take possession of our lodging at Cowes, meaning to follow the first day George is well enough to go.

20 August. – We were rather put into a hurry the day after our arrival at Cowes by an invitation to Norris Castle to dine with the Duchess of Kent and Princess Victoria. The Duchess was extremely gracious to me and enquired much after all those to whom I belong. The Princess Victoria is a very intelligent agreeable little Girl, not handsome but very pleasing.

The fourteen-year-old Victoria discussed naval matters with George: 'She has a *real* not an acquired taste (like the rest of us), for the whole thing,' Katherine observed. 'She knows the name of every rope and every part of a ship.'

The sailing match that followed was frustrating to watch.

KATHERINE TO HARRIET
WEST COWES, 21 AUGUST 1833
... I am writing to you now in such anxiety that I prefer sitting in the house to standing out with the rest of the world seeing the race. George is sailing in the Water Witch for the Kings Cup against all the little vessels. I think the W. Witch has no chance, and that it was a most ill advised thing her starting. There is neither water enough nor space enough here for a vessel of her class and she loses time in turning. It would have been so much

wiser to rest upon her established fame in having beat all the Kings ships out at sea, instead of attempting impossibilities and giving all the other people the triumph of saying they beat her, and all the ladies and people who do not understand it will say the same thing. I now see her off Portsmouth taring away and she will get aground or do some dangerous thing. The gold *cup* given by the King is a small gold *tureen* with a shell for a handle, very beautiful, but it stands in a large round shining gold plateau out of proportion. Mr Weld in the Alarm will get it, and it is just the thing for [a] maigre day, for it is too small for a party of people ...

The Alarm (Mr Weld) has now passed by the window triumphant and is going off the other way to Yarmouth to return.[106] The Water Witch is sailing beautifully a mile behind, but it is like a broad wheeled waggon coming after a gig. Georges face very indifferent ...

As with any British sporting activity, the social aspect of yachting was as important as the competitive.

KATHERINE'S JOURNAL

26 August. – We went to an entertainment at St Lawrence, Lord Yarborough's cottage to meet Her R. H. the Duchess of Kent and Princess Victoria. The day was most beautiful. George and I went in one of the little carriages of the island and arrived about two o'clock. Several of the yachts were at anchor, and together with the fineness of the day and the beautiful scenery made it altogether a very uncommonly lovely sight. We met all the Cowes society and the principal people of the island. We went in the evening to Appuldercombe[107] to stay the night. The moon shone brightly over the sea as we travelled up Steephill. Some of the yachts were in full sail returning to Cowes and the scene was altogether beautiful. I shall look back to this evening with great pleasure. When we arrived at Appuldercombe we found it well lighted up and the pictures and statues seen in their greatest perfection formed a striking contrast between the works of art and the beauties of nature we had just left. In the course of an hour Lord Yarborough, Lady Durham and others arrived, we were very glad to go to bed. The next morning Mr and Mrs Copley and Mr and Mrs Pelham came to breakfast, and in the course of the day we returned to Cowes and found my three dear children quite well and happy.

Three days later George sailed his new boat the *Emily* in the Royal Yacht Squadron's second expedition to Cherbourg, where there was to be a naval review in the presence of King Louis Philippe and a race for an £80 cup. The flotilla had a stormy passage but arrived in Cherbourg without mishap and took shelter in the harbour. On the king's arrival the twenty-six British vessels hoisted their flags and he invited their owners to dine with him in the town. In one of the few surviving letters to his 'dearest K.' George describes the festivities.

GEORGE PECHELL TO KATHERINE
CHERBOURG, 7 SEPTEMBER 1833
... The King and Queen went away yesterday and we are now quiet. 10 of us besides Lord Farnbro and Durham dined with him every day, 150 at dinner they called it, excellent things and in the room where we danced fitted up as when you were there. The King very civil to me and talked ¼ of an hour about Hampton Court etc. and presented me to Madame his sister. This was in the circle before we went into dinner. Lord Farnbro handed out the Queen, who is very *like* ours, and Lord Durham one of the Princesses, who are really very pretty. We sat very little time at dinner, a servant behind each chair in silver lace jackets.

Thursday the people gave a ball to the King at the building called the Baths Louis Phillipe at the entrance of the harbour, where all the mob and national guard were, and we were stuffed and pushed dreadfully. The royal family set at the end of the ball room with a quadrille always kept going, just as our King and Queen and Princess Lieven sit at St James's. The Miss Bushes danced in the quadrille and were much admired. Indeed every body allows that les dames anglaises have created a great sensation, for with the exception of the Princesses there never was such a collection of plain women.

Jerry Codrington danced with one of the Princesses, but I could not push through to do the same which I would have done. The King gave Lord Yarborough a bag of medals silver and bronze to distribute to the yachts, which he has done ...

Mrs Gibson was the only woman who did us little credit. She could not waltz at all and her clothes appeared as if they were put on her by the coxswain. Miss Norbury looked well and had no maid at all!!! ...

The Emily lays due to w[est] in the basin, and I have only been able to shew her off once when the King went to review his fleet, when I manoeuvred her round the French fleet, but the wind and sea were too high to do much. I fired salutes and the King told me in the evening how much he admired L'Emilie ...

The autumn saw frequent movements between Castle Goring and Parham, where Lady Zouche and the Curzons had settled. George no longer absented himself from these gatherings, but there was a breeze between him and his mother-in-law when he asked her not to bring her favourite dog to Castle Goring as it frightened his tame pheasants. George's sister Fanny visited with her husband Robert Tredcroft, and Katherine's old friend Lady Charles Somerset delighted her by fulfilling a promise to come for an extended period. In November the king and queen moved to Brighton, and each time the Pechells dined at the Pavilion Katherine had the gratification of answering the queen's enquiries about her goddaughter's health. Her journal for 1833 closes on a contented note: 'So ends another year, and I am very thankful for the many blessings I enjoy and for the daily improvement of my three dear children, who are everything I can possibly wish them to be.'

Harriet is again largely hidden from view this year, with only a few glimpses in her sister's journal and in a letter from a friend, which reveals that she was very much an invalid. At Christmas she received a letter from Sir George Bisshopp that contrasted sadly with his earlier ones. His wife had died and his own health was shattered.

THE REV. SIR GEORGE BISSHOPP TO HARRIET
CHELTENHAM, 24 DECEMBER 1833
... I am fully aware of having failed in my promise of a visit either to Hagley or Parham during the summer, which had I been differently circumstanced would have afforded me very great pleasure, but the fact is that I have neither had health or spirits for a long time past sufficient to render me an acceptable guest anywhere beyond the circle of my own immediate family.

During part of the summer, when I was in London, I was so unwell as to be obliged to have recourse to medical advice, from which, as I expected, I derived little benefit. The malady was not within the reach of the physician's skill. I afterwards went to Ireland and passed a miserable autumn at Lismore, ill and dispirited. I returned to this place on Saturday last, and am now comparatively happy surrounded by my dear children, who are growing up in every respect as I could wish. Their aunt, Miss Sproule, has indeed proved a second mother to them. My two little girls with their governess are to live with her entirely for the present, and my boys, whom I have placed under the care of the rector of Painswick in Glos'tershire, ten miles from hence, make this their home during the holydays. This is the best plan I could devise for them in the present unsettled state of unfortunate Ireland, and as I hope they will pass their lives in England it is right they should be educated there. It is my intention to be with them always at Christmas and in the summer, so that I can satisfy myself that all is going on right ...

Sir George intended to return to Lismore the following February, but died in Cheltenham four months after these words were written. The baronetcy was inherited by his eldest son Cecil, a boy of twelve, who under the direction of his mother's relatives was educated for the church and died aged twenty-seven while serving as archdeacon of Malta. He was succeeded by his younger brothers George and then Edward, the eleventh and twelfth baronets, and when Edward died without issue in 1870 the title died with him.[108]

1834

During 1833 Robert II had continued his travels, now in the company of a young Leicestershire squire named Sir George Palmer. They made their way south through Italy and sailed for Malta, where they arranged a passage to Egypt. Robert II's adventures there and elsewhere in the Eastern Mediterranean, and his quest to procure manuscripts from ancient monastic libraries, are described in his classic travelogue *Visits to Monasteries in the Levant*. In moments of idleness during his long voyage his thoughts drifted back to England, and it was not at Hagley but at Parham that they came to rest – a Parham enhanced by his fancy.

ROBERT CURZON II TO HARRIET AND ROBERT CURZON
CAIRO, 4 FEBRUARY 1834

... I have built, furnished and lit all the fires at Parham, and shut the curtains and made myself comfortable after dinner in the new dining room in my airy chateau, for about 3 years now, so I am quite at home there, and am convinced that it is one of the nicest old houses that ever was built upon a cloud; and moreover the terrace is so very pleasant in the sunshine after breakfast to walk up and down with your hands behind your back, and look at the deer eating grass in the park on purpose to become fat and make good venison for dinner for my good friends to eat, and then afterwards I shall tell you some wonderfull long stories of foreign lands, and explain to you how that the drawingroom is much more comfortable than an encampment in the desert ...

Harriet, though not given to such romantic flights, would also have liked to live at 'the beautiful and dear old place', as she called Parham, but her husband's heart was in his native county and she was content to make Hagley her main home. After the tussles it had caused between the sisters, the venerable seat of the Bisshopps now stood empty for most of the year.

Contrasting with Parham's somnolence was the teeming life at Castle Goring, where an endless stream of guests added to the hubbub of a family of five. This busy domesticity was interrupted only when the Pechells made social visits or answered summonses from the king and queen, who were still at Brighton. George disliked being called away at short notice, but Katherine always put royalty first. 'George and I went to dine at the Pavilion,' she recorded one day in February. 'He was much annoyed at leaving our company, I was much amused. The King and Queen all kindness. George asked leave for us to go home at ten o'clock, which I much regretted. It was a very pleasant party. We reached home by 12 o'clock, every body gone to bed.' This is as close as she came to criticising her husband.

In March the Pechells' pleasant routine received a nasty jolt.

KATHERINE'S JOURNAL

3 March. – We dined with Sir Richard and Lady Jane Jones at Warwick House, Worthing, and now I write the dreadful misfortune that happened to us. In a very narrow part of the road nearly a mile from home we attempted to pass a wagon, which we should have accomplished without difficulty, but it was laden with sacks, which projected beyond the waggon and broke our carriage window and smashed the lamp. The noise startled the horses, and the coachman being frightened pulled up so suddenly that the reins broke and the horses ran off. George looked out of the front window and from thence climbed upon the driving box in the hope of getting on the pole or the backs of the horses to stop them. In this attempt he failed and either fell or was thrown to the ground.

The horses brought me home very fast. I was much shaken about from one side of the carriage to the other and fully expected I should be dashed to pieces from some impediment we might meet in the road. My anxiety as to what George's fate might have been was intense as I saw him disappear from the box. I had given up all hope of ever seeing my dear home again when the horses suddenly dashed into the gate and brought me in safety to the coach house, where the fence stopped their progress.

I let myself out and was much dismayed at finding myself alone. I soon called up the house and Mr and Mrs Bright and sent in all directions to know what was become of George, when I was told his leg was broken. I did not suppose that was the full extent of the mischief and therefore made preparations to place him in a room down stairs. At length he was brought home on a hurdle into the saloon and laid on the floor. I was so happy to hear him speak and see him, though unable to move, tolerably cheerful that I felt only thankfulness for his merciful preservation, and all injuries seemed light in comparison to greater misfortunes. Dixon soon came and set the leg, then Evans. We had no sleep that night, I stayed on the sopha.

The next few days were a blur of trepidation and weariness. George needed someone with him all night as he was constantly shaken from his slumbers by cramping or spasms. A carriage wheel had crushed his tibia and fibula just below the left knee, and he had wounds and severe bruising from the hip to the foot of the same leg. Even with three doctors in attendance Katherine only left him for short stretches during the first week, and thereafter went to bed very late and rose early. The Dowager Lady Pechell soon arrived, but she had aged considerably in recent years and was unable to help much. In mid-March George's sufferings were aggravated by an attack of gout; the violence of his spasms made him delirious and he called out for his wife even though she was next to him, taking it in turns with a servant to hold down his knee so that the knitting of the bones would not be impaired.

The journal of April and May tells of a slow convalescence with several setbacks, including an inflammation of the periosteum, the fibrous membrane lining the bones. George tried not to be a troublesome patient, putting on a cheery face for his wife, but privately he feared his leg would never be right again. Lady Pechell left after a few days, but friends and neighbours came to raise his morale, and one lent him an invalid's open carriage so that he could take short drives and imbibe fresh air. Another visitor was his brother, who was himself often incapacitated and could sympathise with his condition. Sir John's marriage had turned out well, and Katherine was intrigued to see how his wife Julia handled him: 'She said she was very anxious about Sir John's gout, but was able to go to Lady Grey's soirée, and now she say's she never laughed so much as she did at Miss Berry's dinner the day before and Lady Davy's in the evening … I think she is very clever to make Sir John happy at home and make herself happy out, but *it must* require great strength of constitution.'

In early May it was Harriet's turn to be jolted, in her case by the astounding news that her younger son Edward, an undergraduate at Christ Church and twenty-one years old, had married in secret. To make matters worse he said nothing to his parents even after the wedding on 5 May, and they only learnt of his 'horrid step' from a notice in the *Morning Post*. In despair Harriet asked Katherine to find out what she could about Edward's bride Amelia (Emily) Daniell and her family.

KATHERINE TO HARRIET
CASTLE GORING, 13 MAY 1834
My dearest Harriet – By dint of puzzling and inquiring I have discovered the following particulars as to Edward's Daniells.

Old Daniel, East India director. Behaved very ill and cheated every body, now lives separated from his wife in obscurity.

Mrs Daniel, was Miss Hodges, an East India heiress, her two sisters Lady William Murray (brother to late D[uke] of Athol) and Mrs Something Smith.

Eldest son, very good sort of man, a very lucrative appointment in China under the new arrangement.

Another son, very respectable, captain of an East India man doing very well.

Daughters:

Mrs Ferrars. Mr and Mrs Ferrars very respectable people, live in Leicestershire or some inland county.

Mrs Johnson

Mrs Jenks, a doctors wife at Brighton

Mrs Fowler, a clergymans wife

One gone out to India

Emily

Mrs F. Long

Catherine, a child, who is with her mother

Three out of the above mentioned 7 eloped with their husbands.

Mrs Daniel not able to support her daughter Emily. She lived with her sisters and friends and was married from Mrs Pigots house. Mrs Pigot is Miss Brummell, niece to Beau Brummell, and ran away with Mr Pigot, and is cousin to Miss Daniel. Snugest remembers these Miss Brummell's at Brighton with a Mrs Bradshaw. I understand Edwards Miss Daniel is a most beautiful, accomplished and clever woman of about 28 years old. Old Mr Long, who has just been here, says he should have liked to have married her himself and never saw any body so charming and was frightened for his son.

I write the above from the information of Mr William Frazer, Lady Saltoun's son, an old partner of mine whom you perhaps may remember. He heard I was annoyed about this marriage and came to tell me all he happened to know of them. I feel Edwards duplicity towards you and Bob so deeply that I can hardly bear the subject, and people do not understand this part, and think it is our pride of birth which makes us unhappy ...

Katherine went on to say how she abhorred clandestine arrangements, and she must have reflected that for over a decade she and George had resisted the temptation to which Edward had succumbed in a few weeks. Her real anger was reserved for his bride, who had, she was sure, set out with her family's connivance to foist herself upon him.

This suspicion of a wily stratagem was shared by the Curzons.

ROBERT CURZON TO ROBERT CURZON II
UPPER BROOK STREET, 29–30 MAY 1834
Dear Robert – I am sorry to inform you of what will be a subject of great grief and vexation to you as it is to your mother and me, namely Edwards inconsiderate and most undutiful conduct such as I am convinced you are incapable of. On the 5th of this month he married Miss Emily Daniell against your mothers and my consent and without our knowledge. We had no suspicions of his intentions [and] were thunderstruck when made acquainted with it. How he was induced to commit this unjustifiable act I know not, but the conduct of Mr and Mrs Frederick Long, with whom Miss E. D. lived, in forwarding, being instrumental and keeping what was going on from the knowledge of his parents is disgraceful and dishonorable in the extreme, what no gentleman particularly a relation could be suspected to be capable of.

It is an alleviation in our distress that the girl bears an excellent character. He poor foolish fellow by this unjustifiable conduct has thrown himself out of the class of society he has been brought up in. He is now to take orders, which he is desirous of doing. I hope he will bring down his ideas to the situation he has reduced himself to and look forward with satisfaction to settle himself with his wife as a country clergyman. When this unfortunate event took place I was in the act of paying his debts, which are very great ...

Cowed by his parents' anger, Edward at first showed willing to enter the church, but presently he changed his mind and said he would prefer to study law. 'I am sorry to see,' his father retorted, 'that you are still actuated by the wilful undutiful perverse spirit which has caused so much grief and anxiety to your too indulgent parents.' A legal training was too expensive, he told him, but if he presented himself for ordination he would within three years earn enough to maintain a family, and so 'abstract reasoning' about his lack of a religious vocation was irrelevant. Moreover, there could be no increase in his allowance because of the cost of paying off his debts. Edward had dealt his parents a severe blow, and when Katherine saw them in London a few weeks later Harriet was 'in great sorrow' and Robert 'truly afflicted'. Katherine had her first sighting of Amelia and was not impressed: 'Rather a missish kind of person, and though pretty by no mean's charming enough to account for the sudden and determined conduct of her little foolish husband'.

This was the second half of June, and the Pechells were in London to see the surgeon Sir Astley Cooper about George's leg, which was still acutely painful. In a gesture much appreciated by Katherine, Lady Zouche gave up the ground floor of the house she had taken in Hyde Park Place to accommodate them. Sir Astley's advice was that George should return to the healthy air of Sussex and adopt a regimen of gentle exercise. He did so, but the pain grew no less and in July he and Katherine made a second trip to London, where the surgeon performed a small operation that afforded him some relief. He recuperated at Castle Goring, and with the aid of crutches he joined Katherine on some local visits before venturing farther.

KATHERINE'S JOURNAL

7 August. – George went to Cowes! After five months incessant watching him I felt much at seeing him go off. I accompanied him in the carriage and walked back through the wood. I could hardly bear to part with him, and yet it was the best thing he could do. He was strongly advised by the medical people to go.

12 August. – My dearest George returned home much benefited in every respect by his little voyage.

27 August. – George and I were sitting reading in the evening at half past ten when we suddenly heared a great noise as of some great weight falling or breaking. I thought a beam of the room or the floor was giving way under my feet, these sensations were momentary. We rang the bell and enquired what had happened and if anything had fallen upstairs, but nobody heared the noise excepting Adele Gauchet,[109] who was going to bed in a room not immediately over our sitting room but with the same aspect. She said she thought some one was bursting into her room as the door shook and rattled.

29 August. – George returned to Cowes, and I promised to follow him with the children next week to stay a fort'night. I am glad he is returned to Cowes. He frightens me at home by getting upon the poney, when a sudden jerk might throw him over and break his leg again, for he is still very helpless. The club room at Cowes, with many friends and acquaintances about him, with the additional amusement of an occasional sail, is the best means of whiling away the tedium of his slow convalescence, which to a man must be a still more tiresome state than positive illness. God grant that he may soon entirely recover.

30 August. – I read in the county paper an account of a shock of earthquake having been felt at ½ past ten on Wednesday evening at Chichester, Arundel, Littlehampton and Worthing. George had said in a joke, if nobody can account for the noise it must be an earthquake, but we went to bed and thought no more of it!!

Katherine called 1834 a 'year of difficulties', but there was much to be grateful for, especially in the health and happiness of her children: 'While this consolation is mercifully continued to me, all vexations are light and disregarded.' By contrast Harriet's grown-up children were far from consoling: one had married beneath himself and the other was exposed to the perils of Oriental travel. It was therefore a great relief when Robert II, who from Egypt had journeyed through the Levant, Turkey and Greece, arrived back in England in December after an absence of two and a half years. At his father's suggestion he went straight to Parham to speak with Edward and Amelia, who were staying there while their future was decided. Lady Zouche was there too.

A Sequel to Persuasion

When the Uppercross party travel to Lyme in *Persuasion* Anne Elliot makes the acquaintance of some naval friends of Captain Wentworth who live there. The cheerfully practical Captain and Mrs Harville and the poetry-loving Captain Benwick are unaffected, kind-hearted people who do all they can – a great deal, as it turns out – to oblige their visitors:

> There was so much attachment to Captain Wentworth in all this, and such a bewitching charm in a degree of hospitality so uncommon, so unlike the usual style of give-and-take invitations, and dinners of formality and display, that Anne felt her spirits not likely to be benefited by an increasing acquaintance among his brother-officers. 'These would have been all my friends,' was her thought; and she had to struggle against a great tendency to lowness.[110]

At this moment Anne realises she is yearning not only for Wentworth, but also for a community to which they can belong together, and which only he can provide.

After just a few weeks with the Musgroves and the naval group at Uppercross and Lyme, Anne feels deeply involved with their lives, while the arid preoccupations of her own family in Bath are 'but of secondary interest'.[111] Indeed, when Lady Russell speaks to her of the Elliots she has to exert herself to reply 'with any thing like the appearance of equal solicitude, on topics which had by nature the first claim on her'.[112] The two women's opposite impressions of Admiral Croft, Wentworth's brother-in-law, signal Anne's move away from attitudes she grew up with: 'Admiral Croft's manners were not quite of the tone to suit Lady Russell, but they delighted Anne. His goodness of heart and simplicity of character were irresistible'.[113] Anne is amused when Croft comments a little indelicately on the array of large mirrors in Sir Walter's dressing room at Kellynch. Lady Russell's feelings are not given, but can be imagined.

Anne's distrust of suavity and urbanity, acquired when she learned to love Wentworth, makes her wary of her cousin William Elliot:

> Mr. Elliot was rational, discreet, polished, – but he was not open. There was never any burst of feeling, any warmth of indignation or delight, at the evil or good of others. This, to Anne, was a decided imperfection. Her early impressions were incurable. She prized the frank, the open-hearted, the eager character beyond all others. Warmth and enthusiasm did captivate her still. She felt that she could so much more depend upon the sincerity of those who sometimes looked or said a careless or a hasty thing, than of those whose presence of mind never varied, whose tongue never slipped.[114]

She therefore rejects Mr Elliot and the superficial advantages of a marriage with him and instead becomes Wentworth's wife and the newest member of his circle of friends. Anne 'gloried in being a sailor's wife',[115] and her only regret is not having relations who can appreciate her husband:

> To have no family to receive and estimate him properly; nothing of respectability, of harmony, of good-will to offer in return for

all the worth and all the prompt welcome which met her in his brothers and sisters, was a source of as lively pain as her mind could well be sensible of, under circumstances of otherwise strong felicity.[116]

Katherine Pechell's early wedded life completes the transition to a new community and a loosening of former ties that *Persuasion* foretells for Anne Wentworth. Long before marriage gives her a new primary loyalty, Katherine feels herself slowly pulling away from her mother and sister, and thoroughly alienated from her father. She too likes her husband's family before joining it, and is afterwards more comfortable with his relations than her own. She experiences Anne's 'lively pain' at her family not taking her husband to their bosom, and her social life changes quite as completely: she has not been to Hagley since moving to Castle Goring and no longer sees old friends in the Midland counties. Other attachments wane due to altered circumstances and sentiments, and an unexplained rift ends her intimacy with Lady Verulam. Aside from one or two long-standing female friends, Katherine now has two social circles: her Sussex neighbours, almost none of whom mix with the Parham family; and her husband's sailing companions.

This nautical group is dedicated to yachting rather than the navy, but given the decades of peace after 1815, which neither Anne nor Wentworth, nor indeed Jane Austen, could have predicted, it is possible that Wentworth will also take up recreational sailing and Anne experience private vessels rather than men-of-war. Both women develop a liking for the sea that symbolises their membership of a new community. When Anne arrives in Lyme she makes her way down to the shore and gazes out lingeringly, and next morning she and Henrietta Musgrove walk to the sands before breakfast to see the tide come in: 'They praised the morning; gloried in the sea; sympathized in the delight of the fresh-feeling breeze – and were silent.'[117] Mrs Wentworth will doubtless be as comfortable afloat as Mrs Pechell, who exults in how much better her sea legs are than those of most women.

The brides achieve happiness in marriage, but this is not because their spouses are patterns of perfection. We have already outlined similarities in the characters of Wentworth and Pechell, and closer acquaintance with the latter confirms that he is no less upright, single-minded and energetic than the former. Their faults are such as naturally go with these qualities. Each has a secure faith in his own judgement that makes him strong-minded but also stubborn. Wentworth's ostentatious firmness of purpose is patently excessive, and Louisa Musgrove's imitation of his attitude prompts the precipitate jump from the Cobb in Lyme that nearly kills her. Pechell is equally resolute, and this causes him to be contentious in his disagreements with the Curzons about the inheritance of the Bisshopp estate and the Zouche barony and with John Bright about boundaries and sporting rights at Castle Goring.

Both show hints of pedantry: Wentworth takes a strict view of navy rules about taking women aboard ships; Pechell is particular about household arrangements. Tactlessness too, with Wentworth's remark on Anne's altered looks after eight years akin to Pechell's on the encumbrance of Lady Zouche's jointure and his advice about the management of Parham; one can imagine Wentworth after his marriage giving broad hints on how Kellynch should be run. Wentworth's manner does not suit Lady Russell's notions of good breeding any more than Pechell's suits those of Lady Zouche. Admittedly these ladies have rather exalted notions of gentility, but the men who displease them are a little rough around the edges. Finally, their manliness can show itself as masculine selfishness: while Wentworth loves Anne as much as Pechell does Katherine, he could turn out to have the same taste for male company, acquired during long years at sea, and the same intention of pursuing his hobbies exactly when he pleases.

Katherine evidently likes her husband to be firmly in charge. She seeks to adapt herself to him, avoids interfering with his habits, and even adopts his politics. Her jocular insistence before their marriage that she had 'no ways' for him to contend with turns out to be pretty much true. In repeating his opinions in letters to Harriet she also appears to see nothing that could reasonably give offence, though her sister and mother feel differently. Anne too likes a strong, self-reliant man and will probably take just as mild a view of her husband's occasional departures from decorum, believing as she does in 'the sincerity of those who sometimes looked or said a careless or a hasty thing'. Yet neither woman is simpering or submissive. Anne shows her presence of mind by taking command after Louisa's fall and head injury, when Wentworth and the others go to pieces. Katherine deals with the carriage accident and the injuries that Pechell sustains with authority and stamina.

Nor do the wives fully renounce the values of the families they leave, however strained some of the personal relationships have become. Their husbands usher them into a new circle, but along with highly refined manners they retain the family pride that made their fathers' fecklessness so painful to them. This pride can look like prejudice. In speaking to Mrs Smith about William Elliot's wealthy first bride, Anne asks, 'But was not she a very low woman?'[118] Mrs Smith replies that her father was a grazier and her grandfather a butcher, but that she was a fine-looking woman with a decent education. Katherine is appalled by Edward Curzon's marriage to Amelia Daniell, more so than his mother Harriet. She says it is his duplicity, not her 'pride of birth', that make the marriage distasteful in her eyes, but the tone of her letter suggests it is both.

These alliances are heavy blows to the bridegroom's family, whereas those of Anne and Katherine were no worse than mediocre in social terms when first mooted, and quite creditable when concluded many years later. 'He was now esteemed quite worthy to address the daughter of a foolish, spendthrift baronet, who had not had principle or sense enough to maintain himself in the situation in which Providence had placed him': these words about Wentworth apply also to Pechell.[119] The gains of the ambitious husbands, and the losses of their wives' families, have brought about a shift in relative wealth and status. Still, on the face of it, the naval marriages are not as good as those of the already-married sisters. As Mary Musgrove observes, 'Anne had no Uppercross-hall before her, no landed estate, no headship of a family'.[120] Harriet too could reflect that Pechell, with his rented house, was a poorer match than Robert Curzon.

But will the vigour of Captains Wentworth and Pechell and the slackness of Messrs Musgrove and Curzon lead to a change in fortunes in favour of the younger sister? Not if the elder sister corrects her husband's weakness, but this is no more likely in Mary, who complains she is short of funds but proposes nothing to rectify matters, than it is in Harriet, who later admits she is no good at supervising servants or managing finances. By contrast, Anne helps Lady Russell to draw up a comprehensive scheme of retrenchment for her father when he gets into debt, indicating her practical money sense, and Katherine's careful accounts at Castle Goring show her to be an efficient housekeeper.

And then there is the subject, broached earlier, of raising children. Like the hunting squire Charles Musgrove, who finds it hard to grasp how any man can have different interests from his own, especially if they involve reading, Robert Curzon is alienated by the tastes and pursuits of his bookish elder son. The younger son he and his wife spoil thoroughly, and they will reap the bitter harvest of this error for the rest of their lives.

But we should not get too far ahead of ourselves. Suffice it to say that the rest of our story, which takes us into the Victorian era, contains moral lessons for the sternest Victorian to chew over.

5

Later Years

1835–1839

When Edward Curzon saw how angered his father was by his refusal of a clerical career he took a different tack, expressing despair at the reproaches being heaped on his head and declaring that no one knew what he had suffered when his hopes of forgiveness were dashed. He further lamented that for a long time he had not dared to reveal to his parents the true feelings of his heart and had become quite a stranger to happiness. His father, he said, never spoke to him or looked upon him kindly, indeed seemed no longer to care for him, and he was at a loss to understand what he had done to deserve such a wretched fate. If he must become a clergyman to prove his dutiful disposition he would do so.

In reality a father could scarcely love his son more, and this is what made Edward's barbs effective. For a while Robert continued to insist on ordination, but his sternness soon wore off. It is probable that Amelia was directing Edward's conduct towards him; certainly her own in mollifying his mother was very deft. Harriet could not help being flattered by the meek, confiding manner of this lovely creature, who was not twenty-eight years old as Katherine had thought but a more acceptable twenty-four.[121] The Curzons maintained a show of disapproval by refusing to meet or communicate with her relations, but she did not take this amiss and may secretly have been relieved. 'Amiable, prudent and anxious to please' is how Robert described her, and he began to wonder if marriage might not do Edward good after all, for a sensible wife would overcome his indolence and make him exert himself for his family.

While Edward had no intention of going into the church, he never refused outright, and Robert was confident that he would soon buckle down to the study of divinity. He had let him and Amelia occupy 'a corner of Parham' while the next steps were planned, but before long they had the run of the place, and when a son was born to them in February 1835 their position was entrenched. The sight of Harriet and her daughter-in-law blithely driving round the neighbourhood of Parham together surprised Katherine, who retained a sense of family injury long after those directly affected had forgotten it. She never grew to like Amelia, with her 'Daniel impudence and assurance', but she kept on civil terms with her.

By the beginning of 1836, Edward felt confident enough to suggest that his father rent a house for him in London. He had found one overlooking Regent's Park owned by a widow in financial difficulties: 'There are 8 rooms in it altogether, so we might just get into it.' This, he reasoned, would allow him to look for a job, maybe something at the British Museum or the College of Arms. Robert turned this request down, reminding Edward that the house in Upper Brook Street was available whenever he was in London, but he did not dismiss these new career plans or revert to the idea of ordination. In fact, Edward had no employment at all for many years, unusually for a younger son, though he did at least qualify as a barrister after leaving Oxford.

Any effort to find work was hampered by his delicate health; he suffered from headaches and exhaustion and often retired to bed during the day. This only made him more precious to his parents, who were adoring grandparents to the six children he and Amelia produced. Even with her position secure, Amelia was careful not to overreach herself, and continued to treat her in-laws with humble gratitude. In 1837 she wrote a becoming letter to Lady Zouche, who had been shocked by Edward's marriage, and Harriet, her eager advocate, followed it up: 'Emily begs I will add that she hopes you will not trouble yourself to write to her directly, but is so happy you liked her's. So if you are so good as to write her deux mots sometime hence, any day, it will be very kind.'

Although settling 'the Edwards' at Parham seemed like rewarding them for their false conduct, Robert was glad that an asset so costly to run was being put to use. Before the partition was agreed he had begun to wonder whether he and Harriet were wise to insist on having the house, and once it became her property and his responsibility these fears were confirmed. In Lord Zouche's final decade basic maintenance had been neglected, and it became apparent that much of his earlier work had been shoddy. Structural repairs were urgently required, and to make them Robert engaged Anthony Salvin, a specialist in the renovation of old buildings. The estate needed endless upkeep too, and Robert was soon deep in correspondence with his solicitor and agent about drainage and fencing, repairs to buildings, tenanting the farms, glebe land, tithes, arrears in rent, tax assessments, poor rates and crop blights.

Despite the expense of running Parham and its estate, Robert decided to make fairly substantial alterations to the house. Still with Salvin as his architect, he restored the great hall to its Elizabethan proportions; moved the main entrance to the north front, with a new forecourt for carriages; and replaced the Georgian segmental gables with triangular ones such as the house would originally have had. Much was also done to the outbuildings, especially the stables and dairy range. Harriet furnished the freshly decorated rooms and arranged books accumulated over several generations in the new library, the old one having been turned into a dining room. Lady Zouche sent portraits of her Southwell ancestors to hang in the long gallery.

An exception to the general shortage of matter from Harriet's pen during this and the next decade is a clutch of letters to Lady Zouche in the summer of 1837. Mainly sent from Parham, they show her in the thick of family life and delighting in her grandchildren's winsome ways and the antics of her dog Toby, the successor to the departed Ri. Harriet wrote as she might speak to her beloved mother, who at nearly eighty was still her confidante and best friend.

HARRIET TO THE DOWAGER LADY ZOUCHE
PARHAM, 3 AUGUST 1837
My dearest Snugest – I flatter myself you will not much mind the pence my letter costs you ... The little boy really grows like

Grumpus, only think! In a cap he is positively handsome and *smiles agreeably*. Missy runs about and *talks* and calls pan pan to the peacocks and delights in the gallery. The dear old place looks beautiful today. The rain has been nearly incessant, till this afternoon it cleared up and Emily and I determined to go and see Mrs King, but we did not find her at home. We drove up Windmill Hill the old way and lamented the trees. Your plantations and the 3 trees on the top of the hill are all flourishing. We returned by the approach road and then drove a little about and called upon old Dame Gibbs, who is tolerably well, so is old Dame Skinner. The poor people are delighted to see us and have us back, which is so comfortable. Poor old Dame Kimpshot is dying. Watch is very well, was not sent to the keeper and has not yet eat up Toby, who is now pretty nearly settled in his mind, only cannot bear the post horn, and cannot make out whether Missy is not a rival to him, so sometimes he barks *at* her and sometimes runs *with* her to make friends ...

HARRIET TO THE DOWAGER LADY ZOUCHE
PARHAM, 30 AUGUST 1837
My dearest Snugest – Rimel is very busy sewing at the carpet in your room, which is at last happily displayed. I cannot say I think it very pretty, but it is bright and gay and will enliven the smaller room very much. But as dear Bob *pokes about* every where he has discovered the damp place in your *cabinet* and will have it all wainscotted so as the paint will succeed. I don't know when I shall get rid of the workmen. Perhaps Katherine has told you of our mutual expedition to Slindon Monday ... Lady Newburgh enquired most kindly after you and I was very happy to go there again, but was quite tired and so knocked up I could not write to you yesterday. We were fortunate in a very fine day, yesterday and today it has continually rained. Kate looked very handsome, she had her two children with her. Lady Newburgh was to have a dinner, so we were all stuffed into the tiny room by the conservatory for our luncheon, and she gave me some apricots. She was to leave home today, but I did not understand where she was going. I invited her to come to Parham, which she said she would do in October ...

HARRIET TO THE DOWAGER LADY ZOUCHE
PARHAM, 7 SEPTEMBER 1837

My dearest Snugest – When I wrote you yesterday I forgot the next day would be my birth day, as you so kindly remembered. I am fifty years old. It is a sad thing to think of so long a life and so much sickness and sorrow, time misspent and little left to look back upon with approbation! But I comfort myself in trusting to the merits and mercies of an Almighty Redeemer and hope every day to mend. [*Robert's hand*: She is a great love and few of less occasion to mend.] Dear Bob has just put in the last kind words. Dearest Snugest, how many blessings I have to be thankful for, and indeed I am thankful, altho' sometimes 'my heart is afraid' …

Our little George makes faces with his new teeth coming, and he sometimes looks quite ugly, but sometimes I think him like Grumpus. He has those great light blue eyes. He is very fond of Grandpapa, who nurses and dances him about. Missy is a little afraid of him, but says by herself, by way of reflexion, 'But I love dear good Grandpapa, and I have a great many grandpapas in the gallery.' I wonder how soon that impression is made *to last*. She makes many amusing remarks now and is very intelligent.

I am very glad you proposed to take a walk because it seems like being well, but I hope and *entreat* you will take care to have all your attendants to take care of you my dear Snugest. I will not teize you about coming here, yet still hope perhaps, with fine weather to encourage, you will arrive some day …

Harriet still needed a crutch to walk, and doctors earned fat fees giving her black doses and sal volatile. Robert, now well into his sixties, was rheumatic too, but suffered in silence. They worried about Robert II, who in June 1837 sailed to Smyrna on another manuscript-hunting expedition. Before this he had lived uneasily with them, mainly at Hagley. He had an affectionate nature and wanted to please, just as they wished to forge a bond of sympathy with him, but there was mutual incomprehension. Robert II's interests were literary and antiquarian, whereas his mother's knowledge of such things was superficial and his father's non-existent. Like many clever young men he was not clever enough to conceal his arrogance, and he unsettled his parents with verbal sallies and caustic humour. Their mistake was trying to make him adopt their lifestyle despite his evident boredom with country pursuits and jogging round the big houses of Staffordshire. 'All I want,' he wrote to Walter Sneyd, 'is some one with a congenial spirit, who would care for an old book, or a picture, or a quaint old thing of any sort, for I am terribly lonely.'[122]

His second voyage, like his first, is recounted in *Visits to Monasteries in the Levant.* He acquired over twenty manuscripts on Mount Athos and various treasures from the Coptic monks of Egypt before returning overland through Europe and arriving home in September 1838. When he unpacked his hoard scholars rubbed their eyes. 'My MSS astonish all the wise men,' he boasted to his father, 'and we find out something more extraordinary in them every day. I have discovered part of an unknown Greek classic in one, giving a description of the pyramids, labyrinth and famous people of the antient world, which is highly curious and interesting. There is also a suspicion of a new apocryphal book of the Old Testament in another MS, but this has not yet been clearly made out.' One wonders what the elder Robert made of all this.

*

Information on the Pechells is scanty for the second half of the 1830s. Extant family letters for the period following the partition of the estate are almost all to or from the Curzons, and in August 1834 Katherine's journal lapses for fourteen years – possibly because volumes are lost, possibly because her 'business doing, hard working life' left too little time for it. We hear briefly of her charitable activities, of her research of Parham's history, of a trip to Brighton with George to wait on Princess Augusta, and of a feud between George and Colonel Wyndham, the notoriously disputatious son of the Earl of Egremont. The best-documented strand of their lives is George's political activity.

After the disappointment of 1832 he resolved to try again for one of Brighton's seats, both held since that contest by Radicals. In late 1834 a dissolution was expected and George hoped his more moderate brand of progressive politics would prevail this time. He formed a committee, published letters to the electors, and set about canvassing. As before he presented himself as the court candidate, somewhat anomalously as the king's ministers were now Tory. His leg was still painful, and for a few days in December it confined him to his hotel. Nonetheless he won the election, held in January 1835, with almost two fifths of the vote and was returned with one of the sitting Radicals, who came a distant second. Years afterwards the travel writer Lord Albemarle recalled a humorous exchange with the poet Horace Smith to the effect that George's injury had assisted him by limiting his contact with electors, who might have liked him less if they had seen him more: '"His broken leg," I observed, "has served him in good stead." "It was," replied Horace, "the only leg he had to stand upon."'[123]

In his speech after the returning officer's declaration George promised to attend to local interests, and this, rather than seek fame for himself, is what he did. The defence of coastal fisheries from French and Dutch exploitation and the abolition of tithes on turnips fed to sheep were among the concerns of his constituents that he took up, and for his work on the latter a delegation of Sussex agriculturalists presented him with a piece of plate designed by Rundell and Bridge. Larger causes he supported included a national education system for all sects and an extension of the franchise, and his voice was often heard in debates about the mercantile marine and the navy. It would have been natural for George to work on naval questions with his brother, but uncertain health had made Sir John give up Windsor in 1834, and the formation of Peel's Conservative government in the same year ended his work at the admiralty.

The election of 1837, occasioned by the death of William IV, saw George again at the head of the poll, this time with almost half of the votes. But if the Brighton electors liked his politics, his wife's relations did not. Harriet told Katherine she had only skimmed over a speech printed in a newspaper 'as you know I would abuse George', and Elizabeth Curzon was so appalled by his views on religious toleration that she asked her nephew Robert II to write to him 'and beg him to compose another address more acceptable to a true upright Protestant'. Still, he was useful as a provider of franks. With neither husband nor son in parliament, Harriet had no way of sending letters without charge to the recipient, but at least when she and Lady Zouche wrote to Katherine they could enclose a letter to each other to be addressed and forwarded by George.

King William's passing brought Princess Victoria to the throne, the eighteen-year-old whose progress Katherine had watched with reverent benevolence. A few months after her accession she saw her again.

KATHERINE TO THE DOWAGER LADY ZOUCHE
CASTLE GORING, OCTOBER 1837

My dearest Snugest – I languish much to write you a long letter, but I am so unequal to keeping pace with other people that I have not had a moment to do so, and I have not yet told you circumstantially of our expedition to Brighton Friday. First of all you know Capt. Brown, who invented and built the Chain Pier and was always bothering George in London about the Greenwich Rail Road etc. etc., was extremely anxious that the Queen should fix a day and hour to see the pier in a regular way and to explain *himself* the wonderful mechanism of the whole thing, and this was to be managed through George, who spoke to the Queen about it the day he dined at the Pavilion, as he had always found her at Cowes and Portsmouth perfectly capable of understanding all works of the kind in the way of shipbuilding etc. etc.

However she never fixed a day, and Capt. Brown kept coming here and writing, and at last on Thursday George was to go to a public meeting at Brighton, and late in the day he applied to Lord Melbourne and the Queen sent down word that she would walk the next morning at *12 o'clock*, and if that was *inconvenient* to Capt. Pechell she would put it off till next week. George of course was glad to receive the first command, gave notice to Capt. Brown and the other proprietors of the Chain Pier instantly, and instead of going to dinner and bed very goodnaturedly drove home in the dark in the gig to see if I should like to go.

So he ordered post horses, and at ½ past nine on Friday morning I was in the carriage extremely cold, for it was a great exertion to me as you may suppose, and at ½ past eleven we got to Brighton and had just time to shake ourselves at the York Hotel and walk down to the pier when the Queen arrived with the Duchess of Kent, Lord and Lady John Russell and Lord Melbourne. The Queen shook hands with me as she went by and walked on with her party to the end, and in the course of the quarter of an hour that Her Majesty was in the pier she found an opportunity to ask after my children, who she remembered in the Isle of Wight, and how far off I lived. She expressed astonishment when I said 14 miles, and seemed to think it was very good natured of George to come so far to amuse her and Capt. Brown.

George introduced me to Lord Melbourne, who stared at me very much and when I proposed to speak turned short off in a shy way like Lord Egremont and Col. Wyndham, which really is quite absurd but you would see what I mean. If it had not been Lord Melbourne I should have described him as a shy awkward man who wanted encouragement. Lady John Russell looked quite plain with a red nose, as if it did not agree with her being out so early. I revived myself with a glass of wine en passant at the York Hotel. The Queen looked really beautiful. She has a sort of intellectual earnest look when she speaks to one, very like Henrietta Howard's look at the same age, and having very pretty eyes and a very clear complexion her face bear's examination and her countenance lights up beautifully ...

This letter contains the first mention of the 'rail road' that so revolutionised personal mobility. George played his part in getting the London and Brighton Railway Bill passed in 1837, and three years later he made the first rail journey recorded in the family papers. It followed a visit to his mother at Hampton Court Palace and took him from nearby Kingston to Nine Elms, the London terminus of the still incomplete Southampton line being built by the London and South Western Railway. Some unspecified seasonal problem, perhaps leaves on the track, made for an uneven motion: 'I was so distressed at the uncomfortable travelling he had from hence by railway,' Lady Pechell told Katherine, 'that I ventured a note of remonstrance to the director Mr Easthope, who replied with civility that he *should lay my note before the board,* but that he much feared that, however he might regret the cause of complaint, he could not perceive the means of providing an effectual remedy.' Modern passengers would deem such a reply an extraordinary courtesy in itself, but Lady Pechell was not satisfied: 'After this avowal, I shall not recommend the rail road during winter to my London friends'.

George's work as an MP took him away from home even more than his duties as a courtier, which ended with the new reign in 1837. For weeks he left Katherine to run Castle Goring, look after their children and socialise with local families. During Harriet's annual stays at Parham the sisters saw each other frequently and no one would have guessed that they had barely been on speaking terms a few years earlier. The relationship did not regain its former intimacy, though, partly because of the shock it had received, partly because the first objects of each woman's affection were her husband and children. They also had different social circles located in different parts of the country.

Lady Zouche enjoyed visiting Parham until a bout of influenza in early 1837, after which she rarely left her house in Hyde Park Place. Towards the end of her life we see her only as reflected in her daughters' letters and brief mentions elsewhere. The nervous anxiety from which she began to suffer in the 1820s became more acute, and Harriet often had to soothe her mind, but she was still full of gossip and keen to know about the work being done at Parham and her great-grandchildren's progress. In 1838 Robert II dined with her and found her 'in great force'. However, back pains made it hard for her to move, and doctors could do little beyond alleviating her discomfort. In August 1839 she gathered her remaining strength for a short visit to Parham. At the onset of winter Harriet and Katherine learnt that she was seriously ill and hurried to her bedside. She died aged eighty on 10 December; a week later she was buried at Parham.

'Well acquainted with sorrow' is how Lady Zouche described herself, and her unhappy marriage and the deaths of her sons in early manhood tested her severely. However, just as she had been the light of her mother's life, so Harriet, her 'first of loves', had been the light of hers, and while her darling was with her or in her mind's eye nothing could overwhelm her. In her final years she was on easy terms with Katherine and often provided George with a bed when he attended parliament, but she had never loved her daughters equally, not before, and certainly not after the discord between them. In her will she mentioned Katherine kindly and gave her a token bequest, but made Harriet executrix and left her all her property and the lease on her house.

1840–1848

Harriet took up her journal again in 1839, but from now on it is little more than a calendar of events; spans of months and years pass unrecorded, and it is possible that volumes are missing. Her life continued its familiar train, though she and Robert lived more at Parham, returning to Hagley only for the winter and spending little time in Upper Brook Street. Edward and Amelia sometimes came to Parham, but mainly resided in the house just off Connaught Square that Robert, after some cajoling, had engaged for them in 1837. As for Robert II, he spent most of 1840 in Italy and Switzerland. On his return he found that he was expected to tag around with his parents and entertain their guests, and that they would not let him invite a friend to Parham in their absence.

So he took his courage in both hands and told them how frustrated he was that his preferences were never consulted and that he was treated as if he were fifteen rather than thirty. The ensuing discussion did little to clear the air, and when he was offered the secretaryship to the British ambassador to the Ottoman Empire he seized the chance of getting away again. In early 1843, after a year in Constantinople, he made the arduous journey to Erzurum to represent Great Britain at a conference to draw the border between Turkey and Persia. *Armenia*, his second book, records the adventures and misadventures of this mission. In the autumn a bilious fever nearly carried him off, but at the close of the year he was strong enough to start for home. Harriet was afflicted when she heard of his illness and his return the following August was a huge relief. However, the glamour of his travels and brush with death soon wore off, and mother and son fell into their old misunderstandings.

MEMORANDUM BY ROBERT CURZON II
PARHAM, 20 SEPTEMBER 1844

My father and mother came back from Castle Goring. My father received me most kindly, unusually so, asked me how some fish should be dressed and then sat down as usual to the newspaper.

My mother came later by herself. I was in the room with my father reading a book when the door opened and she came in with Toby under her arm. I got up and went to meet her and enquired kindly about her, when she gave me no answer but drew up and said with an offended voice, 'Oh there you are at last.' I stared and said no more presently. She came and sat down opposite to me and after some silence said, 'Well, where did you sit when I was away.' 'In this room (the library)', said I. 'Oh, indeed', said my mother. 'Why', I replied, 'where did you suppose I should have sat.' 'Oh', said my mother, 'I do not think it necessary that the whole house should be lit up for you.' I was very much taken aback at such a reception, and said, 'I do not know how I have offended you, for you speak unkindly to me. What have I done?' When after saying something quickly which I did not hear, she said, 'I am sure I shall not be choosing my words for you', upon which I being quite astounded said, 'This is very unkind. If I have done anything against you tell me, for if I am to be treated in this way I had rather go away and no longer live here.' She said, 'Oh you may go then, I am sure', and I went out of the room.

However I immediately returned as my father was there and begged my mother's pardon if I had in any way offended her. I found her playing with one of my brothers babies and seemingly quite unconscious that anything had happened. My father was walking about the room and said something to my mother when the nurse went away, and then she said she did not mean to be unkind and also something else which I did not hear, for being very unhappy and upset with such an unfeeling reception, and feeling my head turn, I went away and lay down, and then afterwards wrote this.

As a rare direct account of family life this is valuable, but background information is clearly missing. It is also curious that while Robert II documents grave tensions with his mother, her journal contains no hint that anything was wrong, and his father's letters to him, even where they address disagreements, keep up a cordial, unruffled tone. Perhaps Robert II was morbidly sensitive, perceiving slights where none was intended; or perhaps the Curzons, renewing the stance they had earlier taken with the Pechells, avoided open confrontation while ceding no ground and communicating their displeasure implicitly. They liked to have things their own way, but without sound and fury, always hopeful others would come round to their point of view.

One problem was that Robert II, unlike his parents, could not forgive Edward for his marriage. 'You know my ideas are very aristocratic,' he told his father, 'more so perhaps than they ought to be in these days of mob government, so my pride has received a check which I can hardly get over.' He was also ungenerous in resenting that Edward and Amelia had been set up at Parham and in never going there when they were in residence. More warrantably, he was alarmed at how easily his brother could persuade his parents to fund his extravagant lifestyle and pay off his debts. Despite his allowance and his house in London, and despite the near sinecure as registrar of copyright designs that was obtained for him in 1842, Edward never lived remotely within his means.

This brings us to the heart of the matter: Robert II realised his parents were whittling away their fortune. Edward's profligacy was a major cause of this, but not the only one. Running two country houses and a substantial London home cost more than they could afford, and the renovations at Parham stretched them further. Income from landed estates was depressed in the 1840s, and correspondence with their Sussex agent shows the Curzons to have been generous landlords, ready to accept late payment of rent from struggling farmers and to employ needy labourers in winter. Gradually their debts mounted. They had borrowed against the value of the Zouche estate almost from the moment the deed of partition was signed, and later they raised large sums on both Parham and Hagley.

Robert and Harriet were not particularly extravagant, but they had a weak grip on their finances. In the early part of their marriage Robert had given the impression of being a fairly capable man of business, but even then he was better at initiating things than seeing them through. Paying too much for some plate, underestimating the cost of repairs to Hagley, neglecting maintenance on his Staffordshire estate, mislaying a document needed for the Sussex partition, getting in a muddle about the terms of that partition: all minor in themselves, but building up a picture of someone who was vague about details. Harriet was much vaguer, a poor housekeeper by her own admission who found it 'such a bore having to look over and after all things'. Not surprisingly, pilfering was rife among their domestic staff.

Repeatedly Robert II asked his father how things stood, but the answers he received were evasive. Robert's one idiosyncrasy was that he liked to run his affairs without interference or even advice. He did tell his elder son that money was tight, that his allowance would never be increased, and that if he married his wife must have a good portion. He urged him to overcome his distaste for serving under other men and seek another diplomatic posting. Finally, he said he had laid out £30,000 on Parham mainly to oblige him in his love for the house he would one day possess along with his mother's barony. These were fair points, but the fact remains that Robert was mismanaging what he had inherited from his father and his son expected to inherit from him. In 1846 Harriet admitted to him that because of their difficulties the underused house in Upper Brook Street and Parham's own farm were to be let.

When Robert II read this letter he was again in Italy. The pleasures of travel had long since palled, and he went abroad to escape his family. It was a bad policy, for his absences allowed his brother and sister-in-law to strengthen their position. Sometimes Edward let the mask fall, but Amelia was always ingratiating and made sure her children wrote charming little letters to their grandmother. Both liked Robert II as little as he liked them, and they probably had a hand in his parents' withdrawal of affection from him. Their rewards were Scarsdale House, Kensington, leased from the Kedleston branch of the family and far larger than their previous London abode; and the granting of power of attorney to Edward at Parham, where his seemingly skilful operations earned him much praise. 'I wish my father had had so clever a helper as you are to us!' Harriet told him in 1847.

The paradox of Robert II's life is that he was a misfit at his parents' hearth but well liked everywhere else. He had a large circle of friends and was on good terms with his relations on both sides, including the Pechells. According to a member of the Grosvenor clan, he was 'most especially agreeable, so much information and knowledge and imagination and taste, and such pleasing manners'. He was a great favourite with his Aunt Elizabeth, to whom he wrote witty, erudite letters from all over Europe and the Near East. She was a kindred spirit: prickly and aristocratic, clever and articulate, but much more resolute. She had the ear of her brother Robert, not least as she supported both of his sons, and although she was Edward's godmother her growing disapproval of his expensive lifestyle led her to take up Robert II's cause.

*

The turbulence among the Curzons contrasted with the smooth course of the Pechells' lives. In 1841 George won his third mandate in Brighton, again at the head of the poll. A London clerk staying in the town wrote his young daughter an account of the festivities that followed the victors' nomination: 'The Members were preceded by a boat, fitted up like a Ship of War, decorated with a variety of flags. There were two little Boys in the boat, one the son of Captain Pechell, and the other the son of Mr. Wigney, the successful candidates, who, as they passed, bowed to the people and appeared to enjoy the scene very much. Then followed a carriage, in which were Captain Pechell and Mr. Wigney, and some of their friends, and this was drawn by sailors, who laid hold of a long rope for that purpose. This was meant to shew how pleased the people were with their having succeeded in carrying the Election according to their wishes.'[124]

Later in 1841 the Dowager Lady Pechell died at Hampton Court Palace. To the end she had been a great lady of the eighteenth century, and above all a daughter of Sir John Clavering, a man whose equal she declared she had never seen in all her long life; she observed the modern world, with its reformed parliament and its railways, from a great height. But she was very fond of Katherine and approved of the way she was bringing up her children. She corresponded with her more than with George, who liked his pen as little as most of his sex. 'My love to [the children] and to dear George, who need not apologise for not writing oftener,' she told Katherine in her last surviving letter. 'I am quite satisfied of his kind heart towards me, and do not consider a letter more or less as *proof of regard.*'

By this time the Pechells had their own grace-and-favour apartment at Hampton Court, a reward for George's service as Queen Adelaide's equerry. Another had been granted to Sir John Pechell, who had also bought a house in Hill Street, Mayfair, when his work at the admiralty came to an end in 1834 (the same address as Admiral Crawford in *Mansfield Park*, and now the home of the Naval Club). Sir John was a considerable gourmet, and invitations to the exquisite, beautifully-presented dinners that he and his wife gave at their two homes were eagerly sought after. Aside from a second stint at the admiralty in 1839/1840 he played no further part in public life, but was raised to the rank of rear-admiral in 1846. Two years earlier his wife had died, leaving him to resume the solitary habits of his long bachelorhood.

In the spring of 1844 Katherine went with her husband and daughters to Hagley – her first visit for twenty years. After a week William, now thirteen, joined them from Harrow: 'a very happy time to us all', wrote Harriet. The sisters no doubt discussed a burial monument they were planning for Cecil in Canada. Since his death in 1813, a flat tombstone had marked his grave; the Bisshopps had intended to replace it, but the ongoing hostilities caused a delay and afterwards the idea was given up. In the early 1840s Harriet learnt that the tombstone was cracked in three places and asked Katherine to join her in commissioning a replacement. The new monument, finished in 1846, comprises an altar tomb covered with a slab of dolomitic limestone, a paved foundation and iron railings. The inscription records Cecil's career, the grief occasioned by his death, and his sisters' wish to honour his memory. It stands in what is now Drummond Hill Cemetery.

Harriet's journal of the early 1840s notes her frequent visits to Castle Goring, but too perfunctorily to afford a sense of family life there. In fact, all we have is a brief reference in the boyhood recollections of Lennox Tredcroft, the son of George's sister Fanny: 'Every year we paid visits to our uncles and aunts ... We particularly enjoyed our visit to Castle Goring, as our Pechell cousins were of the same age as ourselves. We had great fun with their donkey-chaise and ponies. One pony, "Old Joey", although only 37 inches high, gave me several spills.'[125] In 1844 the Pechells' landlord Sir Timothy Shelley died aged ninety, and Castle Goring became the joint property of his son's widow Mary Shelley, the author of *Frankenstein*, and her own son Percy Florence. They offered it for sale to the sitting tenants who, late the following year, paid the modest sum of £11,250 for it. Katherine and George had the joy of owning their beloved home, and over time they added to the land attached to it.

After the early death of Lennox's father in 1846, George took a paternal interest in the boy. At fourteen he was sent to an army school preparatory to passing into the Royal Military Academy at Woolwich.

LENNOX TREDCROFT TO FANNY TREDCROFT
BROOM HALL, SHOOTER'S HILL, 31 JUNE 1847
My dearest Mother and Sisters – I arrived here quite safe yesterday; uncle George Pechell brought me here from London,

and was very kind, gave me half a sovereign. The guard, as soon as I arrived at Brighton, showed me and my luggage to the London train. When I got to London Bridge I got a cab, and got my bag, &c., without any trouble. I then drove to Spring Gardens; there uncle G. was waiting for me. As soon as I had taken my dinner, we drove to Hill Street, and found uncle John just getting into his carriage. We drove with him round the Park, and under the Wellington Arch. At half-past-four, we went to the House of Commons, where uncle G. got me a capital seat under the Gallery, in a sort of pew, which I had all to myself. I heard Lord Palmerston speak and Mr. Hudson and several others. I saw Sir Robert Peel but he didn't speak. After this, uncle G. took me to the House of Lords, where there were Lords Lansdowne, Stanley, Clanricarde, Radnor, and the Bishop of Chichester. Lord Lansdowne was wearing a swallow-tail coat with gilt buttons. It is a very small house, I can't think where all the Peeresses sit. In the evening, I went with uncle G.'s valet to the Haymarket. I had never been to a theatre before, and liked it very much ... [126]

1849–1855

After another break Harriet resumed her journal in 1849, which seems to have been a relatively harmonious year for the Curzons. In October 'dear Robert' came to stay with his parents at Parham, and in December 'dear Robert' and 'dear Edward' were with them at Hagley at the same time. In the summer *Visits to Monasteries in the Levant* had been published to high acclaim, and a friend told Harriet that it was 'universally admitted to be most interesting' and could be found 'on every table that one approaches'. At the end of the year Harriet proudly noted the appearance of the third edition, with the first six hundred copies already bespoken.

The peace did not last. In the summer of 1850 Harriet and Robert were 'thunderstruck' to learn that Robert II had proposed to and been accepted by Emily Wilmot-Horton. His father reminded him they could do nothing to augment his income and asked nervously if he had spoken to his Aunt Elizabeth. It was an ungracious response, for the young lady in question was a charming, clever member of a distinguished family, linked by ties of friendship to the Curzons; everyone else, including his Aunt Katherine, congratulated

Robert II on winning her. Moreover, the Curzons had expressed regard for Emily in the past, and he assumed they had absorbed his hints that he cared for her. It is true that her fortune was not large, but he had nothing except his allowance.

Emily's widowed mother was incensed and wrote the Curzons a heavily underscored letter containing some home truths.

ANNE, LADY WILMOT-HORTON TO HARRIET
CATTON HALL, 16 JULY 1850

... At 40 and 28 they are at an age to *enjoy* the good things of this world, and they are *both* I think disposed to do so *reasonably*.

We must do our best to assist them. It is natural perhaps that you should have been surprized at the *sudden* announcement. I fear there *has not* been de part et d'autre the *habit* of (what shall I call it) open and unreserved communication. It is not for me to say why or wherefore, but to *hope* that it may no longer be the case where interests and affections are so closely united, and where there is so much *good feeling* on all sides as I am convinced there is in this case. It may sound absurd, but I believe you are both a little afraid of one another! And now having ventured so far I will go one step further on a point to which you *once* alluded to me – your *two* sons, and I *have* from several *quarters* I must admit heard opinions given (as people *will* talk of their neighbours affairs) of *partialities* etc. etc., which I have always stoutly *denied*, but if you were really to do *nothing* in this case after all that has been done in the other, I fear such reports would be confirmed and could not be contradicted ...

Emily called the Curzons' stance 'incomprehensible' and 'chilling'. She was confident that she and her betrothed would find the means to set up home together, but worried about the effect of parental disapproval on his spirits. Soon she could be easy, for once Harriet and Robert had ascertained Elizabeth Curzon's support and received 'multitudes of letters of congrats' from their acquaintance they changed their tune. After further manoeuvring the question of the couple's income was settled, with the bridegroom's parents and aunt and the bride's mother all contributing. The wedding took place in August in a church near Catton Hall, Derbyshire, the seat of the Wilmot-Hortons, and the couple had a fortnight at Parham before travelling to Rome for the winter.

Offering Parham for the honeymoon was the Curzons' first act of conciliation; suggesting that Robert II and Emily make the west wing of the house their permanent home was the second. 'It is just the right place for a new married pair!' Harriet told her son, 'quiet and green and cheerful, and where I hope and pray you may long live to enjoy every happiness together.' She suggested he go there before the wedding to speak with the agent and familiarise himself with the management of the estate. He gladly did so, but Edward, hearing what was afoot, rushed down from Scarsdale House and wielded his power of attorney to prevent interference in what he regarded as his domain. Fortunately he did not reappear during the honeymoon.

On returning from Italy in the spring of 1851 the couple went to Hagley and then Catton, where their son Robert, known as Robin, was born in June. 'My wife has produced an immense fat he baby, with a long nose and a very red face,' announced the new father to Walter Sneyd.[127] For many years they resided mainly in Parham's west wing, the rest of the house being empty except when Harriet and Robert or 'the Edwards' were there; in London they rented or stayed with Aunt Elizabeth in Berkeley Square. Having long pined for a wife, Robert II had found one who suited him perfectly. These were also years of outward success, for the esteem he won with his first book was consolidated by *Armenia* in 1854, and the renown of his manuscript collection had been growing since a *Quarterly Review* article on the subject in 1845. He became a noted expert on old books, publishing articles for the Philobiblon Society and an edition of a sixteenth-century text for the Roxburghe Club.

With their elder son established at Parham, Harriet and Robert lived mainly at Hagley. Harriet was fairly mobile, and they spent much of their time seeing friends, including Lady Wilmot-Horton, with whom the old cordiality had been restored. Robert II came with his family and Edward with his, and in 1852 the Pechells visited again. In London the Curzons stayed at Scarsdale House, Upper Brook Street having been sold in 1850. These family movements appear leisurely and serene in Harriet's journal, but they took place beneath darkening clouds, and the Curzons' unease at Robert II's marriage would not have surprised anyone who knew how disordered their finances were. They were candid about their spending at Parham, which required further work in the early 1850s to keep it sound, but not about Edward's endless extractions.

He had a mania for trying to turn a quick profit and lost large sums in murky business ventures. At the same time he made lavish improvements to Scarsdale House, which he persuaded his parents and aunt to buy for him outright.

In the autumn of 1853 Robert raised £26,000 on the Sussex estate, but before long he needed another £3,000. Harriet, unsettled but refusing to confront the problem, wrote plaintively to Robert II: 'You know I promised you not to charge the estate any more, and now I find I must obey my dear husband and all my efforts are in vain. Write me a few lines dear Robert and forgive me, for I cannot help myself.' Formerly so placid, the elder Robert was losing his nerve. He tried to let out Hagley, but because of its lack of shooting he was unable to find a taker. At almost eighty, and suffering from rheumatism and sciatica, he was in a constant state of agitation, and Harriet begged Robert II not to be unfilial: 'I received your alarmed and angry letter and was sorry. I put it in the fire. You should not be so unkind to your ever indulgent old father who loves you *so much*!'

*

Katherine's journal resumes in the autumn of 1848. A mere skeleton compared with earlier volumes, it nonetheless gives a fuller picture of her life than the sundry sources used to sketch in the preceding decade and a half, and there are a few colourful passages. She and George were as pleased with each other as ever, and their financial position, always secure, was getting stronger. They usually passed the autumn and winter at Castle Goring, the spring in rented houses in London, and the summer at Hampton Court Palace. Sometimes George, who won his Brighton seat for a fourth time in 1847, was in London alone to attend parliament. He continued to advocate the interests of the navy, securing good service pensions and half-pay allowances to categories of officers previously denied them; and he was responsible for adding clauses to legislation to combat the illegal West African slave trade.

The names that appear most in Katherine's journal are those of their three children, who at last come into proper view. Henrietta, known as 'Hen' or 'Hennie', was nineteen years old at the beginning of 1849; William ('Bobo' or 'Will') was eighteen;

and Adelaide ('Ad' or 'Addy') almost sixteen. The girls were taught at home by their mother and by governesses, but beyond the fact that Adelaide sang, sketched and played the pianoforte we know nothing of their aptitudes and attainments. Both were tall, slim and dark-haired like their mother, in character lively and affectionate, showing a warm family feeling born of a happy childhood. Sadly, their letters are without even a trace of the vivacity of Katherine's youthful productions. The difference is partly a sign of the times, for the earnest sobriety of Victorianism had cast its pall.

Of William's childhood we learn little more than that he was sent to Harrow. He grew up to be handsome like his father and embodied the gentle but manly ideal of the age. At eighteen he completed his training at Sandhurst and gained a commission in the 77th (East Middlesex) Regiment of Foot, which kept him from home for most of each year, at first within easy reach at Portsmouth, but later in South Wales, Plymouth, Northamptonshire and Glasgow. Katherine noted his every movement, the arrival of his 'continual' and 'charming' letters, her joy whenever he came home, and her sadness when he went away again. She worried that his military duties left him little time for social functions that would enlarge his acquaintance and bring him into contact with influential men – the question that had exercised Lady Bisshopp in relation to her sons forty years before.

All three of the younger Pechells were on good terms with their Aunt Harriet and Uncle Robert. When they were old enough they visited them at Parham without their parents, and William, who could more easily travel alone, went at least once to Hagley while on leave. They also saw a good deal of Robert II and Emily, who often called at Castle Goring once they had settled at Parham. The elder Pechells still socialised vigorously with their Sussex neighbours, George had his shooting parties, and Katherine took her daughters to church at Clapham or Goring. In London they went to plays, operas and receptions and gave parties at home. Their connection with the court was less intimate than in William IV's reign, but Henrietta and Adelaide were presented to the queen and the family attended a variety of royal functions.

One evening in November 1849 Sir John Pechell's coachman drove from London to Castle Goring with the news that his master had died. George and Katherine felt real grief, for he had been an excellent brother and friend and his death was unexpected, though he had not been strong. The funeral took place at Hampton Church, with George and William as chief mourners. Some years earlier Sir John had sold part of his Irish estate, adding to the money he had accumulated by taking prizes, and his will contained generous bequests, among them £10,000 for his widowed sister Fanny Tredcroft. The rest, 'a noble fortune' in her words,[128] went to George, who also inherited the house in Hill Street with its contents and the baronetcy. He and Katherine were now Captain Sir George and Lady Brooke-Pechell, and Hill Street was their London home.

With her children grown up, Katherine had more time on her hands. She compiled a catalogue of books at Castle Goring and expanded her charitable activity, particularly committee work. In 1851 she saw the Great Exhibition in the Crystal Palace: 'Dear William walked about with me, and I with the rest of the world was all admiration, but found an hour quite enough, the heat and fatigue being great.' In May 1852 William made a two-week trip to Paris, staying at the Hotel Wagram and writing daily letters to his parents, and in July the whole family repaired to Brighton for another election. George was again returned, and the occasion was as boisterous as ever: 'The mob was very noisy, and ended by throwing stones at the windows, but not at the candidates as at the last election.' In December George was promoted to rear-admiral on the retired list.

In April 1853 the Bishop of Chichester opened the rebuilt St Margaret's Church in Angmering, a village on the Castle Goring estate. This was an important event for the Pechells as they had a private pew in the new church and, outside its walls, a family vault. In June they all travelled to Oxford, and Katherine repeated experiences of over forty years earlier by visiting All Souls and witnessing the installation of a new chancellor – this time the Conservative statesman Lord Derby – in the Sheldonian Theatre, 'a most magnificent and interesting sight'. She and George had a quiet Christmas at Castle Goring while their son and daughters went to Parham to be with Robert II and Emily, who had adopted the German custom of erecting a Christmas tree and decorated it with gifts for local schoolchildren.

In March 1854 Great Britain and France declared war on Russia after she refused to withdraw from the Danubian Principalities of the Ottoman Empire. The rumblings of conflict had begun months earlier, and Katherine knew that William might be sent abroad. Having lost her two brothers in uniform, she desperately hoped her only son would not have to fight. The 77th Regiment was ordered to Constantinople in February but, to his parents' relief and his own annoyance, William was among a handful of junior officers chosen to stay behind. Promoted to the rank of captain, he was put in charge of the regimental depot at Parkhurst in the Isle of Wight. For Katherine and George the respite lasted only a few months, and the blow fell while they were staying at a hotel in Cowes and visiting him in his barracks.

KATHERINE'S JOURNAL

28 September. – I was sitting in the window when I saw him arrive at one o'clock, and I at once felt the misfortune he came to announce. It was but too true, he had received the order to proceed to join his regiment in Turkey immediately. He went that afternoon to Woolwich to inquire as to the actual time of his departure. We remained in our sad sorrow till he returned to breakfast the morning of the 30th.

30 September. – We returned to Castle Goring.

3 October. – William came having passed the day in London.

5 October. – My sister and Mr Curzon and Robert and Emily came to take leave of him.

6 October. – We all went to London to make the melancholy preparations for his departure.

7 October. – He went to Greenhithe to see the ship.

8 October. – We all went to see the ship, screw steam transport. We were anxious to go on board previous to the embarkation of the troops she was to take out to the East. I saw the cabin my dear William was to share with two other officers containing three berths. Their names Wombwell and Campbell. I saw his horse too, in the stable in Hill Street, and his servant Stevens. It was dreadful to see all this, but I determined to go through it. This week was passed in daily expectation of the ship's sailing, and in frequent and daily excursions to Greenhithe.

14 October. – He went on board and stayed the night.

15 October. – Sunday he telegraphed to us as the Prince was on the point of departure. We all went to the hotel at Greenhithe. We went again on board the Prince, and we also passed the day walking about with dear William, perhaps for the last time. We went on board an Austrian steamer. We dined together for the last time, and parted with that dearly beloved child who has always been to me most kind, dutiful and affectionate. May God restore him to us and to his home, and preserve him through this expedition of hardship and suffering. I lay down on the bed and slept two hours and then watched the lights of the Prince at dawn. I saw preparations were making for getting up the steam before I went down to watch from the sitting room window, and actually saw her towed away by a little steamer quite out of sight, and when in deep water they were gone. Sir George with Henrietta and Adelaide went out upon the pier and saw the last of all this on this melancholy morning, Monday October 16th. We returned by the early train to London, and at one o'clock proceeded to Castle Goring.

17 October. – All is now blank and dreary. There is nothing to be done but to hope and pray.

Katherine's foreboding is unmixed with expressions of pride in her son's service for his country or of hope that he might distinguish himself. Nor does she mention any such pride or hope in her husband, who is simply recorded as sharing her anguish. The messy, ill-managed war in the Crimea – 'the disastrous war' as she called it – did not stoke the nation's fervour as the existential struggle against Napoleon had done, though even then Katherine had found it hard to celebrate victories achieved at such terrible human cost. She passed the winter in a state of 'intense anxiety' which, with the severity of the weather and a lingering cough, made her listless, and other than occasional morning drives she hardly stirred from Castle Goring between October and March. In April 1855 the Pechells moved to Hill Street, and there Katherine's journal ends, this time for good.

William's letters had been shafts of light in the winter gloom. After reaching Constantinople in early November, he had sailed across the Black Sea to Balaklava and joined his regiment in the British camp besieging the Russian naval fortress of Sebastopol. In describing his life in tents and trenches very close to the enemy, he kept up a breezy tone, but he was shocked at how inept the British operation was, with woeful provisioning and poor communications. Their allies the French managed better, he wrote, and resentment was felt towards the British commander Lord Raglan, who lived in a comfortable house with his own cook, was rarely seen by his soldiers, and showed little interest in their welfare. William also commented mordantly on the differences between the real condition of the troops and its representation in London newspapers. His greatest frustration was that despite many little skirmishes the positions of the opposing forces never shifted.

A few times he enjoyed the company of his cousin Lennox Tredcroft, who, after training as a cadet at Woolwich, had gained a commission in the Royal Horse Artillery and was serving in the Crimea with a field battery. In early June, shortly after his twenty-fifth birthday, William's regiment was involved in a partially successful attack on an enemy position, but a larger assault on the Great Redan, a Russian fortification outside Sebastopol, achieved nothing. For a while all was quiet, and then the British inched towards the Redan again. William's last letter is dated 1 September and reports his role in skirmishes, for which he was mentioned in despatches. On 3 September, six days before the fall of Sebastopol, he received a volley of enemy fire while posting sentries before his trench. 'I have been to the place where he was killed,' Lennox told his mother two weeks later, 'a regular death-trap in front of our most advanced trench. He need not have gone into this rifle pit, as it was not his turn, but he offered to show the way to a new hand.'[129]

BRIGHTON GUARDIAN
12 SEPTEMBER 1855
It is under the most painful feelings that we announce the death of Capt. William Henry Cecil George Pechell, 77th Regt., which sad event appears by telegraphic communication to have taken place on the night of the 3rd September whilst serving in the trenches before Sebastopol ...

The personal regard and high esteem in which he was held by his brother officers, and his kindness and attention to the comforts and health of the men under his command during that dreadful period will cause his loss to be most deeply deplored by them. After the attack on the Redan on 18th June, a gracious offer was made by Prince Albert to place him in His Royal Highness's Regiment of Guards, which would have been the means of expediting his return to England; but the high position he held in his Regiment and the zeal which stimulated him in the conscientious discharge of his duties would not allow him at such a moment to quit the post of honor and of danger to which he had so nobly devoted himself; he therefore requested permission to remain in the 77th, and he had the satisfaction of being informed that his decision was fully approved and appreciated by His Royal Highness. Capt. Pechell's many amiable and estimable qualities endeared him to all who knew him, and to his afflicted and bereaved parents and relatives his loss is irreparable ...

On making enquiries George was told that if he covered the costs, William's remains could be transported home. Accordingly his coffin was borne by ship to Portsmouth and by rail to Worthing, where it arrived in mid-December. His parents had him under their roof for one night before the funeral took place at Angmering Church in the presence of relatives, friends, tenants and labourers. When the coffin reached the new vault George and Katherine were ushered forward to take a parting look before it was lowered, but they were unable to do so and withdrew.

1856–1871
The Pechells spent long hours replying to letters and commissioning memorial tablets for Angmering and Goring churches. Commendations of their son's gallantry appeared in the national press, and the townspeople of Brighton presented them with a condolence book of a thousand signatures and raised a subscription for a statue of the fallen soldier, which was executed by Matthew Noble and placed in the vestibule of the Pavilion. All this might have helped the couple to come to terms with their loss, but it did not. Katherine is silent, but other sources reveal that her broken heart would not mend. 'I grieve to find time brings so little relief to her deep affliction,' Harriet wrote to Elizabeth Curzon in 1857; and another Curzon relative regretted that her thoughts were 'so entirely fixed on the son she has lost'. George was in like case, and a year later Harriet was sad to see how desolate they both were and besought God to revive their spirits. Their daughters did what they could, and through their marriages provided them with dutiful sons-in-law.

Henrietta's husband was Percy Burrell, seventeen years her senior but a good party as the elder son of the great Sussex landowner

Sir Charles Merrik Burrell. Their union must have raised eyebrows, though, for Percy was rumoured to be homosexual. As a young man he had fallen out with his religiose mother and conventionally hearty father and lived abroad in pursuit of his artistic interests. There is such a thing as smoke without fire, but in Percy's case it billowed furiously when John Bowyer, a small attorney, accused him of committing a crime against the person of Daniel Steer, a turner on the Petworth estate, while both were in Paris in 1844. It soon transpired that he was being blackmailed, and rather than pay up he went to law. Bowyer and Steer were plainly guilty of attempted extortion and in 1847 they were transported for life. Whether their scheme was inspired by Percy's reputation or a real liaison with Steer was not investigated and cannot be known, though it was certainly unusual for a simple estate worker from Sussex to be spending time in Paris.[130]

After this Percy lived quietly at home, and from 1850 he often visited Castle Goring. George and Katherine were friendly with the Burrells and must have decided that the stories about him were untrue. Others agreed, and his marriage to Henrietta in August 1856 caused no consternation in the wider family. The wedding itself was not without incident, as Lennox Tredcroft recalled: '[Percy] was a very absent man, so much so that when I gave him his hat, at the altar rails of St. George's Church, at the end of the Service, he thanked me and was walking away towards the Vestry, when Robert Curzon, afterwards Lord Zouche, who was standing next me, called out "Take your wife, man, take your wife." "Oh Lor' bless me," he said and came back and gave the bride his arm, who was wondering what was going to happen.'[131] The Curzons gave them Parham for the honeymoon, after which they settled at Woodgaters, a converted farmhouse a few miles south of Horsham.

A year later Adelaide followed her sister to the same altar in Hanover Square. Her bridegroom was Alfred Somerset, the only son of the late Colonel Lord John Somerset and a grandson of the 5th Duke of Beaufort. At twenty-eight he was four years older than she. He had served with the 13th Regiment of Foot in Gibraltar and owned Enfield Court in Middlesex, which he inherited from a man whose life his father had saved at Waterloo. Harriet, who had never met Alfred, was glad for her nicce's sake to learn that he had an income of £4,000 and other merits besides: 'His high character, and *good looks* as I am told, all combine to give us hopes of this being a most fortunate connexion, as I trust it will prove.' After the wedding the couple spent a week at Hagley at the Curzons' invitation and then made a tour of the Lakes.

In 1858 George became a vice-admiral, and in the year before and the year after he won new mandates from the Brighton electors, but these successes were overshadowed by failing health. Katherine cared for him, but suffered a setback herself when she injured her right arm in a fall at Hampton Court Palace in September 1859. The following summer it still disabled her, and George was getting weaker.

KATHERINE TO HARRIET
HILL STREET, 28 JUNE 1860
My dearest Harriet – I thank you for your letter. You ask after my arm, the hand and fingers very stiff, as if I was wearing a very tight glove, and my arm occasionally very painful. I am desired to use it as much as possible but it is a very tiresome impediment.

George is in a very uncomfortable state. They say a discharge which they continue to keep up with doubtless will be very beneficial and that he will be better after he recovers this than he has been a long time, but at present it is very lowering and worries him to be obliged to eat and drink all day, whether he likes it or not, to keep him up ...

George had been well enough to leave his bed and take daily drives in his carriage, and was not thought to be in imminent danger. But that night his final struggle began, and he died late the following morning, a day before his seventy-first birthday.

KATHERINE TO HARRIET
HILL STREET, 30 JUNE 1860
You will like to know my dearest Harriet and dear Bob from myself. Robert was to write to you yesterday. The previous night was dreadful suffering, and the fatal and awful end to me unexpected.

Henrietta is staying and shares my bed. Adelaide is in the front bedroom staying also, too ill to go home yesterday and stays on. I find myself forced into much exertion as I have every thing to do and to think of. Nothing can be more kind and useful than my dear daughters and their husbands.

I believe I shall have much to do and settle here for a considerable length of time. I know you and Bob feel for me, and I trust it will please you to give me strength to go through all this.

Ever your most affectionate
K. A. B. P.

HENRIETTA BURRELL TO HARRIET
HILL STREET, 4 JULY 1860
My dear Aunt – I write a few words to thank you for your kind letter, and I was going to answer it but Mamma wrote down what she wished and then thought it better to send the paper to you, so I can only repeat how much we feel your kind thoughts in this sorrow. Mamma will I am afraid as days pass get worse in health. At present she has not moved out of her room, that is to say she has looked into Addys on the same floor and into poor Papas, which opens into her bedroom ...

With many thanks and love to dear Mr Curzon ever

Your affectionate
Henrietta Burrell

A week later George took his place alongside William in the family vault at Angmering. The vicar who led the service said that grief at the loss of his son had shortened his life, and his nephew Lennox also believed this to be true. In Brighton there were dignified expressions of sorrow for a man who had represented the town in parliament for twenty-five years. 'It has been said that Sir George may sit in his chair and be returned for Brighton,' a supporter had stated three years before,[132] and thus it was, for his liberal principles, diligence and plain speaking had won him universal respect and affection.

In default of surviving male issue, his baronetcy passed to his cousin George Samuel Pechell.

*

Harriet's tribulations were of a different order from Katherine's, and perhaps worse. In 1856 Robert II, learning that a large amount of timber was to be felled at Parham, pleaded with his father to be frank with him about his finances. Why, he asked, was he raising sums on his estates that bore no relation to his apparent expenditure? In his reply Robert admitted that Edward's debts were the reason for this, but denied being secretive and observed that no indulgences of his own had brought the family to its present straits. In 1857 an angry letter from Robert II prompted Harriet to reproach him for his 'domineering tone' and remind him that his entire income came from them and was regularly paid. We do not know the size of his allowance, but all his life he bought quantities of antiquarian books and other collectable artefacts – his 'gimcracks', as he called them – so it must have been a comfortable sum.

Then Edward turned his fire on his parents for standing by as their servants stole from them. He had got into another scrape, and finding his father unable to help him he inveigled £1,200 from his Aunt Elizabeth. 'I have no pleasure in serving him,' she told Robert II, 'as I fear it will prove but a momentary relief, and he will be wanting more assistance in a few months. In short the whole concern is very melancholy.' The brothers were not speaking, and Robert II denounced Amelia as an 'open enemy' who had poisoned his father's mind against him. For the outside world, however, they all kept up a façade of unity and prosperity. It is kept up too in Harriet's journal, which shows her sentimental and timid, reliant on others, and grateful for every danger averted and difficulty overcome, but makes no mention of money troubles or the rancour they caused. She simply turned away from such things: 'Long discussions always seem to me only to distress the mind and give pain to the heart.'

In 1858 part of the Curzon façade collapsed when Robert and Harriet shut up Hagley, which was heavily mortgaged, and settled at the even more encumbered Parham. Robert II and Emily groaned inwardly, but Harriet had every right to live in her own house. Moreover, while her husband had grown frail, she was stronger. '*The crutch* never appears excepting for church or a *visit*,' wrote Emily tartly, 'and is then only in the way I think, for really Lady De La Z. is *far* younger and more active than most people of her age.' In 1859 Lady Wilmot-Horton rescued her daughter and son-in-law by supplying funds for them to take a house in Arlington Street, St James's. In the same year Elizabeth Curzon died, leaving her favourite nephew £20,000 and the contents of her Berkeley Square house; Edward got £10,000, but in a trust to be managed by his brother. This strengthened Robert II's hand, and the birth of his daughter Darea in 1860 made him determined to insulate his wife and children from the actions of 'these deluded people', as he called his parents and brother.

According to calculations he made in 1861, his father had settled Edward's debts to the tune of £25,000 by that date. Soon afterwards a telegraph company into which Edward had sunk a large sum came to grief. Harriet told Robert II of this fresh disaster but refused to blame her darling and said he would get every assistance: 'Your dear kind father always being anxious with me to help him and preserve him and his from destruction, we have agreed to give a note of hand for 1000£!! as the first step, for alas it is not enough. God grant we may live long enough to repay this debt.' Robert II's reply condemned the 'heartless and cruel system' that Edward used on his gullible parents and warned them that unless he changed his ways there was no knowing what his end might be.

And then another calamity. Harriet had long dismissed Robert II's suspicion that Daniel Diones Geere, the Parham steward, was defrauding them; indeed she trusted him so completely that he was permitted to bank estate income in his own name. He used this practice and other ruses to appropriate large sums, financing a lifestyle that included a wine cellar, a stable full of horses, and the commissioning of a yacht. The first sign of the imminent crash came in June 1862 when the bank returned the housekeeper's wages cheque, and in the next few weeks more irregularities came to light, though Harriet clung to the hope that there was a benign explanation for it all. Robert II intervened forcefully, but Edward, who had appointed Geere, insisted that he had done no wrong. In August the steward, on the point of emigrating to Canada, was arrested for writing another worthless cheque. The shock of exposure unhinged his mind, and he was committed to a lunatic asylum.

Robert was unable to do anything about this humiliation. He had become very weak, and in the spring of 1862 he fell in his bedroom.

HARRIET TO KATHERINE
PARHAM, 22 MAY 1862
… We had a sad alarm about dear Bob this morning, thank God ended well but frightened all. He got out of his bed for some

occasion, lost his balance and was not able to get up from the floor. So at last, for he seems to have [lain] a ¼ or ½ an hour there, en chemise poor dear, he knocked his slipper on the floor, which my maid and I hearing we jumped out of bed and hastened to him, ringing the bell en passant for Foxwell, who came directly, and we got him into bed again, only chilled and surprised, happily not hurt. Meantime I had sent for Dr Mudd, and by the time he came dear Bob was smiling in his bed with some joke, and the alarm subsided. Dr M. assures me it was *not a fit* at all, but only weakness of his limbs preventing his being able to rise from the floor when once he was down. One knows how difficult it is to get up *from the floor* when quite down, without help. I thought of what you said dear Kate, but he is averse to having any one *in his room*, which '*disturbs* him', he says. He fell asleep and got warm in bed, and I am most thankful to say now is much as usual …

Robert remained lucid until almost the close of his long life, and his last years were spent in a state bordering on panic about his deranged affairs. He would rummage busily through drawers in search of a way out of his troubles, and a fragmentary note to Robert II of 1856 reveals his state of mind: 'I have not made a single debt myself. I have only paid the debts of those who have gone before me. With my fortune I supposed my sons would have done something for themselves. But I have had to pay their debts. I had to mortgage Hagley last year to pay Edwards debts. You saw the account of my affairs some years ago etc. You knew that I was living beyond my income, and you have ruined me and married a woman with nothing, and you have ruined me and I have done nothing for myself. I have had to pay the debts of others – all this very incoherent.'

After Geere's arrest Harriet agreed to place their affairs in Robert II's hands. She still refused to sell her husband's ancestral home, but conceded that he was no longer capable: 'It is now imperative upon us all, and for his sake also, to prevent your dear father doing any thing he would himself be sorry for.' Robert II provided him with housekeeping money, for which he was pathetically grateful. In August 1862 Harriet described him as 'puzzled and forgetful', and towards the end his worries may have slipped from his mind. Following a short illness he expired, aged eighty-nine, just after midnight on 14 May 1863: 'About 12 o'clock my own dear Bob died! in a bed where he had laid since Sunday week! So patient, so resigned, pious, and full of faith, sinking by degrees as he passed to Heaven. We are all here and all kind to poor me!' Katherine came from London to be with her sister. A week later, Robert was buried in the family vault at Parham Church.

*

Robert Curzon and George Pechell were very different men, but both had admired, honoured and cherished their wives and were deeply mourned by them. Harriet and Katherine consoled each other after their respective bereavements, and as widows they were together more than at any time since their girlhood, moving back and forth between Parham and Castle Goring and staying each summer at Katherine's house in Hill Street. Their children strengthened the bond: Henrietta and Adelaide were fond of their Aunt Harriet and Robert II of his Aunt Katherine, and they were on easy terms with each other and their spouses. Edward and Amelia remained a little apart, but their grown children were well liked and often present at family gatherings.

The Burrells remained childless but appeared content. They lived at Woodgaters until the death of Sir Charles Merrik Burrell in 1862, when they moved to West Grinstead Park and took a house in Berkeley Square. Whatever Percy's youth may have been, his married life was highly respectable: he was a Sussex magistrate and succeeded his father as baronet and as MP for New Shoreham. Henrietta took up charity work, especially for schools, and tried to improve the welfare of labourers on the West Grinstead estate. Her own family and her Curzon relations often came to stay, as did Lennox Tredcroft, who later remembered with real feeling how kind the Burrells always were to him, in particular when he converted to Catholicism and was more or less disowned by his mother.

The Somersets' marriage was as happy as Harriet had foreseen. They spent most of their time at Enfield Court, which they greatly enlarged. Alfred's career in the regular army had been fairly short, but for much longer he served in the militia, eventually as colonel of a battalion in the Rifle Brigade, and for this he was knighted. His other interests were hunting and driving: he was a master of the Hertford Foxhounds and a member of the Four-in-Hand Club and of the Coaching Club, whose meets in Hyde Park were a highlight of the Season.

He and Adelaide also founded a riding school at Enfield Court. In 1865 their daughter and Katherine's only grandchild Gwendolin was born. Sir Percy Burrell was her godfather.

*

Robert Curzon left his affairs in a convoluted state, and Robert II, his executor, had plenty to do. The main provision of his will was £20,000 for Edward, and to pay it and settle mortgages Robert II sold Hagley to a colliery owner, clearing a smaller sum for himself.[133] Parham was entailed on him, and he filled it with his manuscripts, early printed books, armour and ancient plate; but it still belonged to Harriet, and Edward and Amelia regularly came from Scarsdale House. Relations between the brothers were as bad as ever, and when Emily died aged forty-four in 1866, Robert II accused Amelia of worrying her into an early grave by her spoliation of the family coffers. Edward upbraided him for ungentlemanly conduct and sent copies of his letter to his mother and to Katherine. Robert II apologised for the misdemeanour of writing in anger to a lady, but told his mother he did not wish to see the couple again.

Harriet still sometimes kept a journal, albeit in very attenuated form. At Parham she watched as people came and went, and in London she sat quietly with Katherine or drove out with her. Things were patched up after a fashion between her sons, but she always saw them separately. She now had great-grandchildren, born of the marriage of one of Edward's daughters, and these 'two dear little ones' were her joy. Slowly Harriet and Katherine grew frail. Katherine had painful eyes and episodes of neuralgia, and the lowness caused by George's death reduced her to a 'deplorable state of health' according to Harriet. She recovered, but Robert II thought she looked 'ill and feeble' a few years later. Harriet was plagued more than ever by rheumatism and often felt listless; in 1866 Katherine advised her to build up her strength by eating as much capon, tongue and bacon as she could.

Harriet died first. In April 1870 she fell as she entered the great hall at Parham and damaged her hip. At eighty-two she was too weak to rally, but lingered until 15 May. Her final days, wrote Robert II, 'brought out some beautiful proofs of the innocence of her heart, and her perfect confidence in the mercy of God'.[134]

According to her wishes, expressed in a surviving draft of her will, she was buried 'as quietly as possible' by her husband's side at Parham Church. She left £100 to her maid Patience Brown, her carriages and horses to Robert II, and her plate and the balance of her bank account to Edward. 'I desire my dear sister Lady Brooke Pechell to accept of my Bible that belonged to my dear mother and my Prayer Book as a remembrance of her kindness to me.' All this was written in another hand, and in her own painful scrawl she added a few words for her sons: 'I leave to them my best blessing and thanks for all their kindness to me.'

Katherine now fades from view. Robert II visited her at Castle Goring in March 1871, and in April she was a guest, along with her daughters and sons-in-law, at the second marriage of her nephew Lennox. She died in her eightieth year at Hampton Court Palace on 29 July and was buried beside her husband and son at Angmering.

The journal Katherine began six decades earlier, on her twenty-first birthday, was preceded by four lines of verse in her mother's hand:

> The morn that ushered thee to life, my child,
> Saw thee in tears, when all around thee smiled:
> O may'st thou, sinking in thy last long sleep,
> Serenely smile, while all around thee weep!

There is no Victorian deathbed scene with which to close our story; but the passing of a woman with such resources of love and loyalty, with so much spirit, charm and intelligence was surely mourned by all who knew her.

*

After Katherine's death, her daughters sold the house in Hill Street; Castle Goring passed to the Burrells. Sir Percy died in 1876 and Henrietta followed him only four years later, described in a Sussex newspaper as a woman 'whose name and good work will remain fragrant for a long time to come'.[135] On her death the Somersets inherited Castle Goring but resided mainly at Enfield Court where, in 1885, Alfred founded the Enfield Chase Staghounds and designed its uniform. He and Adelaide had long lives, dying in 1915 and 1920 respectively. Castle Goring became the home of their daughter Gwendolin, who married her cousin Arthur Somerset in 1887, and it belonged to their descendants until very recently.

Robert II had only three years as 14th Baron Zouche and master of Parham, dying in 1873. He spent much of this short period in a frenzy of building, creating a new dining room and the south library and turning the parlour into a billiards room. At Scarsdale House Edward and Amelia quarrelled with each other and their children, and on Edward's death in 1885 Amelia plunged into legal disputes with her sons. An order of chancery gave Edward's creditors the right to claw back some of what he owed them, but they probably recouped little by the time Amelia died in 1892. 'Everyone hated her. She was a terrible woman,' recalled her granddaughter Lady Frankland, whose own grandson Mark Frankland provided a fitting epitaph for Edward: 'a chronic, shameless plunderer'.[136]

Robert II was succeeded at Parham by his son Robin, 15th Lord Zouche, who was hit by the agricultural depression of the late nineteenth century and forced for long periods to let out the house. On his death without issue in 1914 it was the turn of his unmarried sister Darea, 16th Lady Zouche, who outlived him by three years, and then of Lady Frankland, 17th Lady Zouche. Such was the legacy of bitterness between her father and uncle that Darea pared the inheritance to the bone, leaving everything she could to her mother's family and donating her father's priceless manuscript collection to the British Museum. The new baroness found she could not afford to maintain the large, neglected mansion, and in 1921, more than three centuries after its purchase by her ancestor Sir Thomas Bisshopp, she sold it. This was the best thing that happened to Parham in all its long history, for the new owners Clive and Alicia Pearson, who took possession the following year, were intent on restoring it to its Elizabethan glory. Their deep pockets, their taste and determination, and the sympathetic stewardship of their descendants have made it the enchanting place it is today.

History and Literature

Jane Austen was an avid reader of fiction, and her letters contain many comments on novels by other hands. While her praise is variously grounded, her criticism is most often prompted by improbabilities of one sort or another. Here she is on a popular work by Mary Brunton, in which the heroine makes a miraculous journey in an unpiloted boat:

> I am looking over Self Control again, & my opinion is confirmed of its' being an excellently-meant, elegantly-written Work, without anything of Nature or Probability in it. I declare I do not know whether Laura's passage down the American River, is not the most natural, possible, every-day thing she ever does.
> [I will write] a close Imitation of 'Self-Control' as soon as I can; – I will improve upon it; – my Heroine shall not merely be wafted down an American river in a boat by herself, she shall cross the Atlantic in the same way, & never stop till she reaches Gravesent.[137]

In fact Jane Austen avoids such escapades in her novels, which feature no far-off lands, remote epochs or fantastic occurrences. She steers clear even of aspects of current British reality that she is not fully conversant with, and gives instead a vivid picture of the gentry of southern England, its rhythms of life and its social customs. She is scrupulous about factual accuracy, her language is fitting and proportionate, without purple passages or turgid moralising, and her plots, seemingly so simple, are carefully paced and rigorously integrated.

Some early readers found Jane Austen's subject matter and its treatment too mundane, and saw little merit in depicting characters and events that might be observed daily. Others realised that an artist's greatest skill lies in the concealment of art, so that the finished work seems effortlessly produced. The 'silver fork' novelist Thomas Henry Lister makes exactly this point about her, and the poet Robert Southey praises her fiction's closeness to nature. Walter Scott, the most successful novelist of the day, credits her with 'a talent for describing the involvement and feelings and characters of ordinary life which is to me the most wonderful I ever met with', and he praises her 'exquisite touch which renders ordinary commonplace things and characters interesting from the truth of the description and the sentiment'.[138]

The truth Scott appreciates in his little-known colleague is not achieved by what is sometimes called photographic realism. None of Jane Austen's settings is delineated in great detail, none of her plots is based on a true incident, none of her characters is copied from a real person. Her creative triumph rests on a probably unconscious process by which reality is transfigured: she observes the profusion and confusion of life, discerns its essence, and gives this a finished artistic form that is both pleasing and representative. This is why her characters speak, think and behave just as average people would, so that even subsequent changes in manners cannot obscure their fundamental humanity. Furthermore, they are drawn with economy and revealed largely through interaction with other characters, granting them an apparent independence from the controlling hand of the author. As the plot unfolds they become more and more absorbing.

Though the men and women in Jane Austen's novels are not modelled on real individuals, they have themselves an individuality that gives them the breath of life. And because each of them condenses traits that recur perennially, readers can feel they know someone rather like Miss Bates in *Emma* or Henry Crawford in *Mansfield Park*. By the same token, these characters seem to have an existence independent of the fictions in which they appear. We have already quoted Virginia Woolf to this effect, and E.M. Forster agrees with her: 'All the Jane Austen characters are ready for an extended life, for a life which the scheme of her books seldom requires them to lead.'[139] Thomas Henry Lister puts it another way: 'We feel as if we had lived among them.'[140] In the decades after her death the historian Thomas Babington Macaulay, the philosopher George Henry Lewes and the poet Alfred Tennyson all compared Jane Austen with Shakespeare for the lifelikeness of her creations.

It is because Jane Austen's characters are so rounded that we have been able to make comparisons with Katherine Bisshopp and her relations. Of course even a figure as rich as Anne Elliot is produced by selection and arrangement from the quarry of human nature, and is therefore less complex, more coherent, more fully knowable than a real person. Sir Walter Elliot and Mary Musgrove are simpler still, their salient traits exaggerated to the point of caricature. However, even they are vibrant, memorable individuals, not mere stock figures. Several critics have noted that all Jane Austen's characters are carefully discriminated both within novels and across the body of her fiction, so that no two hypochondriacs, prigs or social butterflies are ever quite alike. This is achieved not by making them too eccentric to occur twice, but by delicate touches that make each of them distinctive and normal at the same time.

Do these characters tell us more or less about late-Georgian society than the people who appear in Katherine Bisshopp's biography? The obvious answer is that a biography, which yields real information, should teach us more than a novel, which is the invention of its author. The classic defence of the novel turns this on its head: whereas historians can chronicle idiosyncratic or bizarre conduct and strange happenings as long as they have documents to prove what they write, novelists must stay within the realm of probability to create a suspension of disbelief in the reader. Novels, therefore, adhere to norms of situation, feeling and behaviour, giving them a likeness to reality, a verisimilitude that has a higher truth value than the bald facts of someone's life or a verifiable sequence of events. The distinction is between the general and the particular, the universal and the specific.

Moreover, history is never a simple transcription of the past. Like fiction, it is subject to the logic of narrative. From the mass of available data historians choose what they consider important and suppress the rest. They then order what they have chosen to produce a neat intelligibility that is necessarily reductive. This must have occurred in our portrayal of Katherine Bisshopp, so that she too has been simplified. On the other hand, the minute reconstruction of a minor life is likely to need less shaping than what Catherine Morland in *Northanger Abbey* calls the 'real solemn history' of popes and kings, wars and pestilences.[141] Katherine's story belongs to social history, in which ordinary people are as important as their most famous coevals. Social history can itself address large subjects, of course, but often it stays close to its sources, especially, as here, in the study of specimen lives.

Such lives shine a light on the same features of period and place as the novels of a realist like Jane Austen. We learn little of major events or powerful people, little of great debates about politics and religion, but much about the social attitudes and moral tone of the everyday world: how parents behaved towards children, wives towards husbands, lovers and friends towards each other, how concepts of duty and pleasure were formed and transmitted. The correspondences between *Persuasion* and the story of the Bisshopps, of whom Jane Austen knew nothing at all, simply confirm how unerringly she reproduced the reality of her time. The claim that novel-writing is justified by its verisimilitude is always dependent on the skill and purpose of the writer. The mirror Katherine's biography holds to *Persuasion* supports the widely-held opinion that Jane Austen's fiction is the best, as well as the most enjoyable, guide to the society in which she lived.

One of Catherine Morland's objections to 'real solemn history' is its shortage of women, but this does not apply to social history. If men dominated the public sphere in the early nineteenth century (and other times), women outweighed them in the private realm and in determining the tenor of social intercourse. Also, because they wrote more letters and journals, they left a larger body of material for the sort of intimate family memoir essayed in these pages. Here is another equivalence with the fiction of Jane Austen's day, when most novels were written by and for women, often about questions of female experience. In her own novels plot events are seen overwhelmingly from the perspective of women and reflected in their states of mind. Men's thoughts are infrequently glimpsed, and with the exception of a short conversation between Sir Thomas Bertram and his son Edmund in *Mansfield Park* men are never shown together without a woman being present.

Of all Jane Austen's works, *Persuasion* is the most firmly centred on its heroine; indeed for much of the text her point of view and the narrator's are aligned. Readers are invited to accept Anne's judgements, the more so as she is evidently worthy of admiration: poised and mature, sensitive and intelligent, capable and generous, gentle yet strong, lucid yet deeply emotional. 'Perfection itself' is how Wentworth defines her character; 'almost too good for me' is Jane Austen's verdict.[142] Yet Anne's is the excellence of common humanity, not inimitable genius or saintliness, which is why she can be compared with a real human being like Katherine Bisshopp, who has, if not all, then many of her merits. Katherine's story is also told largely from her own perspective, partly because she provides most of the material, partly because she too inspires confidence that her words honestly reflect the joys and sufferings, the rights and wrongs she experiences.

It is worth asking whether the insights these lives afford into a span of English social history include a sense of the changes taking place within that span. *Persuasion* juxtaposes an enfeebled landed gentry with a vigorous naval circle, just as the ineffectual, lethargic Bisshopps and Curzons may be set against the enterprising Pechells. In *Persuasion* this polarity is accentuated by the harsh delineation of the narcissist Sir Walter Elliot, whose full-length mirrors, interest in cosmetics, catty remarks about his acquaintances, and unpatriotic disdain for the weather-beaten naval men stand for a more general decadence and incapacity to perform the tasks belonging to the patriarch of a small rural community. Sir Cecil Bisshopp's equivalent failings, the markers of his inadequacy in the same role, are his mood swings and temper tantrums. The two men further depreciate their status by failing to keep a grip on their finances, and their chronic indecisiveness prevents them from acting even as the foundations of their lifestyle crumble.

When Sir Walter complains that the navy is 'the means of bringing persons of obscure birth into undue distinction, and raising men to honours which their fathers and grandfathers never dreamt of',[143] he recognises an uncomfortable shift in relative status. Wentworth and Pechell are not exactly of obscure birth, but they are self-made men whose brides leave prestigious but declining families to marry them. In *Persuasion* this shift is symbolised by Sir Walter vacating Kellynch in favour of a newly-rich admiral, who is likely, as Anne sadly acknowledges, to do more for the estate, the parish and its poor than the man he replaces. In Katherine's story, which continues after her marriage, the rise in wealth and status of her public-spirited husband and herself contrasts with the fate of the Curzons, whose torpor and bad management lead them to the point of having to sell their ancestral seat.

So was Jane Austen making criticisms of the landed gentry that Katherine's story corroborates? Some critics believe *Persuasion* offers a progressive vision, the navy men standing for an idealised bourgeoisie with an ethic of work and responsibility, and Sir Walter for a selfish, enervated caste whose status has grown hollow. In this reading, Anne's marriage revitalises England by rejecting a redundant elite in favour of fresh one. Others see the marriage as uniting a representative of the finest aspects of the upper crust, its exquisite manners and sense of obligation, with a member of a new group that makes more compelling claims to wealth and influence. A third interpretation is that the savage treatment of the baronet aims to expose derelictions his class must purge, but no more denigrates that class as a whole than Jane Austen's careerist clergymen represent an attack on the church. Seeing this satirical portrait as a well-meant warning from a conservative gradualist makes sense if we consider that the creator of such model landowners as Fitzwilliam Darcy and George Knightley is an unlikely scourge of the established order.

In a sense it does not matter what the intended message of *Persuasion* is. What matters is Jane Austen's supreme sensitivity to the social forces around her, to the complex tensions that are slowly renewing England, and her ability to distil them in fiction. The story of Katherine Bisshopp illuminates the same forces, and prompts the same impulse to read wider significance into a woman's life. One thing is clear: for both Katherine and Anne marriage is not just a happy outcome in personal terms, but socially and morally good because the merits of the two couples allow them to play a positive role in their communities and to raise a strong new generation.

Notes

Jane Austen's novels appear in these notes as *NA* (*Northanger Abbey*), *SS* (*Sense and Sensibility*), *PP* (*Pride and Prejudice*), *MP* (*Mansfield Park*), *E* (*Emma*) and *P* (*Persuasion*). *Letters* refers to Dierdre Le Faye's edition.

1. The bather was wheeled out to sea in a little hut called a 'bathing machine', from which she emerged and descended a ladder into the water, often helped by two female attendants. Health benefits were ascribed to the 'electric shock' of sudden immersion in cold water.
2. George Frederick Nott, a distinguished clergyman, theologian and Fellow of All Souls (1767–1841).
3. Katherine leaves her own gap unfilled.
4. It should not be confused with Hagley Hall in Worcestershire.
5. Dr Ireland, a local clergyman.
6. *Letters*, p. 64.
7. *NA*, p. 104.
8. *E*, p. 453.
9. *Letters*, p. 351.
10. *MP*, p. 102.
11. *P*, p. 236.
12. *MP*, p. 218.
13. *MP*, p. 219.
14. *P*, p. 236.
15. *MP*, pp. 56–57.
16. *Letters*, p. 71.

17. Mitford, p. 1.
18. *Letters*, p. 296.
19. *Letters*, p. 25.
20. *Letters*, p. 125.
21. *Letters*, p. 25.
22. Forster, *Abinger Harvest*, p. 173.
23. Forster, *Abinger Harvest*, p. 175.
24. *Letters*, p. 89.
25. *Letters*, p. 17.
26. *Letters*, p. 130.
27. *Letters*, p. 94.
28. *Letters*, p. 119.
29. *NA*, p. 103.
30. The sisters' former French governess Marianne La Housse, a lifelong friend of the family.
31. *Letters*, pp. 216–17.
32. 'I can do no more at present' (Italian).
33. *Letters*, p. 275.
34. William Robertson was a prominent Enlightenment churchman and historian. His *History of Scotland during the Reigns of Queen Mary and of King James VI* (1759) long remained popular.
35. 'As usual' (Italian).
36. *Letters*, p. 117.
37. *PP*, p. 152.
38. Lord Whitworth was married to the Dowager Duchess of Dorset, who continued to be known by that title.
39. A daring night-time raid he carried out during the blockade of Rochefort in 1811 is recounted in Carden, pp. 253–54.
40. Princess Charlotte married Leopold of Saxe-Coburg-Saalfeld at Carlton House on the evening of 2 May.
41. The Bisshopps' coach dog. Usually Dalmatians, these dogs were trained to run behind or even underneath a moving coach. Originally intended as a defence against highwaymen, they were by this time valued mainly as companions and fashionable travel accessories.
42. Stapleford Hall, the Nottinghamshire seat of Sir John and Lady Warren.
43. Cassiobury House or Park, the seat of the Earls of Essex, demolished in 1927.

44. Lady Verulam.
45. Prince Pál Antal Esterházy, Austrian ambassador in London from 1815 to 1842.
46. *P*, p. 5.
47. *P*, p. 8.
48. *P*, p. 5.
49. *P*, p. 10.
50. It has been suggested that Jane Austen based Sir Walter Elliot on Samuel Egerton Brydges, the vain, title-obsessed brother of her close friend Anne Lefroy. If this is true, it is unsurprising that Brydges should resemble Sir Cecil Bisshopp just as much. Fascinated by his own genealogy, he spent many years and large sums of money on a claim to the extinct barony of Chandos of Sudeley. This was finally thrown out, and he had to make do after further pleading with a baronetcy in 1814, just before Jane Austen began work on *Persuasion*. Despite his own blatant social climbing, he took a dim view of recent additions to the peerage, 'men who have been advanced from nothing in the last fifty years – they are a miserable set' (quoted in Greene, p. 161). As a result of his extravagance and his determination to live in a noble style, Sir Samuel Egerton Brydges had to flee to the Continent to escape his creditors in 1818 and died in exile in 1837.
51. *P*, p. 39.
52. *P*, p. 78.
53. *P*, p. 189.
54. *P*, p. 34.
55. *P*, pp. 33, 191.
56. *P*, p. 26.
57. *P*, p. 232.
58. *P*, p. 63.
59. *P*, p. 169.
60. *P*, p. 222.
61. *P*, pp. 6, 7, 12.
62. *P*, p. 12.
63. *P*, p. 27.
64. In another coincidence, it has been suggested that Lady Warren is the model for Sophia Croft in *Persuasion*. Jane Austen would have known of the Warrens from her brother Charles, who served under Sir John Borlase Warren on the

North American Station, and whose wife acted as his wife's
companion on a voyage from Bermuda to Halifax. Like her
fictional counterpart, Lady Warren was an intelligent, doughty
woman who enjoyed naval society. Whether she ever helped
her husband negotiate a rental contract or corrected his
driving, as Mrs Croft does, is not known, but the joke in the
navy was that while Sir John was the admiral, his lady was the
commander-in-chief. The tenor of her letters to Lady Zouche,
and her eagerness to guide the progress of Cecil and Charles,
tally with a naval historian's description of her as 'stately, fine
and humane, though somewhat inclined, in the opinion of
junior officers, to think of things for them to do'. (Wilkinson,
vol. I, p. 293; see also Southam, *Navy*, pp. 280, 282).

65. *P*, p. 12.
66. *P*, p. 26.
67. *P*, p. 27.
68. *P*, p. 27.
69. *P*, p. 29.
70. *P*, p. 40.
71. *P*, p. 24.
72. *P*, p. 27.
73. *P*, p. 96.
74. *P*, p. 116.
75. It was a courtesy extended to commanders who had captained
a ship to address them as 'Captain'.
76. How Mrs Bisshopp had come by this nickname is unclear.
77. Now a widow, Sir John Warren having died in 1822.
78. *P*, p. 32.
79. *P*, p. 35.
80. *Letters*, p. 240.
81. *Letters*, p. 124.
82. *P*, p. 35.
83. *P*, p. 41.
84. *P*, p. 41.
85. *P*, p. 36.
86. *P*, p. 61.
87. *P*, p. 181.
88. *P*, p. 25.
89. *P*, p. 218.
90. *P*, p. 32.

91. *P*, p. 41.
92. *P*, p. 55.
93. *P*, p. 29.
94. *P*, p. 56.
95. See Todd and Blank, p. lxi.
96. *P*, p. 165.
97. *P*, p. 158.
98. *P*, p. 175.
99. *P*, p. 225.
100. *P*, pp. 230–31.
101. *P*, p. 232.
102. Quoted in Southam, *Critical Heritage*, vol. II, p. 244.
103. 'Pleasant meadows' (Italian).
104. Presumably the Basilique Sainte-Trinité, the town's most imposing church but not a cathedral.
105. George purchased the *Emily* from Lord Belfast and kept her until 1837. He remained a member of the Royal Yacht Squadron to the end of his life.
106. The *Alarm* did win the race, but was disqualified as Mr Weld had ignored the rule that a boat on a port tack must give way to one on a starboard tack.
107. The home of Baron Yarborough in the Isle of Wight. The usual spelling is Appuldurcombe.
108. The succession of three brothers in turn has caused confusion, and baronetages incorrectly list Edward Cecil Bisshopp as the 11th baronet. Wentworth-Fitzwilliam (p. 87) wrongly states that the title became extinct on the Dean of Lismore's death.
109. The children's recently engaged French governess.
110. *P*, pp. 91–92.
111. *P*, p. 116.
112. *P*, p. 116.
113. *P*, p. 118.
114. *P*, p. 151.
115. *P*, p. 236.
116. *P*, p. 235.
117. *P*, p. 95.
118. *P*, p. 189.
119. *P*, p. 232.
120. *P*, p. 234.

121. We learn this from one of the corrections in Harriet's hand to those particulars in Katherine's letter on the Daniells that show them in a bad light.
122. Quoted in Fraser, *Heir of Parham*, p. 89.
123. Albemarle, vol. II, pp. 306–07.
124. William Cabell to Elizabeth Cabell, 6 July 1841; printed in Djabri, 'Letter from Brighton', p. 94.
125. Tredcroft, p. 88.
126. Quoted in Tredcroft, p. 93. The impossible date is retained.
127. Quoted in Fraser, *Heir of Parham*, p. 186.
128. Quoted in Tredcroft, p. 97.
129. Quoted in Tredcroft, p. 122.
130. The case is reported at great length in the *Brighton Gazette* of 1 April 1847.
131. Tredcroft, p. 35.
132. Quoted in the *Brighton Herald* of 14 March 1857.
133. After passing through various hands Hagley Hall was largely demolished in about 1930. The remaining part was used as an arts centre and finally pulled down in 1985.
134. Fraser, 'Calendar', p. 134.
135. Quoted in Tredcroft, p. 287.
136. Quoted in Frankland, p. 16; Frankland, p. 17.
137. *Letters*, pp. 244, 295.
138. Quoted in Southam, *Critical Heritage*, vol. I, p. 106.
139. Forster, *Aspects*, p. 52.
140. Quoted in Southam, *Critical Heritage*, vol. I, p. 114.
141. *NA*, p. 104.
142. *P*, p. 226; *Letters*, p. 350.
143. *P*, p. 20.

Note on Manuscript Sources

Letters and journals are the heart of this book, which would be nothing without their charm and revelation of character. Reading and reproducing them was facilitated by the sisters' neat writing, though Harriet's in particular deteriorated as she got older. Their mother also wrote legibly, as did Charles Bisshopp and Robert Curzon. The best hand of all is that of Robert II, some of whose letters are as easy to read as a printed page. The second worst belonged to Cecil Bisshopp; the worst – sometimes a mere scrawl – to George Pechell. Deciding what to include was facilitated by the existence, for much of the material, of typed transcripts.

Many of the letters reproduced here are in the Parham MSS. Most of these have been anonymously transcribed and form part of the Parham Papers, of which twenty of the fifty-three volumes contain Bisshopp and Curzon family correspondence. The smaller but also significant Castle Goring MSS, held alongside the Parham MSS in the West Sussex Record Office, have not been transcribed. There are a further twenty-seven letters, mainly from Katherine to Harriet, in the possession of the Somerset family, and these have been transcribed by Marigold Somerset.

Harriet wrote her journal in an assortment of notebooks and printed diaries and on unbound sheets. The most substantial volume records the years 1809–15. Two more narrate her travels of August and September 1815, a fourth covers 1818–19, and a fifth 1830. The entries for 1816–17 are on unbound pages, and tiny volumes, mainly printed diaries, contain the entries for 1807, 1829, 1839, 1841, 1842, 1849–51, 1852, 1857–58, 1862 and 1863–64, with a few stray notes on other years. All this material is in the Parham MSS and there is a complete transcript in the Parham Papers. A further volume for 1843–44 is not transcribed.

Katherine's journal for the years 1812–34 is contained in a very large notebook of which her brother Charles had previously filled two pages with notes on historical events in Europe during the Early Middle Ages. Though a steadier diarist than Harriet, Katherine by no means kept a daily record, and sometimes covered weeks or even months in a single entry. At the end of the volume are a few retrospective entries for the years 1808–16. Laid in are loose pages with further jottings on 1808 and 1831 and an undated letter from Katherine to her mother. The 1808 and 1848–54 journals are separate. All of this material is in the private archives of the Somerset family. In 1926 James Wentworth-Fitzwilliam made a transcript of the 1812–34 journal and gave copies to the Pearsons of Parham and the Somersets of Castle Goring. Other transcripts are by Marigold Somerset. I was allowed to make copies of these transcripts.

With all the letters and with Harriet's journal, but not with Katherine's journal, I have used the original documents. In presenting primary matter I have aimed at authenticity while removing obstacles to comprehension and readability. Faulty grammar is left untouched, as are spellings specific to the period or wrong at any time. Vagueness about such things was widespread in the early nineteenth century, and cleansing the text would create a false impression, as would inverting the common practice of using apostrophes for plurals but not possessives.

On the other hand, punctuation has been modernised, especially by replacing long gaps, commas and dashes after sentences with full stops. It also seemed pointless to reproduce the arbitrary and inconsistent use of capital letters, which is somehow less obtrusive in a handwritten than in a printed text. Rational paragraphing is introduced, ampersands and contracted or abbreviated words are expanded, superscript letters lowered to the line, obvious slips of the pen silently corrected, and missing words and explanatory insertions placed in square brackets. Underlined words appear in italics.

Excisions from letters and within journal entries are indicated, and the dating of both is standardised. Where writers omit dates contextual evidence is used to supply them. Quotes from printed sources have references, but to avoid a proliferation of notes I do not give information on persons mentioned in passing. Street addresses refer to London.

Bibliography

Manuscript Sources

West Sussex Record Office

Castle Goring MSS. Bisshopp and Pechell family letters, commonplace books, scrapbooks, legal documents, pedigrees, photograph albums etc.

Parham MSS. Bisshopp and Curzon family letters and journals, commonplace books, notebooks, scrapbooks, memoranda, wills and other legal documents, accounts books, polling books, pedigrees, sketches etc.

Parham Papers. Bound volumes containing a large selection of transcripts of material from the Parham MSS

Add. MSS. Small amount of material on Sir Thomas Pechell, Henrietta Burrell etc.

Clapham, West Sussex

Transcript of journal of Katherine Bisshopp prepared by James Wentworth-Fitzwilliam

Letters from Katherine Bisshopp to Harriet Curzon with transcript of the same prepared by Marigold Somerset

Parham, West Sussex

Parham Papers (volumes missing from the set at the West Sussex Record Office)

Katherine Bisshopp's catalogue of portraits at Parham

Knepp Castle, West Sussex

Burrell MSS. Correspondence relating to the youth of Percy Burrell; marriage settlement of Percy Burrell and Henrietta Pechell

Worthing Library
George Bason Files. Published and unpublished material relative to the Pechells and Somersets of Castle Goring, collected by George Bason

Archive Centre, King's College, Cambridge
Ian H. C. Fraser, 'Calendar of 506 Letters from Robert Curzon to Walter Sneyd' (typescript)

Hertfordshire Archives and Local Studies
Earls of Verulam Estate MSS. Journals of the Earl and Countess of Verulam

Petworth House Archives, West Sussex
Correspondence relating to George Pechell

Arundel Castle Archives, West Sussex
Letter from Robert Curzon II to Harriet Curzon

National Archives, Kew
Will of Sir Thomas Brooke-Pechell

Printed Sources
1) The Bisshopps and Related Topics
Anon., 'Parham. Sussex', *Saturday Magazine*, 21/648 (6 August 1842), p. 50
Anon., *Extracts from the Public Journals Relating to the Death of Captain Pechell, 77th Regiment, Before Sebastopol; with Reports of the Several Meetings of the Inhabitants of Brighton* (privately printed, 1856)
Anon., *A Bundle of Sticks, Being Some Account of the Pechell Family, Collected by a Twig, from Various Sources* (Winchester: Warren, 1914)
Albemarle, G. T., Earl of, *Fifty Years of My Life*, 2 vols (London: Macmillan, 1876)
Allen, R. S., ed., 'The Bisshopp Papers During the War of 1812', *Journal of the Society for Army Historical Research*, 61/245 (Spring 1983), pp. 22–29
Bamford, F., ed., *Dear Miss Heber: An Eighteenth Century Correspondence* (London; Constable, 1936)

Barnard, Lady E. et al, *Parham, West Sussex* (Wymondham: Heritage House Media, 2009)

Carden, J. S., *A Curtail'd Memoir of Incidents and Occurrences*, ed. by C. T. Atkinson (Oxford: Clarendon, 1912)

Cruikshank, E., *The Documentary History of the Campaign upon the Niagara Frontier*, 9 vols (Welland: Lundy's Lane Historical Society, 1896–1908)

Djabri, S. C., 'A Letter from Brighton – 1841', *Sussex Family Historian*, 11/3 (September 1994), pp. 92–100

Djabri, S. C., A. F. Hughes and J. Knight, *The Shelleys of Field Place: The Story of the Family and Their Estates* (Horsham: Horsham Museum Society, 2000)

Djabri, S. C. and J. Knight, *The Letters of Bysshe and Timothy Shelley* (Horsham: Horsham Museum Society, 2000)

Frankland, M., *Child of My Time* (London: Chatto & Windus, 1999)

Fraser, I. H. C., *The Heir of Parham: Robert Curzon, 14th Baron Zouche* (Harleston: Paradigm, 1986)

Gash, N., 'The Influence of the Crown at Windsor and Brighton in the Elections of 1832, 1835, and 1837', *English Historical Review*, 54 (1939), pp. 653–63

Goodall, J., 'Downland Treasure: Parham House, West Sussex', *Country Life* (27 July 2011), pp. 39–45

Guest, M. and W. B. Boulton, *The Royal Yacht Squadron: Memorials of its Members, with an Enquiry into the History of Yachting and its Development in the Solent* (London: Murray, 1903)

Hussey, C., 'Parham Park, Sussex' (London: Country Life, no date)

Kirk, J., *Parham: An Elizabethan House and its Restoration* (Chichester: Phillimore, 2009)

Mitford, M. R., *Letters*, ed. by R. B. Johnson (London: Bodley Head, 1925)

Parker, S. E., *Grace & Favour: The Hampton Court Palace Community, 1750–1850* (Hampton Court Palace: Historic Royal Palaces, 2005)

Ponsonby, A., 'Katherine Bisshopp (Lady Pechell)', in A. P., *More English Diaries* (London: Methuen, 1927), pp. 170–78

Russell, C., Lady, *The Rose Goddess and Other Sketches of Mystery and Romance* (London: Longmans, Green, 1910)

Somerset, M., 'The Journal of Katherine Annabella Bisshopp', *Sussex County Magazine* (1955), pp. 114–18 and 217–22

Tredcroft, C. L., *Recollections of 70 Years and Memoirs of My Family* (Guildford: Stent, 1904)

Wentworth-Fitzwilliam, J., *Parham in Sussex: A Historical and Descriptive Survey* (London: Batsford, 1947)

Wilkinson, H. C., *Bermuda from Sail to Steam: The History of the Island from 1784 to 1901*, 2 vols (London: Oxford University Press, 1973)

2) Jane Austen

Auerbach, E., *Searching for Jane Austen* (Madison: University of Wisconsin Press, 2004)

Austen, J., *Northanger Abbey*, ed. by Marilyn Butler (London: Penguin, 2003)

Austen, J., *Sense and Sensibility*, ed. by R. Ballaster and T. Tanner (London: Penguin, 2003)

Austen, J., *Pride and Prejudice*, ed. by V. Jones (London: Penguin, 2014)

Austen, J., *Mansfield Park*, ed. by K. Sutherland (London: Penguin, 2014)

Austen, J., *Emma*, ed. by F. Stafford (London: Penguin, 2015)

Austen, J., *Persuasion*, ed. by G. Beer (London: Penguin, 2003)

Austen, J., *Letters*, ed. by D. Le Faye (Oxford: Oxford University Press, 2011)

Austen-Leigh, J. E., *A Memoir of Jane Austen* (London: Folio Society, 1989)

Barchas, J., *Matters of Fact in Jane Austen: History, Location, and Celebrity* (Baltimore: Johns Hopkins University Press, 2012)

Burrows, J. F., '*Persuasion* and Its "Sets of People"', *Sydney Studies in English*, 2 (1976–77), pp. 3–23

Butler, M., *Jane Austen and the War of Ideas* (Oxford: Clarendon, 1975)

Copeland, E., and J. McMaster, eds, *The Cambridge Companion to Jane Austen* (Cambridge: Cambridge University Press, 1997)

Deresiewicz, W., *A Jane Austen Education: How Six Novels Taught Me About Love, Friendship, and the Things that Really Matter* (New York: Penguin, 2011)

Duckworth, A. M., *The Improvement of the Estate: A Study of Jane Austen's Novels* (Baltimore: Johns Hopkins University Press, 1971)

Forster, E. M., *Abinger Harvest* (Harmondsworth: Penguin, 1974)

Forster, E. M., *Aspects of the Novel* (London: Hodder & Stoughton, 1993)

Gard, R., *Jane Austen: 'Emma' and 'Persuasion'* (Harmondsworth: Penguin, 1985)

Gay, P., 'The Romanticism of *Persuasion*', *Sydney Studies in English*, 5 (1979–80), pp. 15–30

Gooneratne, Y., *Jane Austen* (Cambridge: Cambridge University Press, 1970)

Greene, D. J., 'Jane Austen and the Peerage', in I. Watt, ed., *Jane Austen: A Collection of Critical Essays* (Eaglewood Cliffs: Prentice-Hall, 1963), pp. 154–65

Grey, J. D., ed., *The Jane Austen Handbook* (London: Athlone, 1986)

Harding, D. W., *Regulated Hatred and Other Essays on Jane Austen*, ed. by M. Lawlor (London: Athlone, 1998)

Horwitz, B. J., *Jane Austen and the Question of Women's Education* (New York: Lang, 1991)

Johnson, C. L. and C. Tuite, eds, *A Companion to Jane Austen* (Chichester: Wiley-Blackwell, 2009)

Jones, H., *Jane Austen and Marriage* (London: Continuum, 2009)

Lane, M., *Jane Austen's World: The Life and Times of England's Most Popular Novelist* (London: Carlton, 2005)

MacDonagh, O., *Jane Austen: Real and Imagined Worlds* (New Haven: Yale University Press, 1991)

Mahony, S., *Wealth or Poverty: Jane Austen's Novels Explored* (London: Hale, 2015)

Monaghan, D., *Jane Austen: Structure and Social Vision* (London: Macmillan, 1980)

Monaghan, D., ed., *Jane Austen in a Social Context* (London: Macmillan, 1981)

Nardin, J., *Those Elegant Decorums: The Concept of Propriety in Jane Austen's Novels* (Albany: State University of New York Press, 1973)

Olsen, K., *All Things Austen: An Encyclopedia of Austen's World*, 2 vols (Westport: Greenwood, 2005)

Pinion, F. B., *A Jane Austen Companion: A Critical Survey and Reference Book* (London: Macmillan, 1973)

Roberts, W., *Jane Austen and the French Revolution* (London: Methuen, 1979)

Sales, R., *Jane Austen and Representations of Regency England* (London: Routledge, 1994)

Selwyn, D., *Jane Austen and Leisure* (London: Hambledon, 1999)

Selwyn, D., *Jane Austen and Children* (London: Continuum, 2010)

Simons, J., ed., *'Mansfield Park' and 'Persuasion'* (Basingstoke: Macmillan, 1997)

Southam, B. C., ed., *Jane Austen: The Critical Heritage*, 2 vols (London: Routledge, 1995)

Southam, B. C., *Jane Austen: 'Northanger Abbey' and 'Persuasion'* (Basingstoke: Macmillan, 1976)

Southam, B. C., *Jane Austen and the Navy* (London: National Maritime Museum, 2005)

Spacks, P. M., 'In Praise of Gossip', *Hudson Review*, 35 (1982), pp. 19–38

Sturrock, J., 'Dandies, Beauties, and the Issue of Good Looks in *Persuasion*', *Persuasions*, 26 (2004), pp. 41–50

Tanner, T., *Jane Austen* (Basingstoke: Macmillan, 1986)

Thompson, J., *Between Self and World: The Novels of Jane Austen* (University Park: Pennsylvania State University Press, 1988)

Todd, J. ed., *Jane Austen in Context* (Cambridge: Cambridge University Press, 2005)

Todd, J. and A. Blank, 'Introduction' to *Persuasion* (Cambridge: Cambridge University Press, 2006), pp. xxi–lxxxii

Tomalin, C., *Jane Austen: A Life* (London: Viking, 1997)

Watkins, S., *Jane Austen in Style* (London: Thames and Hudson, 1996)

I have also drawn on countless works of reference, including bibliographies, biographical dictionaries, the *History of Parliament*, peerages and baronetages, guides to Sussex, and the researches of local historians and others published online.

Timeline

1782 Marriage of Sir Cecil Bisshopp and Harriet Anne Southwell (27 July)

1783 Birth of Cecil Bisshopp (25 June)

1784 Birth of Charles Bisshopp (September)

1787 Birth of Harriet Anne Bisshopp (7 September)

1791 Birth of Katherine Annabella Bisshopp (1 December)

1805 Marriage of Cecil Bisshopp and Lady Charlotte Townshend (6 April)

1807 Death of Lady Charlotte Bisshopp *née* Townshend (3 October)

1808 Death of Lady Bisshopp's mother Annabella Southwell (April)

Death of Charles Bisshopp (10 May)

Marriage of Harriet Bisshopp and Robert Curzon I (14 October)

1810 Birth of Robert Curzon II (16 March)

1812 Birth of Edward Curzon (8 November)

1813 Death of Cecil Bisshopp in Canada (16 July)

1815 Sir Cecil Bisshopp becomes 12th Baron Zouche (1 August)

1817 Auction of Parham's contents (February)

1820 Death of Assheton Viscount Curzon (21 March)

Marriage of George Bisshopp and Catherine Sproule (17 May)

1821 Return of George Pechell to England after a 3½-year absence (December)

1822 George Pechell promoted captain in the navy (26 December)

1824 Katherine Bisshopp and George Pechell become engaged (6 June)

Death of Lord Zouche's brother Hugh Bisshopp (10 August)

1825	George Pechell takes out a repairing lease on Castle Goring
1826	Death of Mrs Hugh Bisshopp (23 April)
	Death of Sir Thomas Brooke-Pechell (18 June)
	Marriage of Katherine Bisshopp and George Pechell (1 August)
1827	The Pechells' expedition to Dieppe (15–21 September)
1828	Death of 12th Baron Zouche (11 November)
1829	Harriet Curzon becomes 13th Baroness Zouche (13 January)
	Birth of Henrietta Pechell (4 April)
1830	Birth of William Pechell (26 May)
	George Pechell becomes gentleman usher to Queen Adelaide (June)
1831	George Pechell appointed equerry to Queen Adelaide (April)
	The Pechells' expedition to Cherbourg (25–30 August)
1833	Birth of Adelaide Pechell (5 January)
1834	The Pechells' coaching accident (3 March)
	Death of Sir George Bisshopp, 9th Baronet (22 March)
	Marriage of Edward Curzon and Amelia Daniell (5 May)
1835	George Pechell elected MP for Brighton (January)
1839	Death of Harriet Anne Bisshopp, Dowager Lady Zouche (10 December)
1845	The Pechells buy Castle Goring from Mary Shelley (November)
1849	Death of Sir John Brooke-Pechell (3 November)
	George Pechell becomes Sir George Brooke-Pechell, 4th Bart
1850	Marriage of Robert Curzon II and Emily Wilmot-Horton (27 August)
1851	Birth of Robin Curzon (28 June)
1855	Death of William Pechell before Sebastopol (3 September)
1856	Marriage of Henrietta Pechell and Percy Burrell (26 August)
1857	Marriage of Adelaide Pechell and Alfred Somerset (24 September)
1860	Death of Admiral Sir George Brooke-Pechell (29 June)
	Birth of Darea Curzon (13 November)
1863	Death of Robert Curzon I (14 May)
	Hagley Hall sold to William Harrison
1866	Death of Emily Curzon *née* Wilmot-Horton (11 March)
1870	Death of Harriet Curzon, Lady Zouche (15 May)
	Robert Curzon II becomes 14th Baron Zouche
1871	Death of Katherine, Lady Brooke-Pechell (29 July)

Index